Dangerous Passions,
Deadly Sins

DANGEROUS PASSIONS, DEADLY SINS

LEARNING FROM THE PSYCHOLOGY OF ANCIENT MONKS

Dennis Okholm

BrazosPress

a division of Baker Publishing Group
Grand Rapids, Michigan

© 2014 by Dennis Okholm

Published by Brazos Press
a division of Baker Publishing Group
P.O. Box 6287, Grand Rapids, MI 49516-6287
www.brazospress.com

Printed in the United States of America

Library of Congress Cataloging-in-Publication Data is on file at the Library of Congress, Washington, DC.

ISBN 978-1-5874-3353-5 (pbk.)

Scripture quotations are from the New Revised Standard Version of the Bible, copyright © 1989, by the Division of Christian Education of the National Council of the Churches of Christ in the United States of America. Used by permission. All rights reserved.

14   15   16   17   18   19   20   7   6   5   4   3   2   1

Dedicated to
Robert C. Roberts
whose invitation to friendship I am
reminded of every time I read
Wallace Stegner's *Crossing to Safety*
and whose invitation to a scholarly
community began my study
of the deadly sins I commit

Contents

Acknowledgments

I began this investigation years ago at the invitation of Robert Roberts to join a think tank that provided me the opportunity to examine ancient wisdom about gluttony. That was followed by a generous grant from the PEW Evangelical Scholars Program which supported further research beyond the first sin on the list. Sabbaticals provided by Wheaton College and Azusa Pacific University added leave time to do more work on this project.

I am also thankful that several churches responded positively to presentations of what these ancients taught on these topics. Among others, this includes First Presbyterian of Glen Ellyn (IL), St. Barnabas Episcopal Church (Glen Ellyn, IL), St. Andrews Presbyterian (Newport Beach, CA), and Community Presbyterian Church (Palm Desert, CA). Students in classes at Wheaton College and Azusa Pacific University also listened to, read, and provided feedback on this material, many times with questions and insights that added clarity.

There are individuals who have helped in one way or another with the research, including Morse Tan, Joseph Tsang, Chris Waks, Cory Anderson, and, though it was only a short meeting in his office and over lunch at St. John's Abbey and University,

Columba Stewart. (Though he would probably not remember our meeting, his generosity and insights into Cassian provided me with a compass and course correction that were crucial to this project.) Most significantly, my wife, Trevecca, whose practice of *hypomonē* (see chapter 7) through forty years of marriage would make St. Benedict smile, has not only put up in monastic silence with my hours at the desk, but has been an invaluable sounding board so that what is written is more clear and relevant. (Because it is characteristic of her, she is also the *virtuous* example I used in chapter five.)

Chapters 2 and 6 contain material that previously appeared in the *American Benedictine Review* as "Gluttony: Thought for Food" 49, no. 1 (March 1998), and "Envy: The Silent Killer" 59, no. 2 (June 2008). Chapter 2 also contains material that previously appeared in "Being Stuffed and Being Fulfilled," in *Limning the Psyche*, edited by Robert C. Roberts and Mark R. Talbot (Grand Rapids: Eerdmans, 1997). Adapted by permission of the publisher; all rights reserved.

Chapter 5 is adapted from "To Vent or Not to Vent? What Contemporary Psychology Can Learn from Ascetic Theology about Anger," originally published in *Care for the Soul*, edited by Mark R. McMinn and Timothy R. Phillips. Copyright 2001 by Mark R. McMinn and the estate of Timothy R. Phillips. Used by permission of InterVarsity Press, PO Box 1400, Downers Grove, IL 60515. www.ivpress.com.

One always has to say that, despite the people who responded to my talks, provided feedback on previously published material, or helped with the research and writing, the deficiencies and any errors are my responsibility. One always has to say that . . . because, unfortunately, it's true.

1

*

Getting Oriented

The Psychology of Monks

> The greatest difference between classical and modern psychology probably lies in the former's heavy emphasis on free will.
>
> Gabriel Bunge, *Despondency*

In the 1995 movie *Seven*, after killing six people who represent the first six of seven deadly sins, "John Doe" delivers a speech explaining his actions to the two detectives who have captured him. After recounting the sin of each person he has murdered, he spills out his rationale: "We see a deadly sin on every street corner, in every home, and we tolerate it. We tolerate it because it's common, it's trivial. We tolerate it morning, noon, and night. Well, not anymore. I'm setting the example. What I've done is going to be puzzled over and studied and followed . . . forever."[1]

I was stunned by this speech when I first heard it because the shocking murders that the movie portrayed (a movie not for the squeamish) turned out not to be gratuitous Hollywood fare, but graphic illustrations of the point captured in these lines. We *do* tolerate the deadly sins, not just because they are common, but, in some cases, because they have become virtuous: we celebrate the consumption of five dozen hot dogs in ten minutes in an annual July 4th contest; we dispense coffee from a self-serve urn on which hangs a sign declaring that the vendors "proudly" serve this brand; we pitch food products in commercials that show women erotically engaged with sandwiches or soft drinks; we accumulate so much "stuff" that we have to store the extra in rented storage units that are as large as the average American home of the 1950s.

So what *really* are these "common" sins? Who "invented" them? What have they got to do with our lives today beyond the fact that we tolerate them?

The story begins with a desert monk named Evagrius of Pontus (c. 345–99). He came up with a list of eight evil thoughts (*logismoi*)—generic thoughts that are common to all humans and which Evagrius occasionally reduced to three fundamental thoughts—gluttony, avarice, and vainglory.[2] The others on the list are lust, anger, sadness (*tristitia*), despondency (*acedia*), and pride. These thoughts are not sins to begin with, but can be turned into passions and *then* into sins by the freely willed consent of the one who entertains them—"freely willed," that is, when "demons" use these thoughts as allies that end up distorting human nature as God created it. (Actually, Evagrius sometimes used "demons" and "thoughts" almost interchangeably.) The common root in all of these thoughts gone awry is self-love, a point to keep in mind when we discuss the goal of these ancient monks.

In John Cassian (c. 360–435) this list became the eight principal faults.[3] Cassian stood as the link between the Eastern theologian Evagrius and Western Benedictine monasticism. (At the end of *The Rule of St. Benedict*, Benedict advises his monks to go deeper by reading Cassian and Basil the Great.) For our purposes this is significant especially because the third key figure in our investigation of the psychology of these early monks is a Benedictine who became the first great pope—Gregory I (540–604). He modified Cassian's list and enumerated the "seven principal vices" by placing pride in a category by itself as the root of all sins, adding envy, and merging spiritual lethargy (*acedia*) with sadness (*tristitia*). These became our present-day list of the "seven deadly sins."[4]

Calling all of these *deadly* sins is not entirely accurate. As Thomas Aquinas makes clear in the *Summa Theologica*,[5] Gregory's seven *are* capital or chief or cardinal sins, but they are not necessarily always mortal sins. That is, each is a cardinal sin in part because it is the parent of "daughter" sins (not that "sons" are any better, but that is the language that Gregory used). For instance, Gregory teaches that gluttony breeds foolish mirth, scurrility, uncleanness, babbling, and dullness of mind with reference to the understanding; anger propagates an army consisting of strifes, swelling of mind, insults, clamor, indignation, and blasphemies.[6] But whether each cardinal sin is mortal or venial depends on the degree to which it is opposed to the love and grace of God.

The order in which these thoughts are discussed reflects the fact that the eight were viewed as interconnected.[7] For example, Cassian groups the vices in pairs; the deadly thoughts form alliances against us.[8] Anger is often the bedfellow of envy. It is frequently aroused by frustrated greed and lust. These connections observed between the vices and sins in everyday life is the genius of ascetic theologians like Evagrius, whom one translator calls "the anatomist of the passions of the psyche both in their manifestations in behavior and in their intrapsychic activity."[9] Evagrius called for careful observation, description, and analysis of the precise nature of our thoughts in order for this knowledge to work to our advantage as we struggle with or against these thoughts, or even the memories of them.

The first two, gluttony and lust, involve the body and the soul; they are the carnal sins. They are the first to be conquered, and, along with avarice, they belong to the concupiscible (*epithumikon*) part of our existence. Anger is the first on the irascible (*thumikon*) list, which also includes dejection and *acedia*. Finally, vainglory and pride belong to the third category of principal thoughts—the rational (*logikon*). This arrangement helps to understand why Evagrius could sometimes reduce the eight to the three in the front lines of each grouping—namely, gluttony, anger, and vainglory.

Which ones were the more important depended in part on the context in which one lived. Gluttony and lust were especially threatening for ascetic theologians in monastic environments. Given the architectonic nature of a mature medieval society, pride's individualism might be perceived to undermine the authority of God, the church, and the entitled. There is evidence in the twelfth and thirteenth centuries—in artistic depictions, for instance—that avarice was the worst of the seven.[10]

Before going further, we need to see how this discussion of thoughts or faults fits into the monastic understanding of the soul's health and the ultimate goal of the monk. This context will be important to keep in mind as we discuss these dangerous passions that can become deadly sins.

These early monastic theologians described the health of the soul as *apatheia*. Though they were influenced by Stoic and Neoplatonic philosophies, they adapted (rather than adopted) the Stoic concept of *apatheia*.[11] This is not simply the leveling out of human emotions or the extirpation of the passions.[12] Christian ascetics like Evagrius and Cassian took from the Stoics, Clement of Alexandria, and Egyptian sources such as Anthony, and put their own stamp on this concept.[13] For them *apatheia* is an abiding sense of peace and joy that comes from the full harmony of the passions—an *habitual* state developed through discipline (*ascesis*), which is why we can refer to it in terms of virtue. Through various exercises a person trains herself to be in full possession of her affective faculties so that disordered desires are held in check and rightly ordered, and one can experience a state of deep calm—a "repose," as Cassian calls it.[14] According to Evagrius, one of the marks of the presence of *apatheia* in a person's life is the ability to remain calm and peaceful even when he has memories of situations or events that tend to stimulate and disorder the passions.[15]

This harmonious integration of the emotional life always remains exposed to the attacks of demons, as we mentioned, so emotional health—*apatheia*—must be maintained with effort. Of course, this is to be expected: good health is never a given; one must work at it with care. This implies that *apatheia* can be had (or lost) by degrees; one continually grows in it. Furthermore, it is subject to the limitations of one's unique constitution.[16]

Evagrius teaches that the offspring of *apatheia* is *agapē*. Maintaining the harmony of one's passions enables the person fully to love others and God, because the acquisition of *apatheia* can stamp out anger, sulking, lust, resentment, envy, and all other impediments to self-giving love. It gets at that root of self-love. Without love for others and God *apatheia* alone is of little value. Evagrius reminds us that the absence of distracting thoughts itself is not true prayer: "It is quite possible for a man to have none but the purest thoughts and yet be so distracted mulling over them that he remains the while far removed from God."[17] Gregory gets quite specific and illustrates for us in his practical teaching about fasting that acquiring *apatheia* cannot be divorced from *agapē*:

> In this matter we must consider how little the virtue of abstinence is regarded, unless it deserve commendation by reason

of other virtues. . . . To sanctify a fast is to show abstinence of
the flesh to be worthy of God by other good things added to it
[such as giving to the poor what one has abstained from]. . . .
A man fasts not to God but to himself, if he does not give to
the poor what he denies his belly for a time, but reserves it to
be given to his belly later.[18]

Evagrius puts the equation succinctly: "*Agapē* is the progeny of
apatheia. Apatheia is the very flower of *ascesis.*"[19] And, again,
it is this love which counters the self-love that is the root of the
deadly sins.

What does all of this have to do with us in the twenty-first
century? My contention is that it has everything to do with us.
For one thing, as Gabriel Bunge points out, these "vices which
plague humankind are the same from time immemorial and
everywhere; only their concrete forms vary according to people's
particular conditions of life," all of which, he reminds us, are
in play for the adversary of the human race.[20] If that is the case,
and if psychology (as well as sociology) is analysis based on
the observations and interpretations of human behaviors and
thought patterns, then these ancients are no less psychologists
than are our contemporaries who have the credentials. Gabriel
Bunge, for one, refers to Evagrius as "a thinker equipped with
a rare sense of psychology and an analytical, penetrating insight" who "owes his unusual knowledge of the human soul to
solitary introspection and to innumerable confessions of the
heart."[21] Some even go so far as to claim that there are passages in Evagrius's *Praktikos* that contain insights that have
taken our contemporaries decades to rediscover and record in
psychoanalytic literature.[22] And Thomas Oden gives specific
examples of how Gregory's *Pastoral Care* anticipates much
modern psychotherapy.[23]

The question is this: What happens when we listen to these
members of the Christian family who lived 1500 years ago?
Will we find them to be naïve or ill-informed because they are

not "scientific"? Or were they on target in their recommendations of how to live the Christian life and remain psychologically and emotionally healthy? What happens when we listen to premoderns who did not know they were doing theology *and* psychology at the same time?

Some time ago *Christianity Today* ran an article assessing the status of the Christian counseling movement.[24] It included a "tree" diagram detailing some of the current branches of Christian psychology. The "fruits" were names most of us would recognize. The trunk included Narramore, Tournier, and Menninger. Certainly the list above ground level is selective and debatable. But below ground, where the *roots* of Christian psychology lay, the "pioneers" included Rogers, Jüng, Freud, Maslow, Skinner, and Satir. If the diagram was accurate, it is lamentable, for the roots surely determine the meat of the fruits, even if they are polished on the outside with a Christian veneer to make them attractive to the consumer. Contemporary *Christian* psychology is a tree that might properly include *grafts* from Rogers, Freud, and Skinner, but its roots should be found elsewhere.

I wish that the *Christianity Today* article were a relic of a bygone era, but when, for my ordination in the Anglican church, my wife and I were required to be assessed by a newly licensed psychologist who had received her training in a reputable Christian graduate school of psychology, she had no idea of the Christian heritage we are about to unpack in the following pages. The names, let alone the era, were completely unfamiliar to her. And when I pressed her further, sadly, her training and knowledge verified what the *Christianity Today* article demonstrated.

The fact is that, except for a few lone voices, ancient and early medieval Christian sources have been virtually ignored in the area of practical theology, even by contemporary Christian psychologists (as well as by the church as a whole).[25] Even when these sources are taken into account it is often through the filter of modern paradigms that distort the teachings of the ancients.[26]

It isn't that we haven't heard the cries of neglect. Sometimes the reprimand has to come from within the discipline, even if it comes from outside the Christian camp. Solomon Schimmel, a Jewish psychologist, reacted toward his own tribe of psychotherapists, admonishing his colleagues to learn from classical, Jewish, and Christian theologians and moralists: "Modern psychology's disdain for the teachings of the great moral traditions is an example of intellectual hubris."[27]

My contention is that ascetic theologians and monastics of the fourth through seventh centuries (particularly Evagrius, Cassian, and Gregory) provide the church with a psychology which is not only specifically Christian in its orientation, but relevant to modern people if taken seriously. At the same time, quite often the claims ascetic theologians and monastics[28] make about life issues are borne out by the empirical observations of contemporary psychology.

So what I hope to accomplish in this book is twofold. First, I intend to bring forward the insights of early church monks in order to offer what one might call a *truly* Christian psychology rather than the more typical approach that *begins* with the template of contemporary understanding from the social sciences and then attempts to *insert* Christian concepts to make them fit the alien structure.

Second, I intend to make a bit of an apologetic case for the priority of this Christian psychology over against the presumption of moderns that we are the first to understand the etiology and treatment of the disorders and unregulated passions that will be discussed. And this also serves the purpose of demonstrating that in many cases what we *do* understand and deal with in the realm of psychology today (such as in the case of eating disorders or depression) was insightfully handled by deeply thoughtful Christian psychologists 1500 years ago (such as in the case of gluttony or sloth). There are even cases, such as in the chapter on anger, in which our contemporaries reversed previous recommendations because they had come to see things (unwittingly) the way the ancients correctly understood them. There is simply much wisdom from these early Christian writings for our spiritual and psychological health today.

Lest I be misunderstood, let me say that I am not approaching the topic with the attitude of the gentleman who phoned me for advice and then, when given the advice, told me that he did not believe in psychology. The discipline of psychology has much to offer, and therapists have helped and will continue to help many cope with and remedy much that ails us human beings. My main appeal is to Christians in the discipline and in the profession who might not be familiar with their own heritage, and, secondarily, it is to those outside the Christian community who might find wisdom in this tradition that will help them.

Before we investigate the first of the dangerous passions and deadly sins, some procedural comments and confessions are in order.

I have tried to include an example, either real or fictionalized, that specifically and practically illustrates the relevance of this ancient wisdom for recognizing, understanding, and prescribing remedies for each of these passions. There is no specific case study for the final chapter on vainglory, in part because all the preceding examples would fit this sin from which all others derive. (Cassian will provide us with an example for the sixth—sloth.)

In each case but one, I have paired the "deadly sin" with discussion of a specific pathology or addiction. The exception is avarice, since, as I explain, we hardly think of it as a vice; in that chapter there is, instead, more of a conversation between the ancients and some contemporary thinkers.

By way of confession, I am a theologian (though that is not a sin . . . most of the time), not a professional psychologist. In making the apologetic argument in this book I do not profess to be an expert in the social sciences, but only to give *indications* where practitioners and researchers in the field touch base with the psychology of ancient monks. I have tried to be responsible in representing a contemporary discipline that is not my own, and where I am deemed inadequate I hope that that will serve only to generate more dialogue. All that said, it is reassuring that neither the ascetic monks of the past nor psychologists of the present have systems of thought that are impervious to correction and internal contradictions. Evagrius's schema is not rigid, because he recognized variations in human experience. And even the advent of the *DSM-V* (which, unfortunately, had just come out when this book was written and therefore is not referenced) has been met with disgruntled reviewers. Human life is messy and often difficult to figure out—whether you live in 400 or in 2100.

2

✳

Gluttony

Thought for Food

He who controls the stomach diminishes the passions; he who is overcome by food gives increase to pleasures.

Evagrius, *On the Eight Thoughts* 1.2

Why Gluttony?

When a person mentions that he is writing a paper on gluttony, the reactions can be surprising. The monks at one abbey seemed a bit threatened and engaged in playful teasing, perhaps feeling self-conscious about the twenty-odd varieties of cold cereal boxes in their refectory. A graduate school librarian giggled; it probably *was* an unusual topic of research at a Protestant school. A bank employee asked for a copy of the paper—a heartening response, but one that makes me suspicious given all of the others.

Why *would* a person want to research gluttony? Initially I was curious why it was considered a *deadly* sin. After all, I once taught at a college that proscribed the consumption of alcoholic beverages, but it did not forbid overeating in the dining commons. And when one turns to Scripture, there is not much to be found on the topic of gluttony, unless one relies on the imaginative allegorical exegesis of medieval hermeneutics.

The word "gluttony" is scarcely mentioned in the Bible, though Paul implores us to exercise restraint in the use of our bodies.[1] In fact, the biblical writers encourage us to enjoy food as much, if not more, than they warn us against it. Food itself is not shunned in the Christian Scriptures (a distinction from other religions, such as Judaism, Islam, and Hinduism), but it is not supremely important either. One is not to make a god of one's belly, but neither is one to be overly concerned about what one eats.[2]

Suspicions about food seem to intensify after the New Testament period—in patristic sources, ascetic theology, and monastic practice. This might be expected of a Christian church that was contending against an encroaching worldliness and being influenced by Cynic, Stoic, and Neoplatonic philosophies.

So, one might legitimately ask, "What's so bad about gluttony?" Maybe giggling is the appropriate response to a person who takes the topic so seriously.

On the other hand, little reflection is needed to realize the importance of a topic that has been virtually neglected by modern theologians.[3] For one thing, eating is not only an absolute necessity for us, it is also centrally important in our lives. Given USDA statistics, between ages twenty and fifty the average person spends about 28,000 hours eating—over 1160 days. Our daily schedules are often planned around mealtimes. Business deals are cut among people who "do" lunch together. Foods have been adapted to every aspect of our popular culture: we have *TV* dinners, *car* drive-up windows, and *ballgame* tailgate parties.

Of course, eating is crucial in biblical narratives as well. Our first parents plunged the human race into sin by violating a prohibition against eating. The Hebrews were given a sense of identity in a meal that signifies the defining moment in their history—the Passover. The second Adam was victorious over a temptation involving the production and consumption of bread. Christians celebrate their life together in Christ around a family meal initiated by Jesus—one which anticipates an eschatological banquet that will mark the consummation of salvation history. Add to these all of the stories many of us learned from the time we were toddlers: Abraham and his three visitors; Esau and his soup; Joseph and the famine; the prodigal son and his father's banquet; the feeding of the 5,000; Mary and Martha; the couple on the road to Emmaus; and breakfast on the beach with the risen Lord.

This topic cannot be ignored by contemporary theologians for another reason: food is not only centrally important and necessary in our lives, it is also the focal point of some alarming trends today. For example, up to 1 percent of all American girls and women are anorexic. About 90 percent of anorexics are female.[4] And about the same percentage of those who suffer from eating disorders get them by age twenty. Each day anywhere from 45 to 125 million Americans are dieting (statistics vary depending on sources).[5] At the time he published his book *Fast Food Nation* in 2001,[6] Eric Schlosser stated that the annual health care costs in the US stemming from obesity approached $240 billion while Americans spent more than $35 billion on weight loss schemes and diet products. In 2010 the dietary industry earned $60.9 billion.[7] If Karl Barth is to be taken seriously for insisting that a good theologian has a Bible in one hand and a newspaper in the other, then theologians (which ought to include all Christians) cannot afford to neglect sin, vice, and virtue in the matter of food consumption.

A study of gluttony is even more to the point if one wants to explore ascetic theology and its intersection with psychology. For one thing, fasting and abstinence are perhaps most often associated with ascetic theology (and for good reason). Further, gluttony is a unique "deadly thought": it is one of only seven cardinal sins and only one of two that *necessarily* involves soul *and* body—very apropos for people who are into holistic thinking. Finally, some aspects of the claims ascetic theologians, monastics, and Aquinas[8] make about gluttony are borne out by the empirical observations of contemporary psychology, while other aspects, though consistent with these observations, spring from a distinctively Christian orientation. This will get us started on the apologetic task of this book.

In this chapter we want to know if there are insights from ascetic and monastic theologians that tell us what it means to be a healthy human being with regard to the consumption of food. And along the way, we will want to know how this squares with modern thinking about food. As promised, we will find that our predecessors were quite perceptive in their diagnosis of the human situation and prescriptions for cures, and that their observations should be heeded by a modern culture—including the church—that has ignored them.

Not only has classical theological thought about gluttony been ignored to our detriment, it has also been misunderstood. For instance, as we shall see, labeling gluttony a "*deadly* sin" can be something of a misnomer. So, if we are to raid the banquet table laden with the ancient wisdom about this central issue of human life, we first need to understand fully what gluttony is.

The Recipe for Gluttony

Obviously, gluttony has something to do with the consumption of food, countered by the practice of fasting or abstinence and the virtue of temperance. But it is not simply about *over*consumption. In fact, gluttony is sometimes involved with *under*consumption. Nor is gluttony to be equated with the modern "sin" of being fat. Some fat people are not gluttonous and some thin people are gluttonous. This may be difficult for us to understand because of our cultural and media-induced bias that often depicts fat people as less healthy and virtuous than thin people. This attitude is not unlike that of some of my students who insist that the first thing we must do with the homeless on the streets is to evangelize them; such a recommendation belies a bias that poor people are uncoverted sinners (or they would not be poor) and overlooks the fact that Jesus himself was homeless. Similarly, we must tread carefully through a minefield of biases to understand what gluttony is in the context of our culture.

While we are correcting misunderstandings we should note that the vice of gluttony is not just about food, though this chapter will be confined to that topic. We may be gluttonous about all material goods and physical pleasures. This wider dimension is crucial for a society that thinks of self-indulgence as the number one virtue and self-denial as the root of all that is wrong with us.

Gluttony was on Evagrius's original list of eight evil thoughts (*logismoi*)—those thoughts with which demons tempt us, which can become cardinal sins that pass from the venial stage to the mortal. In the case of gluttony, a person who merely eats more than is necessary or appropriate has committed only a venial sin; but he commits a mortal sin when he is so taken by the pleasure of gluttony that the delights of the palate turn him away from God and his commandments. In effect, gluttony is deadly when a person makes a god of his belly.[9]

Of the seven sins, gluttony seems the least culpable sin for a very important reason that will color much of our subsequent discussion and to which we will explicitly return at the end. Gluttony is a vice that arises from the constitution of our nature.[10] We will always require food, and food usually brings pleasurable sensations to the palate. For this reason, one can never be fully rid of gluttonous thoughts or temptations. In the wilderness Christ was tempted through the same passions as Adam in that such passions were part of his constitution as designed by God.[11] The temptation to gluttony occurred precisely because Adam was created a physical human being. It seems to follow, then, that a gluttonous act is a lesser sin due to its connection with the body's need for nourishment and the necessity of taking in proper amounts of food. Gluttony is not merely a perversion of something good in human nature, as is true of every sin; it is a perversion of something that is necessary to live.[12] There may be an inverse proportion of guilt for sins that are due in part to physical givens.[13]

Nonetheless, though often the least culpable, in ascetic theology it is the first to be faced in the battle schema. Cassian compares our battle with the eight principal thoughts to Olympic and Pythian games with their qualifying heats. In the "rules and laws of conflict," gluttony is the first to be defeated.[14] At one point Cassian compares it to the Hebrews leaving Egypt: they must forsake it and go from it in order to take possession of the seven nations in Canaan.[15] If one cannot conquer a deadly thought that has to do with the body, then how can one proceed to more insidious enemies that attack us only in the spiritual arena? Cassian observes that Satan could not defeat Christ through gluttony, so he leapt to the fundamental sins of covetousness and pride.[16]

We should keep in mind that the order in which these thoughts are discussed reflects the fact that these seven were seen as interconnected.[17] So, for example, Cassian groups the vices in pairs; the deadly thoughts form alliances against us.[18] Accordingly, the first two on the list—gluttony and lust—belong together. One who gives in to gluttony is a goner for lust; conversely, one who conquers the former should have less trouble with the latter. The reason for this particular connection sounds laughable to us: it was thought that a full belly put pressure on the genitals and excited them: "when the one is inordinately pampered, the other is doubtless excited to wantonness."[19] But the alliance is not lost on our modern culture: food and sex are often associated in our commercials, for instance. Consider a Burger King ad in Singapore that pitched the BK Super Seven Incher by depicting a woman set to orally take in all seven inches of the sandwich with the text, "It'll blow your mind away." The fast-food chain Carl's Jr. advertised its hamburgers by having Hugh Hefner declare his preference for a different piece of meat every night, while its cousin, Hardee's, portrayed a megamodel having an erotic relationship with a burger. And these are just the hamburger ads. Cereal, coffee, and soft drinks, to name just a few more products, have been in the mix as well. The long historical connection between food and sex is not lost on Madison Avenue.

We have noted the early Christian awareness that capital sins like gluttony have offspring, are related to other capital sins, and lead to a host of other "thoughts" and grave sins. This is helpful for understanding the debilitating effects of bad habits related to food consumption. For example, to ensure a constant supply of food to satisfy our appetites beyond the body's needs, we might engage in undesirable activities which bring harm to ourselves (such as bulimic episodes) or to others (such as contributing to world hunger). We might find ourselves working harder and longer to earn the money to indulge our appetites. We might be envious of others who can afford more food or dine on the exotic. We may be searching for the ever new taste sensation (something to which the food companies appeal with perennially "new and improved" or repackaged products). Food can become a status symbol as we try to top the last dinner party or treat each other to the most exclusive restaurants. For food we sacrifice the psychological serenity that comes with moderation and simplicity. And to ice the cake, it seems that the more we eat, the less we enjoy.[20]

The connections observed between these vices and sins in everyday life is the genius of ascetic theologians like Evagrius, and they become increasingly clear when we explore the features of gluttony.

As we said, gluttony is more than simply overeating and it is not merely fatness. Nor does gluttony merely consist of our desire for food, the consumption of it, or the pleasure we derive from eating it. The sin of gluttony has to do with the *manner* in which we consume food, involving *inordinate* desire and *immoderate* pleasure.[21] To be more specific, Evagrius, Cassian, Gregory, and Aquinas all delineate several aspects of gluttony that we can reduce to six.[22] They involve both acts and thoughts (or attitudes). One has to do with what we commonly think of as gluttony: *gorging ourselves* and not savoring a reasonable amount of food. A second involves timing: *eating at any other time than the appointed hour*. For the eremitic monk this usually involved the one meal at *none* (i.e., 3:00 p.m.) or later. For the cenobite this involved eating with the community at the prescribed times. The third aspect is *anticipating eating with preoccupied, eager longing*. The hermit who had his desires under control would not be checking the angle of the sun every fifteen minutes. A fourth aspect was *eating expensively*— consuming costly foods. A fifth aspect of gluttony involved discontent with common food—*seeking after delicacies*. Since nutritional values of foods were not known, it was considered unnecessary and distracting to seek variety in one's diet. Being a "fussy eater" who is not satisfied with three varieties of cereal at hand might be a modern variation of this. These last two aspects are especially concerned with being content with what we have (cf. Phil. 4:11). The final aspect of gluttony involved *paying too much attention to food*. While this last is not what we typically equate with gluttony, it certainly applies to our contemporary situation, perhaps even more so than gorging ourselves, for it informs us that it is as gluttonous to be overscrupulous about the food we eat (and how our body looks) as it is to overindulge ourselves. In fact, this overconcern can become idolatry of the creation. One can see, then, that the evil of gluttony lies not in food itself nor in our need to eat it (with accompanying sensations of the palate), but in *how* we go about our eating and in the *thought* (or lack of thought) we give to our eating.

In her thoughts and activities, the glutton is also at fault in her relationships to others. This is especially significant for our culture which preaches entitlement to self-centered indulgence. What is increasingly important as we move from the desert monk Evagrius to Benedictine monasticism is the communal dimension of the principal thoughts like gluttony. This is implicit in the six aspects listed above. For example, gluttony can foster dislike of the monastic community. The symptoms of this might include an unwillingness to eat at the times appointed for communal meals, dissatisfaction with the food that is served to all, or a lack of concern for others by seeking more or better for oneself. When it comes to eating there is to be concern for the community rather than for one's own self-centered food requests: one is to eat what is offered as it has been prepared so as not to offend, shame, or annoy other members of the community.[23] Even if a monk is voluntarily fasting and guests arrive who need refreshment, he is to eat charitably with the guests.[24]

All of this is crucial in our contemporary situation, for we have come to realize that disordered eating often reflects disordered relationships (with ourselves, others, the earth, God). As Bringle puts it, eating disorders fester in private:

> When I cannot, or do not, or will not eat with my fellow creatures—or, when conversely, I cannot or do not seem to be able to stop eating—I am bodying forth the brokenness of a fallen world and of a distorted will. . . . Not only am I refusing and defying companionship; I am also refusing the carnal medium through which these gifts of grace appear.[25]

There *are* compassionate and charitable community-oriented gluttons. But, as Schimmel notes, "there is some correlation between a preoccupation with food and neglect of other responsibilities"—to significant others, to society, and to God.[26]

We have seen that gluttony involves the way that we desire and consume our food, particularly in the context of the communities in which we find ourselves. In an ultimate sense, gluttony refers to a desire or a longing that seeks filling. It is an "exaggerated and misplaced longing"[27]—the "inordinate desire" of which Aquinas speaks. As Gerald May points out, if we were looking at the *deadly* sin of gluttony from a psychodynamic perspective, we could speak of displacing our longing for God upon other things like food; it provides a way of trying to satisfy our longing for God that seems to protect our sense of personal power and demand the least sacrifice, though, in the end, gluttony does neither for us.[28] It can begin as a venial sin, disguised as enjoying God's good gifts, and rationalized by our contemporary ideology of self-indulgence.

Gregory seems to describe the contemporary experience of some who are gradually led into dysfunctional eating habits: "Gluttony is also wont to exhort the conquered heart, as if with reason, when it says, God has created all things clean, in order to be eaten, and he who refuses to fill himself with food, what else does he do but gainsay the gift that has been granted him." What follows is a "howling army, . . . [W]hen the hapless soul, once captured by the principal vices, is turned to madness by multiple iniquities, it is now laid waste with brutal cruelty."[29]

Nonetheless, the temptation to commit gluttonous acts (what May might call a God-given propensity to addiction) can teach us about ourselves and what it will require to maintain our health. The question now is how best to take what Bringle calls "the gift of hunger"[30]—that desire for necessary nourishment—and make it serve us in our relationships with others and God, rather than be enslaved to it. That is to say, what cures us? What restores and maintains our health?

The Remedy for Gluttony

Posing the question this way—using the metaphors of cure and health—is not to assume that all gluttonous eating habits and contemporary eating disorders are symptoms of an underlying biochemical problem beyond a victim's control. Actually, no one truly understands what causes anorexia, for instance, and treatment approaches vary with the etiological theories. There is not even agreement on the definitions of and the distinction between anorexia nervosa and bulimia. It is a complicated issue.[31] The assumption I am making is that eating problems have medical *and* moral dimensions, similar to most addictions.[32]

Ascetic theologians use the medical metaphor (e.g., see Evagrius, *Praktikos*, 56 and 79), but they differ from some of our contemporaries who use the language of disease to encourage the belief that people are not responsible for their vices and the disastrous consequences of their actions. This misuse of the medical metaphor lessens the feelings of guilt and discourages the development of self-control. The contemporary view is attractive because most of us would rather be sick than guilty. But the ascetic used the language of sickness, not to excuse us from responsibility for our vices, but to advise us as the soul's physician to change our habits before it is too late. In fact, if gluttony is a bad *habit*—a deadly sin—then it is so because the contemporary medical model is not exclusively true.

The ascetic theologian described the health of the soul as *apatheia*.[33] Though early monastics were influenced by Stoic and Neo-platonic philosophies, they adapted (rather than adopted) the Stoic concept of *apatheia*.[34] It is not simply the leveling out of human emotions or the extirpation of the passions.[35] Ascetics like Evagrius and Cassian took from the Stoics, Clement of

Alexandria, and Egyptian sources such as Anthony, and put their own stamp on this concept.[36] For them *apatheia* is an abiding sense of peace and joy that comes from the full harmony of the passions—an *habitual* state developed through discipline (*ascesis*), which is why we refer to it in terms of virtue. Thus, it fits in nicely with what we have said above about the misguided or inordinate desire that gluttony involves: through various exercises a person trains herself to be in full possession of her affective faculties so that disordered cravings for foods are held in check and rightly ordered, and one can experience a state of deep calm—a "repose," as Cassian calls it.[37] According to Evagrius, one of the marks of the presence of *apatheia* in a person's life is the ability to remain calm and peaceful even when he has memories of situations or events that tend to stimulate and disorder the passions.[38]

This harmonious integration of the emotional life always remains exposed to the attacks of demons, particularly in the case of gluttony, which, as we have said, trades on the necessity of nourishment and the pleasurable sensations from which we will never be free.[39] So emotional health—*apatheia*—must be maintained with effort. Of course, this is to be expected: good health is never a given; one must work at it with care. This implies that *apatheia* can be had (or lost) by degrees; one continually grows into it. Furthermore, it is subject to the limitations of one's unique constitution. This last point should not be overlooked when it comes to the medical side of eating disorders; we will take this up in a different vein when we discuss discernment in a moment.[40]

Evagrius teaches that the offspring of *apatheia* is *agapē*. Maintaining the harmony of one's passions enables a person fully to love others and God, because the acquisition of *apatheia* can stamp out anger, sulking, lust, resentment, envy, and all other impediments to self-giving love. Without love *apatheia* alone is of little value. Evagrius reminds us that the absence of distracting thoughts itself is not true prayer: "It is quite possible for a man to have none but the purest thoughts and yet be so distracted mulling over them that he remains the while far removed from God."[41] Gregory gets quite specific and illustrates for us in practical terms how even acquiring *apatheia* cannot be divorced from *agapē*:

> In this matter we must consider how little the virtue of abstinence is regarded, unless it deserve commendation by reason of other virtues. . . . To sanctify a fast is to show abstinence of the flesh to be worthy of God by other good things added to it [such as giving to the poor what one has abstained from]. . . . A man fasts not to God but to himself, if he does not give to the poor what he denies his belly for a time, but reserves it to be given to his belly later.[42]

Gregory refers here to a discipline, namely fasting, by which one gets a handle on gluttonous thoughts and redirects the appetite. It is *ascesis* that leads to *apatheia*. Evagrius puts it succinctly:

> *Agapē* is the progeny of *apatheia*. *Apatheia* is the very flower of *ascesis*. *Ascesis* consists in keeping the commandments. The custodian of these commandments is the fear of God which is in turn the offspring of true faith. Now faith is an interior good, one which is to be found even in those who do not yet believe in God.[43]

Let us see how the discipline of fasting, as understood by the ascetic theologians, might be applied to a contemporary imagined case of one who is on the verge of developing an eating disorder.

The Case of Frieda

Suppose Frieda, a college professor, stashes food in her office, takes advantage of every free all-you-can-eat meal and reception at the college, and goes for frequent visits to the vending machines and campus coffee shop. Eating has a way of relieving her stress, comforting her, and picking up her spirits. The problem is that when she comforts herself "too much" she feels depressed. (Recall Gregory's observations about the "howling army.") She does not consider herself anorexic or bulimic . . . yet; she is smart enough to know about the symptoms and rational enough to want to avoid developing debilitating (and eventually fatal) habits.[44] But she is becoming aware of disturbing patterns. Add to this the guilt she feels. For one thing, she has been known to cancel appointments with students who need her help because she fears missing a generous spread of delicacies at receptions for retiring faculty, the brownies and cookies a half-hour before faculty meetings, or the unlimited supply of food at free luncheons to which she has been invited. She can rationalize her attendance at these functions because, after all, they involve associating with her colleagues and she is not bingeing in private at these times. Nonetheless, all of this hints to her that something might be up. And then there is the poor self-image she has from gorging on food that is loaded with calories and fat; in fact, she has become preoccupied with reading food labels when shopping and calculating the caloric and fat content of foods she consumes, even though this preoccupation does not stop her from bingeing. The food that sometimes gives her comfort and a sense of control now more often causes her to experience anxiety, shame, guilt, and feelings of failure.

Frieda is developing the vice of gluttony. She exhibits four features of this "deadly thought" that our ascetic theologians have identified. She gorges herself and eats more than what is necessary. She anticipates eating, and she eats far more often than the "appointed" times (not that there is anything virtuous in three meals per day, though there might be something virtuous about some regularity to our eating schedule; at least monks think so). And she pays so much attention to her eating that it preoccupies her mind (and time) inordinately, keeping her from pursuing tasks that have to do with her gifts and calling in life and from spending time with others. She knows she has a problem—that she is in danger of "making a god of her belly." So she decides to explore the disciplines of fasting and abstinence.

She discovers that fasting is not what Jenny Craig and SlimFast mean by dieting. There are some similarities: controlling what you eat or don't eat; substituting alternative activities for eating. But it is especially her motivation and goal that make this discipline different: simply put, she wants to become a healthy Christian person who is able to love God and others (and herself) as she is commanded. Dieting always tended to put the focus on herself (especially on her appearance) and on cultural idols.[45] While a Christian concern for the body might include a moderate concern for fat and caloric intake and one's weight and appearance, it will be driven chiefly by the spiritual concern to develop attitudes of contentment, gratitude, trust, and patience. These are the aims that radically distinguish the discipline the church has called "fasting" from what our culture calls "dieting."

As she fasts—abstaining from eating between meals (though she does not neglect associating with colleagues) and occasionally even skipping lunch—she meditates on certain portions of Scripture (such as Ps. 119:57–72 and Matt. 6:25–34), as well as on creation through which God manifests himself.[46] She is wise to do this according to ascetic theologians, for the principal thoughts of gluttony and lust require *both* bodily abstinence and a "fast of the soul"—a double remedy for such carnal thoughts. Meditating on Scripture and cultivating a love of certain virtues will help Frieda to fast from thoughts such as anxiety over not fitting cultural expectations and the distrust that she will not find peace of mind without something to munch on. This will make her bodily fast useful and profitable, according to Cassian.[47]

During her times of fasting Frieda gains several insights about herself and God. Through fasting itself she understands even better what had been controlling her life; and she finds that the small incremental steps she takes toward controlling her eating passions give her some mastery over other areas of her life. Furthermore, she discovers that underlying her anxiety about food is a lack of trust in God: a fear to live according to God's commandments, a fear to be content with the way that God has made her, and especially a fear that there might not be adequate food for her to consume (a common irrational fear among bulimics)—something with which her meditations on Psalm 119 and Matthew 6 help her, for they teach her about a Lord whose earth is filled with God's steadfast love and a caretaker who watches over even flowers and sparrows.[48] The bonus in all of this is that her love for God is growing, since she is learning in various areas of her life what it means to trust God as one trusts a good parent; *and* she is displaying loving behavior toward her students in a way that she had not been able to because her bad eating habits had interfered. She now keeps her appointments, does not feel the need to rush through interviews in order to get to her stash or a reception, and is even more intent on what students are communicating because her mind and her body are not filled with food. She has entered the arena of spiritual contest and is beginning to experience victory over the first opponent. Other victories will come in time, such as the defeat of envy of the trim female colleague down the hall. As Cassian puts it, the soul is made more vigorous by the course of triumphs.[49]

Frieda has discovered what Christians from Evagrius to Dallas Willard have taught: the remedy for deadly thoughts is the application of an opposite behavior, a positive counterpractice.[50] In Frieda's case the counterpractice involved fasting and abstinence, accompanied by an amateur's attempt at spiritual reading (*lectio divina*). But for such discipline to have life-transforming effects Frieda must also attend to other aspects of the ascetics' therapeutic prescription.

First, we return to the emphasis on community in ascetic theology—an emphasis that gains momentum as we move from Egyptian eremitic (solo) monasticism to Benedictine cenobitic (communal) monasticism (though it is not absent from the former). In fact, it is inherent in the nature of ascetic and monastic wisdom itself, for one learns about the dangers in eating habits and the way to combat them and the connections such behaviors sustain to other sins through the collective wisdom of those who have experienced the same faults and have overcome them. These are the *abbas* in the desert to whom one goes for advice. Later this becomes the abbot who directs his monks with the wisdom that has been passed on.[51] Furthermore, in the monastic coenobium virtues are modeled; as Cassian puts it, we find Christ "bit by bit in all."[52] Frieda will need to depend on the wisdom of those who have gone before her, whether through spiritual direction (similar to the *abba* in the desert or the abbot of the monastery) or the modeling and support of the community (or, indeed, both). She has already done this to some extent by meditating on Scripture, particularly since monastic rules claimed to be doing nothing more than handing down the wisdom of Scripture as that had been lived out by various successful individuals. But she might also confide in a trusted and wise friend, a counselor, or a pastor. If her problem has progressed to the point of true bulimia, she will need a support group related to eating disorders. As we have seen, Evagrius insisted that insights which come from self-knowledge, observation, tradition, and the wisdom of our forebears give us power to deal with our deadly thoughts.[53] If it is true that eating disorders appreciate their privacy, the obverse seems to be true from monastic experience: eating can be ordered in and through community. Certainly this is the experience of contemporary twelve-step groups. The wisdom of the "masters" (those who have successfully dealt with their problem) and communal accountability and support are crucial.

Second, temperance is the virtue Frieda is cultivating.[54] This coincides with another emphasis in ascetic theology which evolves as one gets closer to Benedictine spirituality—namely, the emphasis on moderation. Despite stereotypes of ascetic and monastic theology, Cassian, Benedict, and Gregory denounce the monk's attempt to become a spiritual superhero. With different degrees of emphasis, from the desert to the *Rule of Benedict*, the focus is on moderation and balance in life. A monk is to take what the body needs, while avoiding the vice of satiety. These Christian psychologists observed that it is easier to be a total abstainer than one who is moderate and balanced in her life. In fact, Gregory's observations on this point are worth citing:

> And sometimes, while we endeavour to oppose our desires too immoderately, we increase the miseries of necessity. For it is necessary for a man so to maintain the citadel of continence, as to destroy, not the flesh, but the vices of the flesh. For frequently, when the flesh is restrained more than is just, it is weakened even for the exercises of good works, so as to be unequal to prayer also or preaching, whilst it hastens to put out entirely the incentives of vices within itself. For this very man, whom we bear outwardly, we have as the assistant of our inward intention, and both the motions of wantonness are within it, and there also abound in it the appliances of good works. But often, whilst we attack an enemy therein, we kill a citizen also whom we love; and after which we spare, as it were, a fellow citizen, we nurture an enemy for battle. For our vices become proud upon the same food, on which our virtues are nourished and live. And when a virtue is nourished, the strength of our vices is frequently increased. But when unbounded abstinence weakens the power of vices, our virtue also faints and pants.[55]

In *Pastoral Care* Gregory offers advice on counseling *both* the gluttonous *and* the abstemious; he reminds us that "vices commonly masquerade as virtues."[56] Anticipating Gregory, Cassian voices a similar insight that corresponds exactly to what we find in contemporary cases of bulimia. Cassian warns us against too severe fasting because it easily leads to unnecessary relaxation regarding eating after the fast is over: "A reasonable supply of food partaken of daily with moderation, is better than a severe and long fast at intervals. Excessive fasting has been known not only to undermine the constancy of the mind, but also to weaken the power of prayers through sheer weariness of body."[57] Ascetic theologians, such as Cassian, know that gluttony is often incited by severe fasting. This is precisely the pattern of bingeing and purging that is seen in eating disorders. Obsessive dieting and self-restraint often result in compulsive eating, not in response to physical hunger, but in response to stress and anxiety. The one who is overly scrupulous about caloric and fat intake and weight loss (recall one of the six aspects of gluttony) is more often the one who compensates (in private) by overindulging.[58]

To understand this better, we might call attention to another dimension of this emphasis on moderation found in Benedict's rule where Benedict insists that the monk is not to engage in an unusually austere fast because of the damage it might do to his spiritual life (e.g., it could lead to pride). If he really wants to engage in such a fast, he can do so only with the permission of the abbot. Why? Because discernment is needed in *each individual* case. Benedict never had in mind that souls are to be mass produced. Each has different needs, and in the monastic community the abbot is the one who is qualified (and given the terrifying responsibility) to know the condition of each of his sheep and prescribe for them just what they need to remain healthy and grow spiritually.[59] Since Benedict begins his rule by insisting that only those who have advanced in the coenobium (the "*schola* for the Lord's service") can go alone into the desert to fight the demons as hermits, we must assume that after a period of time the discerning qualities of the abbot will have been internalized by the monk, so that his own reason can make proper judgments about how to combat the deadly thoughts and the demons who use them in their attacks. Again, the parallels to contemporary psychology should not be lost on us at this point.

Cassian refers to this discernment as the "judgment of conscience," insisting that such discernment does not allow hard and fast rules.[60] All of us are attacked by these faults, but not in the same way. Gregory instructs the counselor to adapt the same doctrine to the character and needs of each individual, as a skillful harpist plays with a variety of strokes to produce a harmonious melody.[61] Cassian finds that this applies especially to gluttony and fasting, because, unlike other vices and virtues, this one has to do with the body; so the time, manner, and quality of refreshment depend upon the condition, age, and sex of the person's body.[62] This has direct application to some of the current thinking about eating disorders.

Our culture imposes a cookie-cutter standard on everyone regarding eating requirements and weight-to-height ratios. "RDA" lists on cans and boxes become gospel for people watching their fat and caloric intake; insurance companies determine who is "*over*weight" based on charts that have not always taken into account ethnic and gender differences. (One standard chart was based on white males, but the standards were applied to all insurance applicants.)[63] Even the term "overweight" is presumptuous if it ignores the current theory that each person has a *set point* for his or her weight—the weight that is right for each person (who has a certain metabolism, number of fat cells, and so forth due to a nexus of inherited predispositions, environmental influences, and individual responses) which the body works to maintain against extremes at either end.[64] The set point can *increase* if a person engages in roller-coaster dieting. What we need is not for the media, the diet industry, and the modeling and entertainment businesses to dictate to us what a healthy person *looks* like; we need discernment to know our own bodies well enough that we feed them what they *need* and apply the remedy that fits our specific compulsions. If Frieda compares herself to a trim colleague whose set-point weight is lower than hers or if she buys into the culture's definition of what spiritually and physically healthy people *look* like, her guilt and shame may be fueled for illegitimate reasons. She must come to know herself as God has fashioned her and learn to accept herself in a way that might even be countercultural. We are all attacked by gluttonous thoughts—but not all in the same way.

Frieda needs to move toward health step-by-step, certainly a fundamental principle of twelve-step groups, but nothing new since the observations of Cassian and Gregory. For instance, as a twist on what we have just said about cultural standards dictating our self-image, both theologians suggested that the deadly thoughts are connected in such a way that vainglory might be used to deal with gluttony as a first step. Cassian notes that this works only in the coenobium, not in the desert, for in the latter nobody is around to see you fast and support you with praise, whereas in the former one grows fat on the notice of others. When gluttonous thoughts are under control, vainglory can be dealt with down the pike; there is less harm in it, but it is more difficult to escape.[65]

For instance, Frieda might be motivated to get a handle on her gluttonous thoughts at first because she does not like the way that her relation to students has been going due to her preoccupation with food. Perhaps she is embarrassed by her teaching evaluations: "Professor is not available" . . . "She did not keep three appointments." Once Frieda gets a handle on her eating habits and her relationship with students improves, she may find that she no longer needs to be motivated by her professional reputation, since good habits have indeed been established, and since she finds her improved performance as a professor to be intrinsically rewarding. In fact, her victory over gluttony may serve to steel her for the later battle against vainglory.

Given what we have said before, Frieda must be vigilant to maintain the harmonious integration of her passions, especially those having to do with eating, since, according to everyone from Evagrius to Aquinas, we are especially prone to succumb to the sensation of touch associated with the palate. Furthermore, Gregory suggests that enemies are incited by triumphs. This is echoed in the basic tenet of groups like Alcoholics Anonymous and other twelve-step groups: one is always a *recovering* addict. This has been challenged by a program called Rational Recovery, a secular alternative to traditional twelve-step programs: "In Rational Recovery, members recognize their 'addictive voice,' called 'the beast,' and learn how to ignore or confront and defeat it. They believe that at some point they have recovered from drinking or using drugs, and can stop attending meetings."[66]

The interesting question, of course, is whether the ascetic theologians ever believed that they had arrived and could "stop attending meetings." There is enough in the sayings of the desert fathers and ascetic and monastic theologians to suggest that in *theory* it was possible to arrive, while in *practice* it never happens. Evagrius certainly would not have rejected the first of the twelve steps in favor of Rational Recovery's assumption of inherent rational power over addictions. While reason's control of the passions is taught by these theologians—a point we will develop in the next chapter—they insist that the *first* thing we must understand is that we cannot win these battles in our own strength; humility must be cultivated.[67]

A conscious human being can never be free from the temptation of the deadly thought of gluttony. In fact, Cassian is adamant that while we must cut out the roots of the other principal faults, we cannot possibly cut off occasions of gluttony.[68] As Dallas Willard argues throughout *The Spirit of the Disciplines*, we were created to be embodied beings, and there is nothing that we do spiritually that does not involve the body. God has chosen to deal with us through and in our bodily existence; to ignore that fact would be to join what Bringle calls a "new gnosticism." Though the ascetic theologians were sometimes suspicious of the body, they did not disparage it or adopt some gnostic dualism that might have ignored the body's needs to serve the soul. Martha is needed so that Mary can sit at the Lord's feet:

> A brother went to see Abba Silvanus on the mountain of Sinai. When he saw the brothers working hard he said to the old man, "Do not labor for the food which perishes (John 6:27). Mary has chosen the good portion" (Luke 10:42). The old man said to his disciple, "Zacharias, give the brother a book and put him in a cell without anything else." So when the ninth hour came the visitor watched the door expecting someone would be sent to call him to the meal. When no-one called him he got up, went to find the old man and said to him, "Have the brothers not eaten today?" The old man replied that they had. Then he said, "Why did you not call me?" The old man said to him, "Because you are a spiritual man and do not need that kind of food. We, being carnal, want to eat, and that is why we work. But you have chosen the good portion and read the whole day long and you do not want to eat carnal food." When he heard these words the brother made a prostration saying, "Forgive me, abba." The old man said to him, "Mary needs Martha. It is really thanks to Martha that Mary is praised."[69]

An adequate theology to undergird any discussion of eating habits must neither oversacralize nor desecrate the body.[70] It is not wrong to attend to the needs of the body nor to enjoy sensations from what touches the body. At times, however, it is difficult to discern when our enjoyment exceeds necessity, particularly, as Gregory suggests, when we think of inordinate pleasure as a necessity. This is especially pertinent for us moderns—including some psychologists—who see self-indulgence as not only a need, but a right. In Gregory's words, "Those things must therefore be taken, which the necessity of nature requires, and not those which gluttony suggests."[71] Gregory admits that this is easier said than done, and it is precisely why a person must know her body as well as her soul if she is going to keep her passions in order. When people like Frieda eat only at regular intervals, slowly, and without being overscrupulous, they tend to savor even the ordinary, and the pleasure they receive from eating has a lasting and healthful effect.

Final Thoughts . . . and a Preview of What's to Come

The majority of us do not suffer from clinically diagnosed eating disorders. But we are not beyond the advice of ascetic theologians when it comes to gluttony. In some ways the goal of *apatheia* seems a second cousin to one of the three vows that a Benedictine monk takes: stability. Specifically, the vow of stability commits a monastic to the same community for the rest of his or her life. As the desert fathers put it, "Stay in your cell, and your cell will teach you everything." One who stays in her community is open to the transforming effects of God's grace, because, as in a long and good marriage, one eventually cuts through the superficial-ity, the guile, and the confusion in such a way that a deep and quiet love can flow. And this is precisely what the *ascesis*—the exercise of the disciplines—is meant to do. The disciplines are a spiritual angioplasty that keeps a person open to receive the life-transforming grace of God so that it can eventually flower into the love of God and neighbor. There is something extraor-dinarily ordinary about all of this, but it is as revolutionary in our present culture as virginity and lifetime monogamy. Stability calls us to regulate our desires and impulses, to be satisfied with the food that is set before us, to avoid an inordinate preoccupa-tion with what is in the package or how it is going to make us look, to refuse to succumb to the constant titillation of "new and improved" taste sensations, and to reject making food a status symbol. Then we might stop long enough to dwell on our hungers to experience how tasty the faithfulness of God is.

In fact, if we have learned nothing else from these ascetic theologians, we should understand that our appetites are linked, so that an ordinate appetite for food might not only help us to learn to savor what we read with moderation and to pray less as consumers and more as lovers, but it might also sharpen our appetite for the kingdom of God and God's righteousness. We need to hunger between meals and instead of meals in order to be empty long enough to realize we are dependent and vulnerable, biodegradable creatures of necessity, who need God's sustaining grace and the loving support of others. Bingeing on pleasure and voraciously seeking new stimulations can keep us from savoring the awareness of God's faithful presence in the daily bread that can satisfy the necessities of our bodily existence. By entering deeply into the tedious necessity of eating we might take pleasure in just the way God made each one of us, and we might recognize what will eventually fully satisfy our hunger. That is indeed the lesson of the Eucharist: our gratitude to God is expressed in our reception of the tiny morsel and swig that is given us, for such a small amount taken after the fast at once both sharpens and satisfies our hunger and thirst for God.

3

※

Lust

Abstinence Resistant

> But what advantage is it to restrain the flesh by con-
> tinence, if the mind is uninstructed to expand itself
> by compassion in the love of our neighbor?
>
> Gregory, *Morals on Job*

Food and Sex

According to the tradition of the monastic elders, after gluttony
the second battle is "the spirit of fornication," three types of
which Cassian lists and the last of which we would call "lust"—
the kind of thing that Jesus said is conceived in the heart (Matt.
5:27–28).[1]

As we saw in the last chapter, in the thinking of these premoderns gluttony and lust—food and sex—are related to each
other more closely than simply the fact that one is listed after

the other. For instance, Evagrius contends that "he who controls the stomach diminishes the passions; he who is overcome by food gives increase to pleasures."[2] Cassian ascribes one of three causes of "nocturnal discharge" (what we ordinarily call "wet dreams") to immoderate eating: "the vice of covetousness of the mouth, that is, of voracity and gluttony" that precedes the fast. As he explains, excessive eating "naturally and necessarily" causes humors to form that are expelled on the occasion of "some itching or fantasy."[3]

Centuries later Aquinas recognized what Carl's Jr. and Hardee's have since advertised, that the stomach and the sex organs are "neighbors." Aquinas argued that there is a biological connection between the emission of semen and a surplus of food: "the nutritive power"—as excessive as it might be—is needed for "the work of the generative power."[4] Of course, Aquinas notes an important distinction: while both gluttony and lust are mortal sins, one act of intercourse that leads to a conception out of wedlock would, in Aquinas's reckoning, hinder the good of a future child, while one meal does not necessarily alter the whole condition of a person's life (unless it's the kind of "meal" that Adam ate!).[5]

The connection that Cassian and Aquinas make, albeit based on what Terrence Kardong describes as "quaint pre-scientific notions of human biology,"[6] is corroborated by recent studies on sexual addiction, similar to a connection that we found in eating disorder studies in the previous chapter.

Though conditions such as alcoholism, smoking, drug abuse and compulsive gambling were thought of and treated in isolation from each other, by the late 1990s the coexistence and interaction of multiple addictions was accepted along with strategies that were developed to treat them.[7] This included overconsumption and under-consumption in both eating disorders and sexual addiction. (There *is* "sexual anorexia," just as there is anorexia as an eating disorder.) Patrick Carnes (who coined the term and concept of "sexual addiction" in 1983)[8] studied one thousand inpatient sex addicts and found that 38 percent of them reported having eating disorders, while another study (whose subjects were women only) found that sex and food addictions ritualized together ran a close second to the combined addictions of sex and alcohol or drugs.[9] And just as we saw in the previous chapter, it doesn't take a professional psychologist to recognize the connection; our culture encourages it with adages such as "The way to a man's heart is through his stomach" and "Take her to a nice restaurant and you can have her for dessert."

The good news is that the person struggling with food disorders, sexual addictions, or both does not have to give up either food or sex. The goal is to avoid extremes—to eat well and have healthy sexual relations. In fact, as we will see, Cassian is very realistic when it comes to this vice, especially since lust, like gluttony, has to do with our embodied existence as well as our heart. For that reason, he observes that few can claim complete victory over the lust that begins at puberty and "does not cease until the other vices have been conquered."[10]

Irrational Sex

In his conferences on fornication, chastity, and "nocturnal illusions," Cassian is actually more realistic and less embarrassed than the Victorian translators who refused to translate his teachings in the three chapters on the subject in the *Nicene and Post-Nicene Fathers* series that was published in the late 1800s. (They even left untranslated the sentences of preceding chapters that led into these discussions. They must have assumed that only those adept at translating foreign languages are spiritual enough to deal with lust!) For one thing, Cassian insists that perfect chastity does not imply sinlessness. He insists that no one can be without sin, whether it is through ignorance, negligence, design, impulse, forgetfulness, or, as we will clarify later, sleep.

(He also says we can be "surprised" by a sinful thought.) He is adamant: the only immaculate one—the *only* one without sin—was Jesus.[11]

Cassian's realistic approach also acknowledges natural biological faculties and processes without trivializing them, and, as we will see, he deals with mundane bodily particulars without being prudish. As Terrence Kardong puts it, "Although he was an ascetic who had 'fled the world,' he was aware of the same basic facts of life as we are, but he comes to different conclusions from the data."[12] In fact, he recognizes that our libido has its place in overcoming lethargy; the struggles of the body are useful for us, as is demonstrated in the contrary case of eunuchs who are slow to pursue virtues because they believe they are in no danger of violating a chaste disposition.[13] He encourages his monks to satisfy the natural demands of the flesh "without arousing desire" and to get rid of excess humors "without any harmful prurience and without necessitating a struggle for chastity." As was the case with gluttony, so with lust: one should maintain "a balanced and moderate fast" to ensure that "immoderate relaxation" does not prevent one from experiencing a "state of tranquility."[14]

A similar attitude is required to overcome sexual addiction. As Patrick Carnes notes, sex addicts "often come from highly repressive families and carry damaging myths inside them," so that recovery requires "restructuring the belief system by acquiring adequate information and accepting one's own sexuality."[15] As if echoing Cassian's advice about our inescapably embodied existence, Carnes states, "Unlike an alcoholic who can abstain and maintain sobriety, the sexual addict has to face the fact of his or her own sexuality. Like the overeater, recovery does not mean the elimination of fundamental human processes. Celibacy does not resolve the problem."[16] As we will see, this last sentence is even more profound when we read it in the context of what Cassian teaches about chastity.

What Cassian's approach implies is that we must distinguish temptation from sin—something like Martin Luther's quip that we can't keep the birds from flying over our heads, but we can keep them from building nests in our hair. As we have implied in the previous chapter, how we were created, what we are now in our fallen condition, and what we are to become is taken into account by the tradition that Evagrius left to Cassian, Gregory, and even Aquinas. For instance, in the *Morals on Job*, Gregory teaches that in our present human condition we are struck by wrong thinking against our will. These thoughts can come from our senses or our memory, such that they can become *instruments*, but not the *source* of sin. In themselves they do not defile the rational part of the soul that ought to be in control. But when we consent to the wrong thought and take delight in it, we have moved from temptation to sin's reign in us. Gregory insists that as long as we live we will never be perfectly and wholly without "unlawful longings," but they do not have to "win an entrance" and gain dominion. Sin touches the mind in thought, but it does not have to master us by our consent. Gregory suggests that to keep from being so mastered we need to keep in mind that we serve the one who made us, a sentiment echoed by Aquinas when he argues that lust uses the body inordinately so that such a person wrongs God who is the Supreme Lord of the body.[17]

Essentially what is argued here is based on an understanding of the soul whereby its lower levels are to be controlled by the higher rational faculty. (See the appendix for a more detailed explanation.) But when the "demons" make use of "thoughts" (*logismoi*) that are good in themselves, what was good in nature (such as our sex drive) can be warped, and we succumb to lust. The progression is from thought, which is linked to sensory impression, to which consent is then given, so that what *was* a thought has now become a "passion" and, if given into habitually, becomes a deadly sin.

Aquinas makes this clear in his definition of "lust": "The more necessary a thing is, the more it behooves one to observe the order of reason in its regard; wherefore the more sinful it becomes if the order of reason be forsaken. . . . Now lust consists essentially in exceeding the order and mode of reason in the matter of venereal acts."[18] And the temptation is strong because "venereal pleasure" is "intense and connatural to humans" and thus very desirable.[19] Almost echoing Evagrius verbatim, Aquinas says that when the lower powers of our soul (the lower appetites—concupiscence) are strongly moved toward their objects, the higher powers (reason and will) are hindered and disordered in their proper activities.[20]

So, in the end Aquinas nicely brings us back to where Evagrius began: passions are not the direct nor even the sufficient cause of sexual sin, but only its occasion. The direct cause of such sin is when one fails to resist a passion by the use of reason, either because one did not think it through ahead of time or because after one *did* think it through the lower impulses won out.[21] And Aquinas recognizes that when it comes to sex we *do* tend to be *more* impetuous and *less* inclined to listen to reason than is the case with pleasures of the palate, so that greater "chastisement and restraint" is needed.[22]

Again, there are parallels with aspects of addiction as Carnes describes it: "First, addiction taps into the most fundamental human processes. Whether the need is to be high, to be sexual, to eat, or even to work, the addictive process can turn creative, life-giving energy into a destructive, demoralizing compulsivity."[23] Translating this into ancient monastic characterizations of the soul with its lower and higher faculties would not be difficult. And Aquinas's description of impetuosity and the inferior strength of reason anticipates the psychological description of "impulsions" as unrelenting urges that demand immediate gratification, are acted upon without forethought of longer-range consequences, and are difficult to resist despite knowledge of potential adverse consequences (such as, in the case of sexual activity, STDs, arrest, bodily harm, etc.). If the impulsive behavior to produce pleasurable effects becomes a pattern (or is repeated *compulsive* behavior to evade painful internal states) then it warrants the label "addiction"—or, for ancient psychologists, "deadly sin."[24]

Battling Lust on Two Fronts

Lust, like gluttony and like sexual addictions, has to be countered on two fronts—mind and body. It is a sin committed either in thought or deed. Citing 1 Peter 1:13, Gregory tells us, "For to 'gird up the loins' of the flesh is to withhold lust from accomplishment, but 'to gird up the loins of the mind' is to restrain it from the imagining thereof as well," warning that the crafty enemy "defiles by secret thought" when he does not succeed with the deed.[25]

On the physical front Cassian tells us to flee—to engage in "bodily fasting." This is the opposite counsel he gives with regard to other vices, such as anger, for those are cured *by* provocations experienced in the human community. They are "cured by the very committing," because "the more frequently these faults come to the surface and are rebuked, the more quickly they are healed." But in the case of sexual sin, Cassian admonishes "solitude and distance from others."[26]

Terrence Kardong says that this indicates Cassian is not optimistic about the cultivation of chastity in the context of cenobitic (community) life.[27] That said, Cassian may not concur with the advice of sexual addiction therapists who recognize that recovery from addictions happens more readily when family members are involved in the treatment, particularly if they are "co-addicts."[28] (We *have* seen, however, that temporary isolation from one's social nexus is often part of the treatment in severe cases of eating disorders.) And on the flip side, it is the addiction itself that leads to distance from others, as Carnes articulates: ". . . the more intensely involved in compulsive sexual life the addicts become, the more alienated they become from their parents, spouses, and children. Without those human connections, the addicts paradoxically lose touch with their own selves."[29] This was vividly and sadly portrayed in the movie *Shame* in which Brandon, a sex addict, was unable to sustain a healthy relationship with his sister or with a woman with whom he desperately desired to be in love. Recovery requires establishment in a caring community—"the reversal of the alienation that is integral to the addiction,"[30] and seemingly the reversal of what Cassian would suggest.

Cassian even counsels the monk to avoid lingering over the thought, let alone being in the presence, of women who are relatives—even mothers and sisters. This sounds strange, but his concern has to do with how the presence of even female relatives might lead us to think of *other* women and so bring on lustful thoughts.[31] Gregory shares this concern about the power of memories or mental images that tempt us to the point that the "shield of resolution . . . lies pierced with the javelin of self-indulgence" so that we give in to lustful thoughts as if we had never resolved not to, even bearing as punishment irrepressible memories of illicit acts we once did that we had considered to be pleasure.[32]

Because Gregory realistically knows that it involves a great struggle to "unloose the image of a shape once bound on the heart," he argues that we cannot be too careful in foreseeing what would trigger a lustful desire. As he puts it, the one who wants to remain chaste must make a "covenant with his eyes, lest he should first see without caution what he might afterwards love against his will." To keep purity of heart we must "discipline the exterior senses."[33]

It is precisely the care to "close the windows of the body as against a plotting enemy" that might have kept the Louisiana

Pentecostal preacher and televangelist Jimmy Swaggart from a second episode, let alone the first that led to his 1988 televised confession to his family and congregation for sexual indiscretions. As a charismatic preacher with a worldwide television ministry bringing in $140 to $150 million annually, pastor of a 7,500-seat worship center, and founder of Jimmy Swaggart Bible College, he was confronted by church leaders with pictures depicting him with a prostitute. As one reporter put it, "Less visibly, he was fighting a secret war with Satan and it is now clear—he was losing it."[34] After denominational rebuke and subsequent excommunication from the denomination, once again he was found in the company of a prostitute about three years later. Of course, sadly, Swaggart's case is not exceptional, but it helps to make the point that Cassian's and Gregory's advice to flee with foresight might be a strategy that would help save a multimillion dollar worldwide ministry from imploding.

It would be wrong, though, for those outside the monastic enclosure to flee in such a way that they end up becoming "sexual anorexics." This was the cautionary advice given at the end of a report on a study of evangelical clients who self-identified as sex addicts. Because they struggled with sexual behaviors considered to be immoral or sinful, some dealt with feelings of guilt and shame by depriving themselves of *any* sexual contact, even if moral and virtuous. This not only might become as problematic as the sexual behavior the client *had* been struggling with, but it also might risk subsequent sexual bingeing, not unlike what we discussed with regard to eating disorders and the monastic caution against severe fasts.[35]

Though we have been focusing on strategies involving the body, it should be apparent that the body cannot be separated from the spirit or mind. Cassian *does* make a point of arguing that "bodily fasting" alone is not what enables us to acquire or retain perfect chastity "unless we also have a contrite spirit and persevere in prayer against this filthy spirit." And this must also include constant meditation on Scripture (something Evagrius practiced with the strategy in the *Antirrhetickos*–categorized lists of Scripture verses to counter sinful thoughts),[36] "spiritual understanding," manual labor to keep the fickle mind from wandering, and true humility ("the foundation without which no vice can ever be conquered," and about which we will have more to say later).[37]

One strategy that Cassian mentions is very insightful. He teaches that we should not try to rid ourselves of passionate desires. (Again, *apatheia* is not simply "passionlessness.") Like driving out a nail with a nail, we should *replace* illicit desires with wholesome ones:

> The desire for present things cannot be repressed or removed unless we replace the harmful things we want to remove with healthy ones. The soul cannot exist in any vital way without some feelings of desire or fear, or joy or sorrow. This must be turned to good account. If we chase carnal concupiscence from our hearts, we should immediately plant spiritual desires in their place so that our soul may always be occupied with them and have a safe base from which to reject the enticements of present and temporal joys.[38]

And he appeals to Psalm 16:8 ("I keep the Lord always before me") to encourage his monks to hone the mind with daily exercises.

In contemporary terms Cassian's instruction is insightful if put in the context of what we now know about the brain's circuitry. The brain works indiscriminately on the basis of do-pamine-enabled "rewards" that result from a substance or an experience, so it can be hijacked by addictions that reward behaviors like eating and intercourse that are necessary for survival. If an addict is made to understand that addictions are unhealthy ways of experiencing the neuro-rewards then the person can be motivated to find other more healthy rewards: "Identifying significant sources of natural highs and healthy reward-producing activities then becomes a major focus of therapy."[39]

An example of this sublimation comes from a self-identified evangelical sex addict who developed an approach for coping with daily temptations. Besides patterning the day with times of meditation and prayer, he articulated this strategy: "You see a beautiful woman, and you say, 'God, thank you for that beautiful woman. I hope she has a nice day. My name is yada yada. I love my God. I love my wife. I love my son. I love my daughter,' and by that time, your mind is turned, and you're away from that."[40]

So in many respects, ancient monks and contemporary psychologists instruct us to engage in similar strategies to deal with the physical and the mental aspects of lust—disciplines that go far, but, like the title of a perceptive book on addiction, *Willpower Is Not Enough*, disciplines are not enough. And with this insight we are led to the most significant teaching about lust that Cassian offers.

Chastity versus Abstinence

Columba Stewart argues that the reason monks practiced asceticism was precisely to demonstrate its limits. The disciplined life can only take a person so far. This has the positive effect of forcing the monk to face his own weakness and need for God's help. Stewart writes: "To deal only with the physical aspects of monastic asceticism is to miss the heart of the early monastic endeavor, which was to take human potential to its limits in order to show those limits to the God who alone could surpass them."[41] Cassian makes this point in one of his conferences, arguing that purity of heart is difficult to attain, so God sometimes even withdraws divine assistance in order for the monk to learn by experience that virtue cannot be obtained through one's own strength and effort alone. Disciplines like fasting, vigils, manual labor, and incessant application to spiritual reading can lead to continence, but perpetual purity cannot be had by these alone, but only by divine grace—a gift of the Lord.[42] Still, we should be clear that Cassian is not instructing the monk to avoid ascetic efforts; instead, with a bit of irony given the topic, he is insistent: "Like someone who very avidly goes after money, so afire with desire and love should a person be in his pursuit of chastity. Like someone who strains ambitiously after the highest honors, or someone who is seized with an unbearable love for a beautiful woman, he wants to consummate his desire with the most impatient ardor."[43]

With his Eastern orientation, it is undeniable that Cassian has an optimistic view of human free will, a perspective for which the West labeled him a semi-Pelagian while the East recognizes him on the Christian calendar with a feast day. We moderns may not be as optimistic given our recognition of the effects of heredity and environment on human abilities.[44] But even with his more optimistic perspective, Cassian admits that it is not willpower that wins the day.

What is ingenious about how Cassian makes the point that the ultimate solution in combating lust is not human effort but divine grace is his appeal to what goes on in our thoughts during sleep—when our free will is not in control. As Stewart puts it, "Only grace can cross the border between waking and sleeping, between conscious and unconscious states. The chaste monk can safely commend himself to sleep, for the disposition of chastity has been assimilated 'in the bones.' Such depth of transformation is impossible for mere continence."[45] While we will later unpack the difference that Stewart makes between chastity and "mere continence," the point is that what is often here translated as "nocturnal illusions" and what we sometimes call "wet dreams" are used by Cassian to make the point that only God can stand the night watch in the heart to keep us completely sanctified: "It will be an excellent sign and full proof of our purity if no lewd image comes to us when we are plunged in sleep."[46]

In other words, we are *not* fully in control when it comes to lust, a point not lost on our contemporaries. Some therapists have discovered that the twelve-steps approach has worked with sex addicts (so that there are groups such as Sexaholics Anonymous),[47] and of course the first two steps require the admission that one is powerless and that a "Higher Power" can restore the addict to health. Cassian would applaud.

There are aspects within our control that have to do with our dreams at night. One of these we implied earlier—an excess of food according to Cassian, Gregory, and Aquinas. But another is our lack of vigilance while we are awake:

> Through the fault of his error and negligence it consequently happens that not only do numerous roving thoughts break into the hidden places of the mind in bold and impudent fashion, but also the seeds of all one's former passions remain there. . . . Therefore, the first thing to be done is to restrain our wandering thoughts, lest the mind grow accustomed to these diversions and, while dreaming, be drawn to still more horrible temptations of lasciviousness.[48]

With the image of preparing for competition in the games, Cassian elsewhere encourages his monks to abstain from forbidden foods, drunkenness, tippling, inertia, idleness, and ennui "so as to increase their strength by daily exercise and assiduous concentration." He even encourages taking a "cold shower," so to speak: "To such an extent do they keep themselves pure from all the contamination of sexual intercourse that, when they are getting ready to contend in the games, they cover their loins with [cool metal] lead sheets lest perchance they be deceived by nocturnal fancies in their dreams and diminish the strength that they have acquired over a long period."[49]

So for Cassian it is what we have done and thought when fully conscious that has much to do with what we think about when left to our subconscious: "The quality of the thoughts, which are guarded negligently during the day because of distractions, is tested during the night rest."[50] Though he insists that the perfect proof of the goal of integrity is "that no movement of the flesh creeps up on us when asleep, and that we have none of the nocturnal emissions to which nature is subject," he does not expect monks to be completely free of how nature has made them in this regard, but to be restricted to "the least frequent and naturally inevitable cases, which for a monk would occur once every two months" (based on experience). But he *does* cite the case of elders who insist it should be less frequent than that, even if something like once every four months sounds "impossible and incredible."[51] Cassian is once again the realist and, perhaps, to our modern ears, the humorist.

Returning to the promise to unpack the difference between chastity and "mere continence"—or what we might more commonly refer to as "abstinence"—we come to one of the most significant points to be made about the deadly sins and about lust in particular. It has to do with Cassian's recognition that *chastity* is the queen of the virtues—"the defining virtue of the perfect monk." As we will see and as Stewart states: "It was the ground of contemplative insight, ecstatic prayer and spiritual knowledge of the Bible. Only the perfection of chastity, [Cassian] claimed, can lead to the heights of love, and only from there can we hope to ascend to the image and likeness of God that is one's birthright."[52] It is one thing to be *continent* (*encratite*), but this "only grants temporary relief to the struggler." It is quite another thing to be *chaste* (*agnos*)—a state of integrity and incorruption exemplified by Elijah, Jeremiah, Daniel, and John the Baptist, according to Cassian. Sanctification is acquired by chastity (1 Thess. 4:3–5).[53]

This crucial distinction that Cassian makes between continence (abstinence, sexual restraint) and chastity can be discussed under three headings: what is necessary to attain it; what motivates it; and what is its end result.[54]

First, abstinence is accomplished by human effort—specifically sheer determination to keep the body disciplined. As we have already mentioned, chastity, on the other hand, is to be desired and sought after in the ascetic life, but is only finally attained by divine grace. This is what the night's subconscious state teaches us.

Second, what motivates abstinence is fear, whether it is contracting STDs, becoming pregnant, getting caught, or anything else that might bring on a sense of guilt or shame. But Cassian insists that the motivation for chastity can only be love, in partnership with all the other virtues. There is an organic bond between chastity and charity such that perfect and perpetual chastity cannot be had without charity in its fullness.[55] Before moving on to the third point—namely, the end result of abstinence—it would be helpful to elaborate this connection between chastity and aspects of charity, such as patient forbearance.

Because it is related to all the other virtues, Cassian repeatedly points out that chastity is connected with patience over against anger (frustration that often results from unsatisfied desires): "The more one grows in sweet patience, the more one grows in purity of body. The further we remove the passion of anger from ourselves, the firmer will be our grasp on chastity. For the heat of the body will not cool unless the outbursts of the heart are restrained."[56]

All of this is because chastity is a social virtue that has to do with human relationships truly founded on love over against selfish desire or vainglorious manipulation. As Evagrius puts it at one point, "flee lust and pursue hospitality."

These connections are illustrated in what probably sounds humorous to us—Cassian's description of the regimen that a monk must follow for six months to see if he is capable of engaging in the disciplined life that leads to chastity: restraint from useless conversation; control of all angry feelings and earthly cares; two biscuits a day; no more water than absolutely necessary; three or four hours of sleep; and, above all, assurance that real chastity is a gift from God.[57] As strange as some of this does appear to us, a thoughtful consideration of these items reinforces the point that chastity is related to other virtues and vices having to do with food, possessions, anger in community, sloth, and so forth.

All of this is not lost on our contemporaries, for anger and human relations play an important role in some sexual addictions. A person who was victimized while growing up might break the rules as a way to retaliate for hurts about which she is angry:

> The anger stems from a set of beliefs, family messages, and self-judgments the addicts use to interpret the world. Most addicts do not connect their behavior with anger. The excitement and arousal of the trance block the feelings, along with the rest of the pain. The greater the anger and pain, the more excitement is required to block it.[58]

Because the addict feels unloved and unlovable (part of the operative belief system), there is rage over unmet needs. And this becomes a cycle because rage about past unmet needs prevents the possibility of expressing current needs since the addict anticipates rejection. Add to this a feeling of being powerless to influence her situation and there is even more proclivity to violence.[59]

Resuming our discussion of the difference between abstinence and chastity in which we have noted that, first, abstinence requires willful determination and that, second, it is largely motivated by fear, we need to ask what abstinence accomplishes. Put succinctly, it wrestles lust to a truce in constant police action over a restive body.[60] As Evagrius says, the demon of impurity "attacks more strenuously those who practice continence, in the hope that they will give up their practice of this virtue, feeling that they have nothing to gain by it."[61]

Evagrius is prophetic when it comes to evangelical efforts to curb sexual activity among single young people. The Southern Baptist Convention "True Love Waits" program began in 1993. Over two million youth had signed the pledge to wait until marriage to engage in sexual intercourse by the time that Columbia and Yale Universities reported the findings of their study in 2004 that had tracked twelve thousand teens who took the pledge. They found that 88 percent of the pledged reported having sexual intercourse before marriage. And rates of STDs were nearly the same for those teens who took the pledge as for those who did not.[62]

Cassian's description of continence over against perfect chastity would probably resonate with these teens:

> For, when something is restrained with an effort, the relief that is offered to the one struggling is only temporary, and there is still no enduring and secure peace after the effort. But when something has been conquered by deeply rooted virtue, there is a calm without any hint of disturbance, and a steady and firm peace is granted the victor. Hence, as long as we feel that we are being afflicted by a disturbance of the flesh, we know that we have not yet arrived at the heights of chastity but are still toiling under a frail abstinence, engaged in battles whose outcome is always inevitably doubtful. . . . For this reason perfect chastity is distinguished from the toilsome rudiments of abstinence by its perpetual tranquility.[63]

An extreme example of the difference between "temporary relief" for the struggler and the peace of the victor is what occurs in cases of sexual addiction. The addict is under the delusion that he is in control of his behavior: "Being able to stop for a period of time provides the illusion of control, which makes it difficult for the addict to acknowledge that there is a problem." Then he fails once again and there is ever-increasing shame. But sexual activity is *not* a choice for the addict because the *addiction* is in control. That is why some therapists are using the twelve-steps program to help the addict to admit his powerlessness and unmanageability: "All those years of trying to control the behavior simply intensified the problem. Giving up control, admitting you cannot stop your behavior, acknowledging that this addiction is destroying your life, asking for help—these are the exact opposite actions of what seems natural to do."[64]

There *are* willful actions that follow the first two steps of admission of powerlessness, just as there are ascetic disciplines that precede and accompany the monk's admission of his need for grace.[65] But, again, it is the necessity of divine help that is the necessary condition without which one cannot arrive at perfect and perpetual chastity. This is illustrated famously in Cassian's explanation of Basil of Caesarea's otherwise obscure comment: "'I know not a woman and yet I am not a virgin!' By this he means that bodily purity consists not so much in foreswearing women but in integrity of heart. . . . a perpetual incorrupt holiness of heart whether from the fear of God or from the love of purity."[66] And this integrity of heart is what is necessary to see God and to attain true knowledge in the freedom and love of God and neighbor with an "abiding tranquility" of peace.[67]

This is the *integritas* which is perpetual chastity. Of such a person Cassian says "stings of flesh" are merely movements of nature, because "perfect chastity is distinguished from the elemental struggling continence by its abiding tranquility."[68] As Kardong puts it, for Cassian the quieting of the spirit is basic to the quieting of the body, and this is the *apatheia* that makes perfect love—*agapē*—possible.[69]

Cassian tells us that this should be a joyful experience, like that of long-married persons who are fully committed: "chastity alone does not consist . . . in austere preventions but rather in the love and the delight in purity itself. As long as some adversity of lust remains, you don't have chastity but continence."[70] He leaves us with a beautiful description of the life of chastity:

> This is the perfection of chastity, that no temptation to lust assault the monk during vigils; that no deceptive dream fool the sleeper. . . . If anyone succeeds in obtaining this place of peace by extinction of carnal passions, he thereby attains the level of spiritual Zion, which is the watchtower of the Lord and the place where he dwells. For the Lord does not dwell among the battles of continence but in the secure tower of virtue.[71]

It is interesting that the *integritas* or perpetual chastity of which Cassian speaks resonates with what is found in discussions of individuals who have sexual issues. Referring to evangelical men with these issues, Kailla Edger cites a study that argued such individuals

> strive to be whole, and this wholeness that they seek is ontological rather than sexual. Feeling complete in oneself as well as being unified with one's life-world is the ontological goal for all human beings. Participants in this study found it difficult to feel whole because their sexual desires did not harmonize with their spiritual beliefs. As they acted out on their sexual urges while continuing to align with a disapproving dogma, they gradually created a separation in their life-world; a division of religious-world and sexual-world.[72]

What Humility Has to Do with Chastity

Before ending this chapter we must return to a theme already mentioned in passing. Before chastity can be secured, there must be a foundation of humility. Humility has to do with discernment of thoughts (*logismoi*) and self-knowledge, something that requires the help of elders. (We call it "spiritual direction" today.) As long as the root of the vice of lust remains hidden in the heart's recesses one cannot attain true knowledge of self or God.[73]

This is advice that might have helped in Jimmy Swaggart's case. After his public confession in February 1988, the Louisiana presbytery of the Assemblies of God initially suspended him from his ministry for three months, followed by the national presbytery which extended it to two years. But Swaggart returned to his ministry after only the original three-month suspension. Since he had not submitted to their judgment, the national body questioned the sincerity of his repentance and defrocked him, taking away his ministerial license—a courageous move on the part of the Assemblies of God denomination, since Swaggart's Baton Rouge church contributed $14 million a year to the national body. He responded by becoming a nondenominational Pentecostal minister. But perhaps those hidden recesses of which Cassian speaks, such as memories and triggers, remained when Swaggart was pulled over in Indio by the California Highway Patrol in October 1991 for a traffic infraction which led to the discovery that he was in the company of a prostitute. This time, instead of confessing, Swaggart reportedly said to his congregation (the Family Worship Center), "The Lord told me it's flat none of your business." What stunned many was that Swaggart was initially "caught" after having been the one who told Assemblies of God officials about fellow ministers Jim Bakker's and Marvin Gorman's sexual dalliances. Some suggested that Swaggart was seduced and self-deluded by his power and fame.[74] No one ever suggested that humility had been his motivation. What comes to mind is a phrase of Gregory's to which we all are susceptible—"corrupted with the luxury of praise."[75]

Whether or not Swaggart fits the description of what Carnes discusses in his book, it is interesting to note that sexual addiction requires the same kind of humility or self-knowledge that Cassian recommended. As Carnes clearly states, addiction begins with "delusional thought processes that are rooted in the addict's *belief system*. That is, addicts begin with core beliefs about themselves that affect how they perceive reality."[76] And the addict's choices are made through the filter of this belief system that includes "denial, rationalization, sincere delusion, paranoia, and blame" that further "closes off an important avenue of self-knowledge and touch with reality for the addict."[77] Recovery requires self-understanding of how all of this works in the addict's life.

Humility—this accurate assessment of oneself—stands in the way of pride and thus preserves chastity. As Gregory put it, "For pride has often been to many a seed-plot of lust; for, while their spirit raised them, as it were, on high, their flesh plunged them in the lowest of depths." The secretly proud spill into the open in a fall engendered by lust: "Lo! the flesh overwhelmed those, whom boastful learning had raised up, and, from the flying of birds, they fell beyond the appetite of beasts, and sank beneath themselves, by the very means by which they appeared to rise above themselves."[78] Gregory later argues that one has to be careful to remain chaste when prosperity comes with its pleasures "as the joy of his heart panders to his wishes." In other words, one is careful to remember that prosperity—whether it is a BMW or an income from contributions of $150 million a year—is a gift of God.[79]

But even if one falls, Gregory reminds us that mercy abounds. In his advice about how to admonish "those who have had experience of sins of the flesh, and those who have not," of the former Gregory is encouraging: if we do not fear God's justice and even harbor contempt of God by our actions, still, we should feel shame in light of the loving-kindness by which God calls us to return. And this perspective is reinforced when he gives advice about counseling the latter, for they should fear ruin even more because the loftier they stand, the farther they fall. They may be satisfied with what they have accomplished bodily without being zealous in spirit, and so they may be put to shame by those among the former group—the fallen—who return to God and engage in good works: "And so it often comes about that the life of one burning with love after having sinned is more pleasing to God than a life of innocence that grows languid in its sense of security."[80]

We should mention that in his advice he iterates what we see repeatedly in the monks' admonitions on the spiritual life: have an eschatological perspective—keep the long view in mind. What comes to mind is a thought I had after driving away from the lunch I had with the parishioner of a church that I served, having heard the story of his wife's recently discovered affair and the mess it had made of the entire family's life. I reflected that, while our society may not hold faithful monogamy in high esteem, I would take it any day over what this man is suffering.

Still, of that latter group to which Gregory gives advice—the ones who have not experienced the "sins of the flesh"—both he and Cassian warn that with the vow of virginity comes the temptation for the pride that sometimes accompanies abstinence.[81] Gregory explains that part of the reason for this is because pride is believed to be less disgraceful than lust and is therefore less avoided. Yet those who fall into lust having been prideful about their resistance end up feeling ashamed: when they believed they were free from lust while allowing themselves to live in the greater sin of pride, they discovered that they were actually guilty of a lesser sin. And Gregory attributes the unleashing of the "Behemoth" of this lesser sin to the "merciful dispensation of God" since he is "conquered by the very means by which he seems to have triumphed." This demonstrates the compassion of God, as Gregory insightfully explains:

> But he who is puffed up by the virtues he has received, is wounded not with a sword, but, so to say, with a remedy. . . . *Because,*

where we make a wound of our remedy, He makes a remedy of our wound; in order that we who are wounded by our virtue, may be healed by our sin. For we pervert the gifts of virtues to the practice of vice; He applies the allurements of vices to promote virtues, and wounds our healthy state in order to preserve it, and that we who fly from humility when we run, may cling to it at least when falling.[82]

Again, Swaggart comes to mind. He had judged others, but then fell by the same sin. Was it pride? In any case, a remedy *for* the wound was offered by the elders, but it was not received. This may be instructive, since for God to make a remedy *of* our wound, there has to be the humility to *receive* it.

According to Kailla Edger's research of the lived experience of evangelical Christian men who self-identify as sexual addicts, this humble willingness for God to use a vice to encourage virtue has been experienced by some. There were some in the sample who, strange as it may sound, felt that their sexual addiction was God's will for their lives. But "others felt that their struggles shaped them to be better Christians and to be closer to God." Here are some of the participants' comments:

> For me, [God] allowed an addiction, and it's because I have this addiction and He didn't take it away that I get up every morning and do my morning meditations . . . and it's because of my addiction that I actually have grown much closer to my God. So in a lot of ways, I feel that I'm blessed I have this addiction because had it not been for this, I wouldn't have had the relationship with my God that I do now. (P[articipant]3)

> That's what God intended for me. God knew that these things had to happen to me for me to have a personal realization that I needed to turn my life and my will over to the care of God. (P4)

> I wish it never happened. It did happen, and I think it has brought me closer to God, but I'm not so thankful for it. (P6)[83]

Edger concluded, "For many, the struggles that had burdened them in the past became blessings because they were better Christians in the present."[84] Gregory stands in agreement. And it means that there is hope for Jimmy Swaggart and for all of us.

One final note before concluding. If chastity is *integritas*, as Cassian has described it—if it has to do with the whole person—then how do we teach our children this truth so that they will grow up to be adolescents who seek perfect and perpetual chastity rather than simply adolescents who take the abstinence pledge? At one point in her description of Benedict's model for peace (and chastity has everything to do with a tranquil body and soul that is no longer "restive"), Joan Chittister asks us to "imagine a world where small children are not jerked down supermarket aisles in the name of discipline."[85] Teaching our children by the ways that *we* treat their bodies—teaching them that true chastity has to do not just with sex, but with the way they think about their bodies as God's gifts to be used as instruments of righteousness—of right-relatedness—may help them to experience the tranquility of body and soul that is chastity.

4

---✴---

Greed

Death by Consumption

> Consumption is not just an economic factor. It emerges as a "way of life." It is an addiction.
>
> John F. Kavanaugh, *Still Following Christ in a Consumer Society*

If, as we will see, sloth is the most religious of the seven cardinal sins, greed may be the least psychological of the seven. In our culture it is not typically considered pathological; in fact it is often considered a virtue.[1] But Roger Wood would not consider it a virtue. His father, Orville, the subject of an *Atlantic Monthly* article, was so miserly that he refused his family members clean unused water for a bath or more than two squares of toilet paper per bathroom visit; yet, his secret hoard at death was discovered to include hundreds of thousands of dollars of treasury bills and certificates of deposit, stocks in blue-chip companies, and cash in seven banks.[2]

Of course, as we will see, greed can manifest itself in compulsive consumption as well as miserliness. And it is just as vicious, as Rodney Clapp points out, arguing that it "militates against all sorts of Christian virtues, such as patience and contentedness and self-denial, but almost always with a velvet glove rather than an iron fist. It speaks in tones sweet and sexy rather than dictatorial, and it conquers by promises rather than by threats."[3]

Though "mammon takes on new forms in every age,"[4] still, greed in its various guises has been with us since Eden.

Ancient Descriptions

Prophets of the Old Testament often scorned greed, particularly when it involved dishonest gain and self-enrichment of the politically powerful through violent means. Elijah, Isaiah, Jeremiah, Habakkuk, Amos, and Micah all denounce this vice that leads to social injustice, oppression, and crime. Ezekiel (22:27), for one, is descriptive in his condemnation of Israel's elite: "Its officials within it are like wolves tearing the prey, shedding blood, destroying lives to get dishonest gain."

Earliest Greek writers did not confine their use of the word "greed" to the desire for more material possessions. Not unlike the Jewish prophets, words like *pleonexia* (consisting of *pleon* meaning "more" and *echo* meaning "have") were used to denote an immoral lust for power. Though they viewed greed as the decisive force in human action and the progress of history, typically they allowed no room for it in a just society.

Though Jesus warned against anxiety over material possessions, it was more often the apostle Paul who referred specifically to greed in the New Testament. In fact, in his list of what the Christian is to "put to death" he equates greed with idolatry (Eph. 5:5; Col. 3:5). It doesn't get much worse than that! It is no wonder that Paul insists that greed must not even be mentioned among Christians (Eph. 5:3); the greedy will not inherit the kingdom of God (1 Cor. 6:10) and folks in the church are not even to associate with the greedy (1 Cor. 5:11).

In contemporary Christian circles it is remarkable that the prophets and the apostle are not taken as seriously when speaking of greed as they are when speaking of sexual immorality. I recall reading an article in a popular Christian magazine about a woman's difficult decision to take 1 Corinthians 5:11 seriously by ostracizing her sister who had committed adultery; I wondered whether she treated the greedy in her church by the same standard. After all, if Paul is to be believed, unlike the woman's sister, greedy parishioners would be committing idolatry.

I broached this same comparison with a dean of students at a Christian college at which I once taught, since as is typical at such institutions he was going on and on about sexual immorality among the students. I suggested that there might be a larger percentage practicing forms of greed, but I was shrugged off because no students had ever come into his office having been caught or having admitted that they were guilty of this vice. Idolaters were running loose on campus and no one seemed to care!

I suspect that part of the reason (though by no means the *only* reason) for this disproportionate attention to sexual sins over against greed is that activities such as fornication and adultery are more easily identified than greed. We are obliged, then, to identify greed. What is it? Once again, the tradition comes to our aid.

What Greed Is

Simply put, greed is loving money and material possessions too much. It is not just having things, but having them inordinately. As Aquinas defines it, covetousness (which is essentially the same thing as greed) is the "immoderate love of possessing" based on the purpose of the things that we use to live well. He does not deny that we need what is necessary to live; there is a certain measure of external goods that a person needs. But evil sets in when one has an excess *or a deficiency* of that measure.[5] Just as it is surprising to learn in the case of gluttony that it may involve undereating as much as overeating, so in the case of greed: Aquinas insists that prodigality is as dangerous as covetousness, since, while covetousness is deficient in giving and excessive in retaining and acquiring, prodigality is excessive in giving and deficient in retaining and acquiring such that one has too careless a concern for wealth.[6] Still, covetousness is a graver sin than prodigality for three reasons: prodigality is closer to giving than it is to hoarding (and is therefore more easily turned into a virtue); prodigality is of use to those who receive the generosity of the prodigal person, while covetousness is of no use even to the coveter; and prodigality is more easily cured since getting older and more needy will curtail prodigality.[7]

Covetousness is particularly deadly when what is coveted is preferred to loving God and when others in our lives have to take a backseat to mammon. Avarice (from the Latin *avaritia* from *aveo*, "I desire") occurs when the motives are selfish or hedonistic, when the means are unjust, and when trust is placed in riches. As Ted Peters puts it, "Our love for shopping becomes a perversion . . . when it marginalizes higher forms of love, when it replaces our love for truth, our love for other people, or our love for God."[8]

That was certainly evident in the case of Orville Wood. He funded his habit of stock purchases by saving money on towels, soap, and lightbulbs that he stealthily acquired from the high school where he taught; he riskily invested money that should have been applied to his mortgage; and he denied his wife access to their funds—all the kinds of behavior that eventually led his wife to severe depression and divorce. Assessing the damage done to Orville's family, William Green observes that "in the real world, old misers seldom learn to cherish their children as much as cash."[9]

Extending Aquinas's terms, Orville was covetous when it came to his family but prodigal when it came to his stock investments. To put it another way, greed manifests itself in different forms—the cutthroat competitor, the workaholic, the swindler, the miser, the gambler. The frugal person might more successfully hide in a cloak of virtue than Orville was able to do, yet he may be as obsessed with money as the spendthrift because he is attempting to alleviate anxiety over his future security and will mortgage his present life to secure a future that is not promised to him. More on that aspect of greed later.

It should be obvious by now that greed can be shapeshifter. Cassian iterates three instances of covetousness, modeled by three biblical examples: Gehazi (over against Elisha) represents those who want to hoard even what they never possessed (such as, in this case, the "grace of prophecy"); Judas typifies those who desire what they had earlier renounced; and Ananias and Saphira are models of those who from a "faulty and hurtful beginning" of "lukewarmness" become greedy "through fear of poverty and want of faith."[10]

Even though at one point Cassian calls covetousness simply the "love of money,"[11] the varieties of greed can go beyond money and possessions. Aquinas admits that the verb "to have" originally seems to have been applied to possessions, but he suggests that it can also be applied to many other things, such as knowledge, esteem, health, spouse, clothing—whatever involves immoderate desire. He consciously cites a homily of Gregory's when he insists that "covetousness is a desire not only for money, but also for knowledge and high places, when prominence is immoderately sought after."[12]

In fact, in his commentary on Job, Gregory specifically says that one can be avaricious for applause and do great works for the wrong reason: the hypocrite does not take external gifts (such as money) from the hand, but desires a word of applause from the mouth, and in the process strives to make others appear wicked in order to make himself look better and more worthy of respect.[13] This is another example of that gangland style of attack, this time by the "demons" of avarice, vainglory, and envy.

Though he does not have as much to say about it, in the end Evagrius calls greed the "mother of idolatry," an identification we have already seen in the apostle Paul (Col. 3:5; Eph. 5:5), and echoes of which we find in the teachings of Jesus (Matt. 6:24; Luke 16:13).[14]

Aquinas is not quite as severe at this point. Not only is covetousness not the greatest of sins,[15] but it is not as bad as idolatry in his opinion, though it bears a certain resemblance to it,

> because the covetous man, like the idolater, subjects himself to an external creature, though not in the same way. For the idolater subjects himself to an external creature by paying it Divine honor, whereas the covetous man subjects himself to an external creature by desiring it immoderately for use, not for worship.[16]

Twentieth-century sociologist and theologian Jacques Ellul finds it more insidious than did Aquinas when he reminds us that we are under the law of the Fall, like a "spiritual law of gravity": "Wealth is temptation because it urges us to put our confidence in money rather than in God. . . . For human beings prefer what they can see and touch to what God promises and gives."[17] It can be argued that any time we place our hope and trust in the material world we have committed a form of idolatry. One who no longer finds his goal or fulfillment in God but seeks fulfillment in himself, his possessions, or his acquisitiveness, creates an idol that strives to subject everything to itself. Jesus was blatant: "No one can serve two masters; for a slave will either hate the one and love the other, or be devoted to the one and despise the other. You cannot serve God and wealth" (Matt. 6:24). And the idol—the master—holds sway over the one who *seems* to control it.

Greed not only overtakes one's life as a master, but, echoing Paul in 1 Timothy 6:10, Cassian and the others recognize that greed is "a root of all evils"—"a regular nest of sins."[18] Aquinas clarifies what is meant by "root of all evils"; it is not to be understood in the sense that all evils always arise from covetousness, but in the sense that "there is no evil that does not at some time arise from covetousness."[19] Referring to the same comment of the Apostle Paul, Gregory vividly portrays what Aquinas later clarifies with the monk's metaphorical description of avarice's effects on the pastoral leader, comparing it to a "pustular disease of the skin that spreads, infects, and disfigures":

> So, too, avarice, while affording the mind of its victim apparent delight, ulcerates it. While filling its thoughts with the acquisition of one thing after another, it kindles enmities, but gives no pain with the wounds it inflicts, because it promises to the fevered mind abundance as the wages of sin. And the comeliness of the members is lost, because this sin results also in the marring of other fair virtues. Indeed, the whole body, as it were, is befouled, since the mind is overthrown by all vices.[20]

This vice which Gregory maintains engenders everything evil extends so far that Gregory even connects it with heretics who covet not merely the minds of those they teach, but their very lives.[21]

In salvation history this selfish amassing has its prototype in grasping the forbidden fruit in the Garden of Eden. Typical of the pairings noted by the early monks, we hear of its associations with other sins—pride, envy, gluttony, lust. The biblical narrative even supports the observation that these cardinal sins give birth to offspring, for murder and injustice are born of greed in the story of Ahab and Jezebel over against Elijah. The consequence is self-destruction and complete isolation from God and fellow human beings—the legacy of Judas Iscariot. And these connections are made in our modern cinematic stories, like *Treasures of the Sierra Madre* and *Fargo*.

Though we have already alluded to it, we need to learn how we acquire this "pustular disease" in the first place.

How We Get Greed or How Greed Gets Us

To get at the origins of greed it is helpful first to consider Cassian's insistence that greed (like envy) is not congenital.[22] He argues that "carnal impulses" (desires such as gluttony and lust) and "pricks of anger" are wisely given to us by the Creator in order to perpetuate the race, raise our children well, and rage at our sins so that we will apply ourselves to virtue, spiritual exercises, the love of God, and patience with others. Even sorrow (*tristitia*), when linked with the fear of God, is a good.

But greed comes upon us later in life and approaches us from without (which is why it can be more easily guarded against, avoided, and resisted—unlike gluttony, for example). It comes from outside our God-given nature and begins with "the free choice of a corrupt and evil will"; it does not issue from natural instincts (such as lust, for instance). As a result, Cassian says that our struggle against covetousness is a "foreign warfare."

At this point we have to ask ourselves if Cassian is entirely on target. That is, if greed is an inordinate desire, is there an *ordinate* desire for material things? Is the desire to have, to acquire, as natural for survival of the species as Cassian claims that lust is? Ted Peters seems to think so when he asserts that "gluttony, lust, and greed are expressions of our embodied creatureliness," though he thinks that at the heart of all three of these (i.e., of concupiscence) is a denial of our own limits in order to eliminate our insecurity in nature.[23] If covetousness began with the consumption of prohibited fruit in the garden, is it "natural" with regard to our "second nature"—our fallen condition— whereas perhaps the desire for food and sex were aspects of our prefallen condition, to be perverted as gluttony and lust when we fell? Perhaps, in part, Cassian's different assessment of greed's origin over against gluttony, for example, is due to the monastic situation: one can renounce possessions, but he cannot renounce food for very long.

Yet, there is agreement of sorts with Cassian's claim that covetousness is learned behavior. Juliet Schor argues that Americans don't spend because it is their human nature to do so; instead, they are locked into a cycle of work and spend. In other words, consumer markets and labor markets are intimately and structurally conjoined. In this way "our daily lives, and indeed our very identities, are structured and regulated by acts of spending."[24]

Add to this what Schor downplays but others insist upon: manufacturers and advertisers have shaped us to be covetous. Clapp narrates the US history that is responsible for this.[25] A huge gap between production and consumption was the result of the nineteenth-century industrial revolution as we produced more cereal, cigarettes, and other products than we could consume. So, instead of cutting production, manufacturers sought to increase consumption—to increase demand to meet the supply. But that would require teaching consumption as a way of life. With money-back guarantees, credit, branding, mail order, and advertisements, the American consumer was trained and habituated—made, not born. New needs had to be created. Clapp quotes Crowell of Quaker Oats: "[My aim in advertising] was to do educational and constructive work so as to awaken an interest in and create a demand for cereals where none existed." The result was "the cultivation of unbounded desire" and the "consumption of novelty." The 1901 *Thompson Red Book on Advertising* put it this way: "Advertising aims to teach people that they have wants, which they did not recognize before, and where such wants can be best supplied." Or more recently, one corporate manager put it this way: "Corporate branding is really about worldwide beliefs management."[26] More than 3,000 sales messages to which the average American is exposed daily help to do the job.[27] William Cavanaugh's conclusion is undeniable: "Consumer culture is one of the most powerful systems of formation in the contemporary world, arguably more powerful than Christianity. . . . Such a powerful formative system is not morally neutral: it trains us to see the world in certain ways."[28] And we can only act in a world we can see.

John Kavanaugh labels this all-consuming worldview the "Commodity Form," with its preeminent values of producing, marketing, and consuming.

> It does not just affect the way we shop. It affects the way we think and feel, the way we love and pray, the way we evaluate our enemies, the way we relate to our spouses and children. It is "systematic." . . . These values are the ethical lenses through which we are conditioned to perceive our worth and importance. They have profoundly affected not only our self-understanding but also our modeling of human behavior (into manipulation and aggression), human knowledge (into quantification, observation, and measurement), and human affectivity (into noncommitalness and mechanized sexuality).[29]

This formation involves not only the wealthy, but all classes of society. In other words, the poor and the rich alike can be avaricious. Just like those who commit adultery in their hearts, Cassian says that it is possible to be poor yet covetous in disposition and intent. Though the opportunity may be lacking, just as it might be for the adulterer, the will for it is not. In fact, Cassian suggests that one might take delight in the advantages of poverty and be resigned of necessity to that burden, yet not take delight in the *virtue* that can be cultivated in the state of poverty. Cassian admonishes the monk—and us—to learn from poverty: "For it is a wretched thing to have endured the effects of poverty and want, but to have lost their fruits, through the fault of a shattered will."[30]

From a more philosophical mind-set, Jacques Ellul agrees that Mammon attacks those who lack money: "The power of money subjects the poor as solidly as the rich. Some are subjected by their savings, others by their desire, worry, discontent—and everyone by covetousness."[31] To the list of sins to which the impoverished are subjected Peters adds envy of the rich as well as "the use of theft or pillage or legislation or revolution or whatever may be necessary to secure one's own livelihood even if it involves denying the livelihood of others who are equally desperate."[32]

While Ellul, in his more sociological bent, suggests that the increase of wealth in the world is one reason that the poor get in on the vice of covetousness, Schor turns to the media to explain why the "culture of desire" is so pervasive today. Some of it has to do with the fact that we are more aware of "reference groups" to which we compare ourselves as consumers: "While spending is certainly a reflection of social distinctions, it does have at least one profoundly egalitarian aspect: just about *everyone* wants in. Desire for Nikes, Evian water, or a BMW can be found at all income levels. Expensive branded goods and designer logos are popular with nearly everyone."[33] She cites research which demonstrates that the more one watches television, the more one spends: "Television viewing results in upscaling of desire, and that in turn leads people to buy—quite a bit more than they would if they didn't watch."[34] Exposure to consumer goods leads to fantasizing, wishing, and rationalizing, followed perhaps by borrowing and then buying.[35] Since 99 percent of US households have *at least* one television set, the exposure to "reference groups" and consumer goods that feeds greed is probably as pervasive among the poor as it is among the wealthy.

Theologically, Ellul is not as certain as Cassian that poverty easily yields virtuous fruit, for he wisely reflects that a "relationship with God is not more *natural* in poverty than in wealth; the poor are not better suited to it. Like the rich, they have a temptation which is difficult to overcome. They are tempted to steal. This is obvious."³⁶ And as Proverbs 30:7–9 makes clear, this profanes God's name:

> Two things I ask of you; do not deny them to me before I die: Remove far from me falsehood and lying; give me neither poverty nor riches; feed me with the food that I need, or I shall be full, and deny you, and say, 'Who is the Lord?' or I shall be poor, and steal, and profane the name of my God.

It would smack of Pelagianism if the poor *were* more naturally inclined to virtue. Ellul is right when he says that "poverty is no justification for sin. Sin is sin, even if it is committed by a poor person." It is for this reason that Ellul goes on to chide with a bit of irony those who want to romanticize poverty: "it is twice recommended not to judge unjustly *in favor of* the poor (Exod. 23:3; Lev. 19:15). The poor have a right to justice and not to injustice in their favor."³⁷

So it is that greed is no respecter of any class, particularly as it begins to fester in the one who begins with a half-hearted, lukewarm commitment to God (or to monastic life, in the scenario that Cassian sketches).³⁸ Gregory unpacks this with a bit more sophistication when he speaks of premature involvement in externals or activities before one cultivates the kind of internal formation that is the result of a long commitment to heavenly desires and a pure, single aim in life. Those without deep roots who engage in good works eventually get blown away or die on the vine because they do such works for the wrong reasons: they are covetous of applause and susceptible to envy and vainglory.³⁹

It might not even be the "fog of applause" (as Gregory puts it at one point) which seduces the ill-prepared toward greed, but a kind of apprehension. Besides pride, Gregory observes that avarice can arise from the fear that one hasn't enough to live on.⁴⁰ According to Evagrius, avarice takes hold when this worried mind contemplates the insecurity of longevity, the future inability to do work, famines, illness, poverty, and "the great shame that comes from accepting the necessities of life from others."[41] Orville Wood is a paradigmatic case: "Wherever Orville went, his fear of poverty followed like a bogeyman," such that he "saved with almost religious fervor."[42]

Cassian unpacks in some detail how this works—the progress avarice makes as it gets hold of the mildly committed monk.[43] It begins by tempting him in small doses with reasonable excuses as to why he should keep some of the money he had vowed to give up: what the monastery provides won't be enough to maintain his health; he may get sick; his clothing is insufficient, and he needs more; he must provide for travel when he leaves the monastery. Orville's excuses were similar. "And so when he has been bamboozled with such thoughts as these, he racks his brain to think how he can acquire at least one penny." He seeks to moonlight without the abbot's knowledge, and thereby he gets some extra income, but then becomes oppressed wondering how to double it and what to buy with it. The more money he gets, the more he craves. Then he worries: What should be done if he lives to an enfeebled old age? So he acquires more and soon engages in lying, perjury, theft, breaking a promise, and "giving way to injurious bursts of passion." These all are the "daughters" of greed to which we have already referred—and which recur in the narrative of Orville Wood's life.

And, finally, there is the fall into idolatry:

> If to any degree the hope of profit slips his grasp, he does not fear to go beyond the limits set by honesty and humility. And so it turns out that, just as other people's belly is their God, in his case it is always gold and the hope of gain . . . you see, then, how ruinous this madness becomes as it increases step by step, so that by the Apostle's words it is even declared to be a slavery to idols and effigies because, bypassing the form of God and his image, which one who serves God devoutly should maintain unsullied in himself, it prefers to love and look up human figures cast in gold instead of God.[44]

The justifications for this fall are not only rational; they also appeal to the authority of Scripture "which they interpret with base ingenuity, in their desire to wrest and pervert to their own purposes a saying of the Apostle or rather of the Lord Himself: and, not adapting their own life or understanding to the meaning of the Scripture, but making the meaning of Scripture bend to the desires of their own lust, they try to make it to correspond to their own views," using Acts 20:35 to lessen the force of Matthew 19:21—in other words, arguing that riches are needed if one is to serve and give to others.[45]

This ploy is as modern as it is ancient. For example, there are many who "interpret with base ingenuity" Jesus's comment about the "eye of the needle" such that it is no longer impossible for the large camel to get through the smallest opening, but only difficult. (Often this interpretation requires the exegete to suggest that there was a low gate in the Old City called the "eye of the needle," though this is simply wishful thinking on the part of the wealthy or those aspiring to wealth.) Apparently the disciples understood Jesus to mean that it is *impossible* for the rich to enter the Kingdom, because they retort in surprise, "Then *who* (if not the God-blessed wealthy) can be saved?!" And Jesus makes it crystal clear that it *is* impossible . . . for mortals. Even if we understand Jesus's radical statement, we often resort to euphemisms such as "stewardship" to justify our accumulation in the face of need.

As Gregory pointed out, it is not just apprehension joined to faithlessness and idolatry that stimulates greed and its justifications. Pride arouses avarice as well. We are not satisfied with what we have. Schor lists many reasons for our dissatisfaction: image, socializing and social rituals, technological change, the need for transportation as we move to the suburbs and shop at the malls, a basic psychological need not to be left out of the national shopping spree, unhappiness at work, or, especially, upscaling.[46] And as Schor puts it, it's no longer simply a matter of keeping up with the Joneses; it's about distinguishing one's self from the Joneses.[47]

Add to all of this our national pride, because consuming is a social act: instead of placing voluntary constraints on competitive spending on everything from athletic shoes for school to family holiday spending, today's society encourages consumption as patriotic and for the good of the collective.[48] This manifests itself in our expectation of an annual rise in the "standard" of living—a socially moving target that has become a "national icon, firmly rooted in the political discourse," according to Schor. What we considered luxuries in the 1970s are now "necessities."[49] And those with higher incomes complain of "not having enough."[50]

How Greed Manifests Itself

So, greed is alive and well. As we have pointed out, it appears in different guises. In fact, at one point Cassian's description of the monk who has been taken in by covetousness sounds very much like Juliet Schor's depiction of the American consumer.

The avaricious monk retains the shadow of humility, charity, and obedience, but in reality is displeased with everything, murmuring and groaning over every bit of work, showing no reverence ("like an unbridled horse"), and discontent with daily food and the usual clothing: "He declares that God is not *only* there, and that his salvation is not confined to that place, where, if he does not take himself off pretty quickly from it, he deeply laments that he will soon die." He is discontent and contemptuous with everything in the monastery such that he wants to flee (*if* the weather is good!). He even complains when he is slighted over against a needy brother, even though he has a secret stash.[51] In other words, this monk demonstrates an instability in his life—a restlessness, always moving on and always seeking more.

Schor asserts that people today are more concerned with what they can't afford than with what they have. In fact, she argues that the "severely addicted person is addicted not so much to the products as to the act of purchasing itself."[52] She cites the sociologist Colin Campbell's argument that a distinctive aspect of modern consuming is that "we have strong desires for products before we have them, but once acquired they mean very little to us. . . . American consumers seem to accumulate large numbers of things in which they subsequently lose interest."[53]

This is corroborated by William Cavanaugh's observation that we are *not* attached to our material possessions; in fact, we are *detached*:

> In consumer culture, dissatisfaction and satisfaction cease to be opposites, for pleasure is not so much in the possession of things as in their pursuit. . . . And the pleasure resides not so much in having as in wanting. Once we have obtained an item, it brings desire to a temporary halt, and the item loses some of its appeal. Possession kills desire; familiarity breeds contempt. That is why shopping, not buying itself, is the heart of consumerism. The consumerist spirit is a restless spirit, typified by detachment, because desire must be constantly kept on the move.[54]

As evidence of this, Schor notes that we are losing space to store all of this accumulated stuff from which we are detached; storage facilities are in high demand:

> What's most impressive is that we are complaining about too much junk even as housing space per person has risen substantially, new homes increasingly boast walk-in closets, and garages are often used as extra storage areas. But then again, maybe that's part of the problem.[55]

Schor pictures this "upward shift in consumer aspirations" colliding with an expansion of "reference groups" (those with whom we identify) to produce the "consumer anxiety, frustration, and dissatisfaction" we see in today's society.

The American consumer which Schor and Cavanaugh describe is Cassian's restless monk that he will describe when we get to the chapter on sloth!

It is interesting that greed not only manifests itself in such excessive desire that is never satisfied, but also in excessive *giving* at the price of despoiling others, as Gregory suggests. This is not unlike the counterintuitive aspect of gluttony that manifests itself in *under*eating or of sloth that manifests itself in *busyness*; even more to the point, it is similar to Cassian's warning against engaging in a severe fast that may engender gluttony. Gregory describes the *indiscriminate* giver as the one who falls into avarice once "want assails them." In this way avarice becomes the child of the virtue "bountifulness," "from which a harvest of sins sprouts." So he counsels that we should admonish such people to hold on to their possessions in a reasonable way and not take what belongs to others afterward:

> For if the root of the fault is not dried out while the growth is profuse, the thorns of avarice, exuberant in the branches, will never be withered. Consequently, the occasion for despoiling others is withdrawn, if the right of ownership is first well-ordered. . . . Obviously, it is one thing to show mercy for sins committed, another to sin in order to be able to show mercy [that is not *really* mercy].[56]

Gregory goes on to note how such people carefully tally how much they give, but neglect to calculate how much they seize; they might even go so far as to offer to God what they withdraw from the needy (perhaps not unlike Jesus's comments about Pharisees who designated their possessions in such a way that they were no longer under obligation to support their parents; see Mark 7:6–16).

It is at this point that we begin to realize the impact greed has as it shows up in the other cardinal sins to which it is related—sins such as vainglory, envy, gluttony, and lust, let alone the "daughter" sins such as murder and injustice. We can see the connection even in our contemporary consumer culture: two of the key phrases that Schor uses are "competitive spending" and "competitive acquisition," concepts that are certainly manifestations of the vainglory and envy associated with avarice.[57] Coordinated with her sociological perspective but from a more theological slant, John Kavanaugh says that what he calls the "Commodity Form" encourages "competition for supremacy, domination, and self-justification," as well as idolatry, the power of which lies in the rejection of our contingency—our creaturehood and our precarious created freedom.[58]

It should not surprise us, then, that our monastic psychologists find that greed ultimately leads to self-destruction and complete isolation from God and fellow human beings. We have noted that Judas is often used as the paradigm for this, but we need not go as far back as two millennia; we see it acted out in movie classics like *Treasures of the Sierra Madre* and *Fargo*, and in real-life examples such as Bernard Madoff, the former stockbroker, investments advisor, and financier who was convicted in 2009 of defrauding thousands of investors out of billions of dollars. And this is true not just of individuals, but of social groups and nations whose greed leads to social injustice, oppression, and crime. At times the appeal *is* made to the message of Old Testament prophets such as Elijah, Isaiah, Amos, and Micah or to Old Testament passages such as Jeremiah 22:17, Ezekiel 22:27, and Habakkuk 2:9. Jacques Ellul states graphically and poignantly what all of these, past and present, are saying about the ramifications of our greed: "The selling of Jesus, first foreshadowed by the story of Joseph sold by his brothers, then by Amos (2:6), shows the constancy of the selling relationship and carries its meaning to the absolute."[59]

The effect on community is a significant aspect of greed's manifestation in our lives. Certainly Orville Wood's wife learned this. She became the victim of power struggles over money, berated for putting too much butter on potatoes and hot water in the bathtub. Her life was endangered by severe depression and more, such that she left a manuscript in which she wrote, "I am left broken down in middle age. . . . Why was my economic status less than that of a servant? My life was tortured because of his love of money, which was his master passion."[60]

Citing Deuteronomy 20:8, Cassian warns against association with the lukewarm brother who should never have taken initial vows of renunciation, because by that one's persuasion and bad example he will turn others back from the perfection of the gospel and weaken them by his "faithless terror." Such should withdraw from the battle and return home, "because a man cannot fight the Lord's battle with a double heart."[61]

In modern life, Cassian's warning against the greedy monk's negative impact on community members is not far removed from what Schor calls the "upscale competitive consumption" that has intensified, leaving families, for example, with increasing levels of debt and more hours on the job. As in monasticism, so in Christian terms generally, fulfillment is not to be construed in individualistic terms. Yet that is the added fallout—beyond the family dynamic—of what Schor identifies: "As the pressures on private spending have escalated, support for public goods, and for paying taxes, has eroded." The result is that funds are squeezed for education, social services, and public safety, which, in turn, increases pressure to spend *privately* (such as to get kids into private schools or go to Disneyland rather than the local playground) and to be unwilling to support programs that transfer resources to the poor, so that poverty conditions get worse. And then our "national discourse focuses on market exchanges, not quality of life, or social health. *Gross domestic product is the god to which we pray.* But GDP is an increasingly poor measure of well-being: it fails to factor in pollution, parental time with children, the strength of the nation's social fabric, or the chance of being mugged while walking down the street."[62]

It is no wonder we turn inward from community to the avaricious individual since consumerism reduces persons to "consumers" whose relation to God, family life, friendships, and every other bond is viewed through the consumerist filter.[63] Humans become things in our consumer society—depersonalized in both the individual and relational spheres. As Kavanaugh puts it,

> We are only insofar as we possess. We are what we possess. We are, consequently, possessed by our possessions, produced by our products. Remade in the image and likeness of our own handiwork, we are revealed as commodities. Idolatry exacts its full price from us. We are robbed of our very humanity.[64]

This shows up in terms of power and sex. It becomes easy to institutionally legitimize violence in the forms of sexism, racism, nationalism, or abortion. When the body is viewed as a commodity our understanding and practice of sexuality affects what should be our most intimate and committed human relationship. Kavanaugh makes the point cogently: "The planned obsolescence of intimacy and marriage covenants is patterned after the career of our automobiles. The average American marriage lasts scarcely longer than the average car."[65]

Greed's tentacles reach deep and wide, notably infecting community life as the individual's understanding of herself is shaped by avarice—something Cassian observed centuries ago that we see now in perhaps more dramatic ways. So how can Cassian and his cohort help us? Actually, their insights for handling greed are extremely helpful.

How to Handle Greed

In her book *The Overspent American*, Juliet Schor makes this recommendation: "The first step [to simple living] is to decouple spending from our sense of personal worth, a connection basic to all hierarchical consumption maps. The second is to find a reference group for whom a low-cost lifestyle is socially acceptable."[66] Perhaps the perfect "reference group" for our purposes are our monastic psychologists, for they have much to recommend about ways to manage greed.

Before we get to that point we must realize that we have a problem with greed in the first place. Of the seven on our list, it may be the most difficult to detect. For one thing, we live in denial. Schor's depiction of this strikes close to home for many:

> Most of our cherished religious and ethical teachings condemn excessive spending, but we don't really know what that means. We have a sense that money is dirty and a nagging feeling that there must be something better to do with our hard-earned dollars than give them to Bloomingdale's. As our salaries and creature comforts expand, many of us keep alive our youthful fantasies of doing humanitarian work, continuing the inner dialogue between God and Mammon. Not looking *too* hard helps keep that inner conflict tolerable.[67]

But, as Schor often reminds us in her book, while we don't look hard at ourselves, we more easily recognize competitive spending and materialism in others, especially if they're in a higher income bracket.[68]

Another reason we don't always see avarice for what it is is simply because we revel in the "Rich and Famous." Donald Trump is considered a hero. But rarely do folks today ask whether the goal of getting rich is commendable, at what psychological or spiritual or relational cost it was achieved, what ruthless or immoral means were used, and what "good" will be done with all of this wealth. The only time folks even intervene when it comes to greed is when it leads to criminal behavior or some extreme disruption of family or personal life. For the most part, our society encourages greed, although people don't call it greed. They call it "financial success," "economic security," "the good life," or "having it all." This culture nurtures avarice, economic warfare, the gospel of pleasure. To be sure, greed and hedonism in a capitalist economy produce greater economic good for a greater number of people, but at what cost?—at the cost of socializing the youth to be avaricious and materialistic, and thus less compassionate human beings. It's the kind of thing that even consumes our time and our energy to find the best price on something we could well live without. But it is fueled by business and advertising in our capitalist society, and, frankly, we like it. Perhaps this helps explain why there are few contemporary therapies for it, because it is rarely perceived as undesirable. Indeed, it's the air we breathe; we experience consumer society as something natural, not created.[69]

Yet again, we fail to recognize greed because of the associations we make with status that trigger symbolic spending. Marketers know the symbols are powerful because they can lodge in our subconscious. Schor notes that we have "profound, if often unrecognized, emotional connections to commodities" about which we must become aware, in part by "laying bare the fantasy," if we are even to recognize how we have been duped.[70]

Heeding Schor's admonition is crucial if we are to take the advice of Cassian and others, for we are not prone to deal with avarice unless we recognize it. She argues that we have to "deconstruct the commercial system," doing so, for instance, by questioning the ads, learning to "read" the commercials, thinking about where and how things are made, realizing that "getting a good deal" is not synonymous with "savings," and questioning why The Container Store and storage business ads are more prevalent than ever.[71]

This leads us to the first recommendation that Cassian and Gregory make to overcome greed. We must realize that greed often leads to the opposite of what it promises.

Gregory makes this point as he describes the one who has "delivered himself over to the law of avarice." He is not able to obtain what he longs for, so he spends the day in idleness and the night in thought, contriving, imagining, scheming. And when he figures out a way to secure what he desires, he schemes for more, even though he still doesn't have what he desires. He even imagines how he will respond to those who will be envious of his acquisition until "the empty-handed disputant is wearing himself out in defense of the thing which he desires" but never really acquires. "Quarreling thoughts" are the fruit of such avarice.[72]

What the avaricious person experiences is that his sin becomes its own punishment. He heaps together all he covets and then becomes anxious over the storage of all that he has amassed (as in the parable of the farmer in Luke 12). Gregory points out that "the mind of the covetous man, which before looked for rest from plenty, was afterwards put to worse trouble for the keeping thereof."[73] He dreads conspirators, fears he will suffer what he has done to others, looks upon the poor as thieves, worries about the disappearance of his hoard lest it be "consumed by neglect": "In all these particulars then, because fear by itself is punishment, the unhappy wretch suffers things as great as he fears to suffer. . . . Consumed first here by the punishment of coveting, afterwards by the trouble of safe keeping, and there at some future time by the punishment of retributive wrath." To put it another way, it seems that the more we have, the bigger the locks we must install.

What Gregory describes resonates with the studies that Schor cites which demonstrate that income not only has no effect on happiness, but that materialists are less content than others with their lot in life and tend to be more anxious, depressed, distressed, not as well adjusted, and experiencing lower levels of well-being.[74] The author of Orville Wood's story poignantly summarizes the end result of the life of misers: "Having hoarded their emotions just as they hoarded their money, they often die friendless, barely remembered by anyone but their brokers."[75]

It seems that what mammon distracts us from is what *would* make us happy. As David Myers puts it, "Wealth, it seems, is like health: although its utter absence can breed misery, having it does not guarantee happiness. Happiness is less a matter of getting what we want than wanting what we have."[76] If it were otherwise then Americans would be much happier today than they were midway through last century when they were half as rich, yet studies indicate they are less satisfied, less happy, and more depressed.[77] How close this comes to Cassian's description of the monk whose labor to acquire leaves him no time to pray and fast, believing that "if only he can satisfy the madness of avarice and supply his daily wants," the fire of covetousness would be extinguished by getting, when, in reality, it is inflamed even more.[78]

Rodney Clapp concurs: consumption is a disillusioning experience and "we modern consumers are perpetually dissatisfied"; and though insatiability is as old as Eden, we have deified dissatisfaction.[79]

We should have known. The monks remind us of Ecclesiastes 5:10–17 which begins, "The lover of money will not be satisfied with money; nor the lover of wealth, with gain." Consumption does not free us. But perhaps it is symptomatic of another hunger. That is what Jacques Ellul suspects:

> A person's hunger for money is always the sign, the semblance of another hunger—for power or rank or certainty. The love of money is always the sign of another need—to protect oneself, to be a superman, for survival or for eternity. And what better means to attain all this than wealth? In our frantic, breathless search, we are not looking for enjoyment alone. We are looking, without realizing it, for eternity. Now money does not satisfy our hunger nor respond to our love. We are on the wrong road. We have used the wrong means.[80]

Not only are we on the wrong road. Cassian warns us to avoid it altogether—a second piece of advice for dealing with greed. We are to avoid greed like the plague. At this point Cassian is echoing the Apostle Paul's stern warnings not to associate with the greedy (1 Cor. 5:11) who will not inherit the Kingdom of God (1 Cor. 6:10), nor even to speak of it among the saints (Eph. 5:3).

To have any victory over such covetousness, Cassian insists that we are "not to allow a gleam from the very smallest scrap of it to remain in our heart"; in fact, there is no hope of quenching its flame "if we cherish even the tiniest bit of a spark of it in us."[81] Alluding to the Genesis account of the Fall, he admonishes his monks to be on guard against the serpent's head, but especially in this case. In graphic language he warns us:

> For if [the serpent's head] has been admitted it will grow by feeding on itself, and will kindle for itself a worse fire. And so we must not only guard against the *possession* of money, but also must expel from our souls the *desire* for it. For we should not so much avoid the results of covetousness, as cut off by the roots all dispositions towards it. For it will do no good not to possess money, if there exists in us the desire for getting it.[82]

We are not to be defiled even by the "least coin."

Cassian goes on to say that the shame and disgrace of it is that we could take some solace in being overcome by avarice *if* it were a strong opponent, yet his assessment is that the adversary in this case is feeble. Perhaps it *was*, but Schor cites expert opinion that addiction to spending—what some call "compulsive buying tendency"—has been on the increase. Indeed, many adults admit that shopping makes them feel good, producing endorphins no doubt. So, although she does not consider this opponent feeble as Cassian did, she offers similar advice for dealing with the compulsion: avoid excessive exposure to tempting situations and impulsive buying.[83] In other words, avoid the mall!

And that leads directly to a third point of counsel. Do not feed greed, because the one thing that will *not* cure avarice is feeding it. Gregory compares it to dropsy: the more one drinks of wealth, the more one thirsts for it.[84] It is like dousing a fire with gasoline.

Perhaps this recommendation could go without saying, since it probably comes as no surprise that statistics and surveys demonstrate that the higher one's income the more one must have to be fulfilled. Desire, expectation, and dissatisfaction are only increased the more we make. As Schor puts it, we are "having more but feeling poorer."[85] Later she talks about the "Diderot effect"—that is, the need for unity and conformity in our lifestyle that keeps the consumer escalator moving upward, so that each new item on our "must have" list requires upgrades and accessories.[86] Indeed, the latest iPad is soon not the latest; one retailer even guarantees to buy back (at a less than retail price of course) the item you bought from them in order to replace it with the newest item that trumps the old.

Even Benjamin Franklin observed that "the more a man has, the more he wants"—an aphorism of his that Orville failed to notice when he copied many of the thrifty man's sayings.[87] And Scripture takes it even more seriously, for Gregory surely had Psalm 78:29–31 in mind when he wrote that "it often happens that when Almighty God is greatly wroth with the covetous soul, He first lets all things accrue to it according to its wish, and afterwards takes it away in vengeance, that it may undergo eternal punishments on account of them."[88]

That provides a bit more impetus for another recommendation that is implied but not explicit in the monastic literature, one that resonates with Paul's exhortation in Romans 8:5: "Those who live according to the flesh set their minds on the things of the flesh, but those who live according to the Spirit set their minds on the things of the Spirit." In other words, we should not seek material wealth at the expense of spiritual poverty. We

must reorient our values, something that Cassian's appropria-
tion of the example of Judas brings home.[89] Like Midas, Judas
touched Jesus with a kiss of friendship so that he became to
the betrayer just thirty pieces of silver. What Judas failed to remember is that money has only instrumental value (something
his religious plotters knew in a perverted way); it is *people* who
have *intrinsic* value. Money does not confer knowledge, skill,
courage, or any other meaningful quality.

What money and goods *do* confer is status. As Russell Belk
puts it, our possessions become our "extended selves."[90] The
problem is, as Jesus put it, where your treasure is (i.e., on what
you invest your money, time, energy, focus) is where your heart
will be. Not only do we express ourselves by what we consume,
but what we consume also shapes what we become.

This adds even more urgency to reorient our values, such as
what the "downshifters" and "simple-livers" do of whom Juliet
Schor writes, making value changes in which time and quality
of life become more important than money, emphasizing function over symbolism, and realizing how our commercialized
culture embodies bad values that lead to personal dysfunction
and environmental harm.[91] But this is not an easy adjustment
for two reasons. First, identity and consumption are deeply
connected such that downsizing and simplifying can be a bitter
pill to swallow when success and identity are attached to what
we own.[92] Second, making it even harder to swallow is the fact
that "advertisers admit that they are no longer selling products,
since we really don't need any more products; they are selling
us the values interjected into them."[93]

One strategy for reorienting values is a further recommendation that is implied by the vowed life of the monastics: reduce
wants. From one perspective wealth consists not in having many
possessions but in having few wants. The problem is that wants
soon become what we "need." My wife and I once gave a ride to
a nun who was attending a "Bread for the World" meeting with

us. She had been cloistered for a couple decades—even without access to television or newspapers—until a recent change permitted the nuns to leave the cloister to visit family, for example. She had taken advantage of this, so I asked her what her impression was after being out of the "world" for so long. With a bit of irony she said, "I went into a department store and didn't know how many things I needed."

The inhabitants of these two different cultures—the cloistered convent and the department store—illustrate that what we desire and what we think we need are conditioned by the social situation into which we are placed. It *is* possible to be in the latter social climate and avoid some of the conditioning. A "simple-liver" that Schor cites thinks before he buys because he has *chosen* to live differently:

> If there's something that I want, I ask myself what's motivating me, why do I really want this, what am I going to do with it? Just about anything. From a tool to a book to a piece of clothing or a chair, what is the life cycle of this thing going to be for me? How am I going to deal with it? I'm not making a moral judgment, it's the reality of what am I getting by buying this, what am I adding to my life by having it?[94]

But asking such questions and being conditioned to define needs over against wants is greatly enhanced if one is accountable to a community. As Schor puts it, consuming is a social act, and so is consuming differently.[95] At this point Cassian makes an explicit recommendation, one which underlies the Benedictine tradition that emphasizes the necessity of the *coenobium* (common life of the monastery) as a "school for the Lord's service."[96]

Cassian teaches that victory over avarice is possible only if one remains in the monastery: "And taking no thought for the morrow [i.e., "what you shall eat and what you shall wear"], let us never allow ourselves to be enticed away from the rule of the *coenobium.*"[97] In sync with Cassian's admonition, Ron Sider warns us that mammon thrives in secret and recommends that those in the Christian community remain transparent with their finances (even to the point of considering exposing their 1040).[98]

But this is difficult in our culture. In what Kavanaugh identifies as the "Commodity Form," we are conditioned to relate to each other as things or, more often, as obstructions. And if that is the case, then accountability to a community becomes difficult.[99]

Relating to one another as commodities or obstructions is one thing, but not relating at all is another. That is, modernity[100] and consumerism have encouraged a highly privatized faith, and the danger is that we think we can accurately assess our attitudes toward money and possessions apart from the wisdom and discernment of others. Rodney Clapp clearly articulates the problem: "With such powerful social forces as the market and the media constantly exhorting us to excesses of consumption, it is ludicrous to think the most viable and faithful response is to face these forces as an isolated individual or family."[101]

But it gets worse. Clapp goes on to say that this creates a taboo in the Christian community such that churchgoers are less likely than the general population to discuss their finances with anyone else, especially with fellow disciples. Clearly, we have to find ways to disclose our finances with trusted Christians if we are to follow the advice of someone like Cassian.[102]

In the end it is the Apostle Paul's imperative that brings us to the final counsel for getting a handle on greed. Paul tells the Ephesian church (in 4:19–20) that the gentiles had become greedy to practice every form of impurity, but that that is *not* the way the Ephesian believers "learned Christ." Indeed, Christ taught that if your eye offends, pluck it out; if your hand offends, cut it off. Perhaps Paul had this in mind. He certainly seems to when he commanded the Colossians (3:5) to "put to death what in you is earthly," including greed.

Evagrius, Cassian, Gregory, and Aquinas are all agreed that, as Evagrius put it, charity and money cannot coexist.[103] So the best way to put to death the "earthly" is to cultivate the "virtue of renunciation of everything" by cultivating the virtue of charity, along with justice.[104]

Aquinas discusses at some length the virtue of liberality (over against covetousness and prodigality) which we might associate with charity. This has to do with using well the things that we just as easily could have used ill.[105] Perhaps a contemporary way of saying this is that we must profane money—deny its power and sacred character, destroy it by grace. Such is charity, as Jacques Ellul puts it so well:

> There is one act par excellence which profanes money by going directly against the law of money, an act for which money is not made. This act is *giving*. . . . Giving to God is the act of profanation par excellence. An object which belonged to a hostile power is torn from him in order to be turned over to the true God (Deut 26:1–11). This act obviously has only a spiritual meaning; it makes no sense at all from a social point of view. . . . [And] it introduces *the one who receives the gift* into the world of grace.[106]

In the same spirit John Kavanaugh asks, "What kinds of behavior are not 'good news for business'?" He follows with a list of activities which are not very "profitable" and are "financially worthless," such as spending time with one's children, praying in solitude, visiting with people, participating in covenanted love with the "economics of intimacy and happiness," or committing to the "economics of the vows" of poverty, chastity, and obedience. Yet these are "the very activities which are held up to derision in our media propaganda."[107]

If we followed this advice of the ancients and the moderns with more specificity—advice to profane and dethrone, instruction in virtues of charity and justice—we might give things away that are of value to us (see Luke 18:18–22), become educated about the effect our level of consumption has on those unseen by us, or, as we mentioned before, open our books for the community to examine. We might begin to look very strange—like we don't belong or like we have come from the centuries of Evagrius or Cassian or Gregory. Kavanaugh describes it best: "In a culture of lived atheism and the enthroned commodity . . . the practicing Christian should look like a Martian. He or she will never feel fully at home in the commodity kingdom. If the Christian does feel at home, something is drastically wrong."[108]

Our home is in the future as the perennial outlook of the monks reminds us. As Paul warns in the Colossians passage and as Jesus's parable of the foolish farmer (Luke 12:20) taught, our riches must always be viewed in light of the eschatological end. Cassian and Gregory put it quite starkly:

> Above all, considering the state of our weak and shifty nature, let us beware lest the day of the Lord come upon us as a thief in the night, and find our conscience defiled even by a single penny; for this would make void all the fruits of our renunciation of the world. . . .[109]

> When these [who strive to increase their resources so that they are caught in the snare of sin] long for the gain of this world and ignore the losses they will suffer in the future life, let them hear what Scripture says: "An estate quickly acquired in the beginning will not be blessed in the end." [Prov. 20:21] . . . They, therefore, who hasten to an inheritance in the beginning, cut themselves off from the lot of the blessed in the end, because, while desiring increase here through evil cupidity, they become hereafter disinherited of their everlasting patrimony.[110]

So, ultimately the cure is to recall how fleeting is this present life and how those who have gone before who acquired riches were unable to keep them and are now receiving their due recompense. In other words, we need to keep the end of

Orville Wood's story before us—burial in a threadbare suit in a veteran's cemetery where the plots and headstones are provided at no expense, and remembered at his funeral by fewer than a dozen mourners that did not include his two children and six grandchildren.[111]

5

***

Anger

To Vent or Not to Vent?

> For the nature of anger is such that when it is given
> room it languishes and perishes, but if openly ex-
> hibited, it burns more and more.
>
> Cassian, *Conferences* 16.27 (cf. Prov. 29:11)

Not long ago while my wife was waiting in line at the grocery
store to pay for her groceries, an older man in front of her yelled
to a female employee at the next counter whom he thought
should be bagging his groceries: "Hey, Stubby, get over here and
start doing your job." My wife was stunned. The words were
so startling that she was not sure she had assessed the situation
correctly, so she asked (with a tinge of sarcasm, since she thought
she probably *had* understood correctly), "Were you joking with
her or were you talking to another human being that way?" He
told her this was none of her business. She replied that it was not

right to talk to someone that way. His response did not match his chronological age: he rattled off a list of insults you might hear on an elementary school playground, such as, "I'd hate to be your husband and wake up to see your face every morning." (It is clear that he not only lacked emotional maturity, but he also had poor aesthetic judgment.) My wife answered these insults by calmly retorting "I feel sorry for you" and "That's very sad."

Should my wife have blown up in response to this man's anger? Is there any place for anger in the Christian's life? Without hesitation many would say "of course." But what happens when we listen to our monastic psychologists?

A Very Deadly Sin

Anger was on Evagrius's original list of eight evil thoughts (*logismoi*)—those thoughts with which the demons tempt us. We have seen that each one on the list gives birth to offspring. In the case of anger, Gregory taught that anger propagates an army consisting of strifes, swelling of mind, insults, clamor, indignation, and blasphemies.[1] And we recall that whether each cardinal sin is mortal or venial depends on whether it is opposed to the love and grace of God. In the case of anger, Aquinas implies that while anger and hatred wish evil on another, anger should wish it according to the virtue of justice, while anger's devolution into hatred wishes evil without measure and for its own sake. Further, anger turned to hatred is long-lasting; in fact, it arises from a disposition—a habit—by which a person considers the object of his hatred to be contrary and hurtful to him.[2] An obstinate racism is a good example of anger that has devolved into a *deadly* sin, both spiritually and physically.

Of the principal thoughts or deadly sins, anger is crucial. Evagrius says, "The most fierce passion is anger"[3] and he mentions it more than the others. If Schimmel's assessment as a therapist is accurate when he says that he spends more time helping clients with their anger than any other emotion,[4] then we should not be surprised that the ascetics likewise identified anger as the predominate temptation of the monk and more detrimental to the sought-after tranquility than almost anything else.[5] Consequently, its management was crucial.

Anger Deconstructed

Evagrius defines anger as "a boiling and stirring up of wrath against one who has given injury or is thought to have done so."[6] This "boiling" constantly irritates the soul, especially when at prayer, such as when the offender appears in a mental picture.

Though they catalog them differently, the ascetic theologians distinguish types of anger, sometimes with different words, but always with distinct characteristics. Some anger rages within, while some breaks out in word or deed; some arises quickly and dissipates quickly, while some lasts for days.[7] The monks also recognize that some outwardly directed anger is irrationally directed at inanimate objects or animals; the former may be an easy target since they cannot talk back, and, if our definition of anger means anything, in both cases the objects of anger are thought of metaphorically as rational animate creatures.[8] Finally, these early psychologists knew that anger could also be directed inwardly, against one's self.[9]

The etiology of anger is often a factor of the connections among the eight *logismoi* or seven sins. Not only do they have in common the characteristic of misplaced desire (with which a psychodynamic theorist could have a field day), but they are also in a kind of causal relationship to one another.

Given the arrangement of the eight *logismoi*, it turns out that anger most often arises from avarice, its predecessor on the list. Desire for worldly attainments and material possessions typically lies at the root of anger. When our desires to possess or control are thwarted (and such desires are usually assisted by envy, vainglory, or pride), then we are enraged.[10] There is more to it than this, but the connection is quickly seen in our culture. The movie *Fargo* gives us a graphic example of a man whose life is consumed with avarice to the point that he destroys the lives of others in outward expressions of anger. Or consider the anger or smoldering resentment that accompanies the news that a "less deserving" colleague received a kudo or merit raise that we desire for ourselves. As we shall see, this will lead the ascetics to prescribe contempt for material possessions as a cure for anger.

Anger can easily lead to its successors as well—dejection (or melancholy) and *acedia* (which we think of as sloth).[11] Once one's life is thrown into turmoil by frustrated avaricious goals, the anger often leads to confusion and melancholy, and one might even simply give up trying. Modern psychology recognizes that sometimes depression may be the sequel to anger.[12]

I recall my feeble attempts to learn the game of tennis when I was a boy. My father would take me to the courts and instruct me. Though I had no illusions of going on the circuit and winning at Wimbledon, I did want to be as good as some of my peers who seemed quite adept at the game. But the more I tried to "possess" the skills before patiently practicing the fundamentals, the angrier I got as the ball would slam into the net or sail over the fence. The only thing I could do was perform antics that would later be imitated by John McEnroe. I was good at throwing my racket down, stomping around the court, and yelling words permitted by my limited Fundamentalist vocabulary. Finally, I gave up in frustration. Anger had won the day and a kind of *acedia* (or giving up) had set in.

Is It Okay to Be Angry?

At this point one might ask if there are any legitimate expressions of anger. It might surprise modern ears to hear Cassian tell his fellow monks that the first remedy for anger is to make up their minds *never* to be angry: "the athlete of Christ who strives lawfully ought thoroughly to root out the feeling of wrath."[13] Ephesians 4:31 commands us to accept no anger as "necessary or useful for us."[14] And the goal in acquiring the virtue of patience consists, "not in being angry with a good reason, but in not being angry at all."[15]

Cassian's interlocutor responds: "There is nothing wrong in being angry with a brother who does evil because God is said to be angry with such people (Pss. 6:1; 106:40)." Cassian bristles, for he and Gregory often mention how easily we misuse Scripture to rationalize our behavior.[16] (Cassian is especially good at seeing this in his treatise on avarice; he would not tolerate the way that Western Christians have rationalized their greed into a virtue.) True, he observes, some try to excuse "this most pernicious disease of the soul" by a "shocking way of interpreting Scripture," ascribing to God the taint of human passion. In the theological argument against the anthropomorphites, Cassian reminds us that Scripture speaks of God metaphorically as sleeping, standing, having parts of the human body, and experiencing human passions. Instead, by God's anger we are to understand "that he is the judge and avenger of all the unjust things which are done in this world"; accordingly, we should dread his judgments and fear to do anything against his will.[17]

Cassian also turns his attention to Ephesians 4:26, which, given its context, some want to apply to unbelievers and blasphemers only—whose attacks on the righteous should be endured—but not to brothers who should know better but have angered another with reproachful words. (Some try to do the same sort of thing by twisting Matt. 5:22.)[18] Again, this is a rationalization that Cassian does not permit.

Then is there no room for anger according to Cassian? Actually, it is Ephesians 4:26 that he cannot ignore. We are commanded to be angry in a wholesome fashion, which Cassian interprets as anger with ourselves and the evil thoughts that arise. In a bit of clever medieval exegesis he explains the verse this way: "be angry at your vices and your rage lest you grow dark on account of your wrath and Christ, the sun of righteousness, begin to go down in your dusky minds and, once he departs, you offer room in your hearts to the devil."[19] Cassian is consistent, even if he does strain credulity in this exegetical maneuver. And he is following the wisdom of Evagrius before him, who insisted that anger "is *given* to us so that we might fight against the demons and strive against every pleasure." In fact, when we are tempted, Evagrius admonishes us not to fall immediately to prayer, but first to utter angry words against the one who afflicts us.[20]

Gregory, who inherited the wisdom of Evagrius and was reared on the writings of Cassian (see *Rule of Benedict* 73.5), would not share Cassian's interpretation of Ephesians 4:26. This is obvious from his insistence that Psalm 4:4 (a verse Cassian also employed in his proscription of anger) is wrongly interpreted by those who say that we should be angry only at ourselves and not with others when they sin: "For if we are bidden to love our neighbors as ourselves, it follows that we should be as angry with their erring ways as with our own evil practices."[21] To illustrate his point Gregory cites Eli, whose lukewarm response to the evil practices of those under his charge led to his demise; he should have been angry with them, and might have been had he distinguished between "the anger which hastiness of temper stirs" and "that which zeal gives its character to" and "is kept under the control of reason."[22] The whole thrust of Aquinas's treatment of anger follows Gregory's, borne out of sorrow at being wronged and out of hope at the prospect of a just revenge.[23]

But even though Aquinas recommends the positive role of anger far more than the earlier ascetics, he echoes their assessment of anger's danger: "of all the passions anger is the most manifest obstacle to the judgement of reason."[24] Citing Gregory, Aquinas recognizes that anger is satisfactory as an appetitive movement that begins in the reason (which he refers to as anger's formal element); but the passion of anger forestalls the perfect judgment of reason since its commotion cranks up the heat that urges instant action (which he refers to as anger's material element). In fact, Evagrius does not limit the debilitation to cases when anger is directed outwardly in the name of justice; even the anger that is given to us to fight the demons and temptation is easily redirected by the demons to worldly desires so that we end up fighting with others and, "blinded in mind and falling away from knowledge, our spirit should become a traitor to virtue."[25] Cassian, who thinks that *nothing* justifies anger, puts it bluntly: "It makes no difference whether gold plates, or lead, or what metal you please, are placed over our eyelids, the value of the metal makes no difference in our blindness."[26]

Why Anger Hinders a Good Prayer Life

If we understand the ascetic's concern about the effects of anger on the practice of discernment, then we will have arrived at the key reason why someone like Cassian proscribes any anger at all. To better understand we need to recall what we said about the goal of the monk.

The ascetic theologian described the health of the soul as *apatheia*—that abiding sense of peace and joy that comes from the full harmony of the passions. Enabled by divine grace, this state was attained through discipline and effort that kept the disordered desires in check, even when memories of situations or events might tend to stimulate and disorder the passions.[27]

With this reminder we begin to see the import of what Gregory cautions when he says that, despite the fact we sometimes act out of a sense of justice, "anger joins it from the side . . . [and] wounds all the healthiness of our inward tranquility."[28]

The anger that "darkens the soul" defiles the mind as much as vivid images of sexual pleasure, so that the mind is otherwise preoccupied during prayer, pure prayer is not offered to God, and the demon of *acedia* falls upon the person.[29] But not only is prayer affected; even reason's ability to appropriately redress injustices is hindered in cases where Gregory and Aquinas have given us permission to be angry. As Aquinas observes, anger does not listen perfectly to reason in meting out vengeance. The irony is that in cases wherein we might even justifiably be angry, "anger requires an act of reason, yet proves a hindrance to reason."[30] Let us examine these two (related) debilitating effects of anger.

First, being angry about injuries done to us interferes with our prayer and prevents us from drawing near to God. This is repeatedly asserted by Evagrius in his *Chapters on Prayer*.[31] If this is true, then Cassian wonders how we can obey God's commands to pray without ceasing (1 Thess. 5:17) and in all places (1 Tim. 2:8; note Paul's reference to anger) if we retain bitterness or allow another to retain bitterness against us.[32] We certainly cannot obey Matthew 5:23–24 in such a case. Believing that anger is dangerous and wrong, Cassian asks how we can endure it in ourselves or in someone else when in either case we cannot pray; God does not allow the gifts of our prayers to be offered to him even if our brother or sister has something against *us, whether we think the other feels this way rightly or wrongly* (because Christ did not say, "If your brother has a *true* ground for complaint"), no matter how trivial.[33] The bottom line for Cassian is that we simply should not pray when angry.[34]

An empirical test bears this out. It may be the case that the psalmist's spiritual maturity is such that his prayer life is not affected by anger, but for us who are still in our spiritual infancy, it is nearly impossible to pray the imprecatory psalms while conscious of being a temple of the Holy Spirit. Once in choir at Blue Cloud Abbey in South Dakota an imprecatory psalm came up in the sequence. I had one of the strangest experiences reciting in a monotone the psalmist's desire that the heads of his enemy's children be dashed upon the rocks; it was all the more strange because as I spoke the words, I also heard them behind me and to my right and left. After the office one long-bearded monk, Brother Gene, approached me. "Does it bother you to pray those Psalms in choir?" he asked. I replied that it did. "It does me, too," he answered. "So I just remember all the people in the world today who are being treated unjustly and might feel that way, and I pray for them." What should be noted is that Gene had to dissociate himself from the anger expressed in the psalm in order to continue praying.

Second, anger affects discernment or discretion and cuts us off from good counsel. Discernment is a crucial aspect of the monk's life in the *Rule of Benedict*, particularly in the administration of monastic life. Cassian leaves no room for doubt about the blindness to which anger can lead: "We can neither acquire right judgment and discretion, nor gain the insight which springs from an honest gaze, or ripeness of counsel, nor can we be partakers of life, or retentive of righteousness, or even have the capacity for spiritual and true light."[35] The list goes on. Apropos in a culture that would find Cassian's remark extreme, he insists that we are in reality cut off from all good judgment *even though* we are thought to be the wisest, most prudent, and knowledgeable.

Even the less strident Gregory zeroes in on the crucial loss of discernment brought on by anger, linking it to a theological concern:

> We must above all things know, that as often as we restrain the turbulent motions of the mind under the virtue of mildness, we are essaying to return to the likeness of our Creator. For when the peace of the mind is lashed with anger, torn and rent, as it were, it is thrown into confusion, so that it is not in harmony with itself, and loses the force of the inward likeness.[36]

Anger does away with wisdom, leaving us in ignorance of what to do. And even if we could discern with good judgment *what* to do, Gregory insists that the mind is still so confused that it cannot execute the action.[37]

So Gregory agrees with Cassian that anger, even born out of a love of virtue, obscures the sight of transcendent objects—which can only be beheld in a state of tranquility (or, to use Cassian's favorite phrase, "purity of heart")—because the mind is disquieted and agitated. But, unlike Cassian, he admits that a brief anger that is associated with a righteous cause can, after a while, enable a person to see *more* of the transcendent—as ointment applied to a diseased eye temporarily clouds vision before it restores sight.[38] The problem, as Gregory later admits, is that it is easy to confuse "furious anger" with a zeal for justice, so that one can end up sinning in the correction of sin by punishing a fault immoderately. Instead of correction, one ends up with oppression. In correcting faults, anger should follow reason as the employed, not the employer. Why then do some overdo it? Here Gregory returns to the foundational reason for the ascetics' concern about anger's effects on discernment: in the end, one cannot see clearly because her eyes are not focused on one thing, but on many things (including the temporarily focused object of anger). Instead of being intent on the love of her Creator alone, many things are desired, and she is distracted with countless thoughts involving transitory cares.[39]

Neither Vent nor Suppress

Cassian nicely summarizes the concern of the ascetic theologians when he says, "wrath that is nursed in the heart, although it may not injure men who stand by, yet excludes the splendor of the radiance of the Holy Ghost, equally with wrath that is openly manifested."[40] Whether tolerated for justice's sake or not, the ascetics recommend neither venting anger nor suppressing it. The insightfulness of this should not be lost on us moderns who have recommended first one and then the other as the appropriate way to manage anger, only for medical researchers and psychologists to now "discover" that the earlier "wisdom" was not the way to physical, emotional, and spiritual health.

Carol Tavris traces the legacy of Darwin (who taught that human anger is just another brand of animal rage) and of Freud (whose followers used an hydraulic model that demanded catharsis) who led us out of the belief that we can and must control anger, to the belief that we *cannot* control it, and then to the current conviction that we *should* not control it.[41] In fact, though she shares a view our early Christian psychologists would hold—namely, that judgment and choice are the hallmarks of *human* anger,[42] current popular thought, even among some clinical psychologists and psychiatrists, is that anger must be ventilated.[43] But beginning in 1956 with studies by Feshbach, followed by Hokanson's very important research published in 1961, the aggression-frustration-catharsis theories were found to be unsubstantiated (though some studies continue to argue the case). A rather conclusive study published by Mallick and McCandless in 1966 demonstrated that, while frustration leads to heightened aggressive feelings, subsequent aggressive behavior does not reduce the aggression, has no cathartic value, and, especially in the case of verbal aggressive retaliation, may actually increase aggression. Surprisingly, it was also demonstrated that when cultural expectations were removed, there were no significant sexual differences in behavioral aggression toward frustrators.[44]

Some might be amazed to learn that the early Christian psychologist Evagrius observed what these studies now demonstrate when he wrote, "Both anger and hatred increase anger. But almsgiving and meekness diminish it even when it is present."[45] While we will deal later with his recommendation of a countermeasure for handling anger, it is important to see that the ascetic theologians did not endorse venting (though the manufacture of foam bats may have made a lucrative cottage industry for the monastery). In fact, Gregory astutely understands our modern tendency to turn the ventilation of anger into a virtue when he writes: "Anger is also wont to exhort the conquered heart, as if with reason, when it says, The things that are done to thee cannot be borne patiently; nay, rather, patiently to endure them is a sin; because if thou dost not withstand them with great indignation, they are afterwards heaped upon thee without measure."[46] Indeed, on the highways we have turned patient endurance into a vice at worst and a naive response at best; afraid of being taken advantage of, we have made a virtue of demanding our own way.

On the other hand, the ascetic theologians did not condone the strategy of suppression. Gregory writes about those whose anger is not displayed in an open frenzy through the hands and tongue, but in whom anger "inwardly burns the worse."[47] In graphic terms Cassian describes those who would not dare or are not able to show their anger openly: "they turn the poison of their wrath back to their own destruction, brooding over it in their hearts and in glum silence digesting it within themselves. They do not at once and with strength of mind cast out their bitter sadness; instead, they mull it over, and eventually as time goes on they deal with it equably."[48] Some of these can only completely satisfy their anger or sulkiness if they unleash completely, so they stew until the opportune moment, retaining their feelings in the hope of an optimal opportunity for revenge.[49]

Whether or not they eventually unleash it in revenge, those who suppress their anger can ruin relationships in the meantime simply by what Cassian and Gregory identify as a feigned patience and a spiteful silence.[50] In fact, this might do more damage to the object of anger and to a relationship than a quick venting of anger. Gregory admits (as we shall see) that the "rigorousness of silence" is sometimes part of an interior discipline (like counting to ten). But sometimes, he observes, "the incensed mind foregoes the wanted converse," and the anger gets transformed into hatred. The angry person finds "louder riot in its silence, and the flame of pent-up anger preys upon it the more grievously." This prohibits the anger from being removed from one's own mind and, at the same time, often feeds anger in the other party. Cassian says that such a person often imagines himself to be patient because he has mistaken the suppression of outward expressions of anger as the fulfillment of God's commands, when God is interested in our resolution of the conflict no matter who initiated it.[51] In fact, this kind of suppression deceitfully mocks the other with its feigned patience (in a manner like Judas's deceitful kiss) and blasphemes God to whom prayers are offered. One blasphemes God, for example, in the sacrilege of a two-day fast that is incited by rage while sustaining one's self on a surfeit of anger, so that in reality one's sacrifices and prayers are offered to the devil (citing Deut. 32:17). These might be people who abuse or misunderstand Christ's command in Matthew 5:39 to turn the other cheek, because they miss the intention of the passage, which is not only to avoid retaliation and strife, but to mitigate the wrath of the striker rather than merely to walk away.[52] Certainly most people who are married can identify with Cassian's description of the one who imagines they are the paragon of virtue when they respond to their partner in "sullen silence or scornful motions and gestures." Gregory and Cassian are right when they observe that such suppressed outward expression only exacerbates the problem.

The description of this person who lacks the virtue of patience but exhibits outward restraint is something like Cassian's description of continence vis-à-vis chastity in his discussion of lust. The latter involves far more than mere abstinence from sex, just as getting a handle on anger is far more than mere suppression. But the difference between dealing with lust and dealing with anger is that, while continence is still commendable even in the absence of chastity, suppression of stored-up anger is not the same as the suppression of stored-up sexual passion. For, in the case of anger such storage harms us (in spite of the fact that moderns also wrongly think that suppressed sexual expression harms us). In fact, Cassian says there is a tell-tale sign that we have not acquired the virtue of patience, though we have stored up anger that is not outwardly directed at persons: "the feelings of passion still retained will spend themselves on dumb and paltry things, not allowing a continuous state of peacefulness or freedom from remaining faults."[53] Certainly, this is borne out in contemporary observations that repressed anger sometimes manifests itself in other ways.

If the ascetic psychologists will not permit us to vent our anger nor to suppress it in order to manage it, what option is left? If anger is so detrimental to prayer and to the maintenance of discernment, both of which are necessary for our health, then how will we manage anger, or, more in the spirit of the ascetics, how will we rid ourselves of it?

Curing Anger: Cultivating Patience and Humility in Community

The primary antidote for anger is to cultivate the virtue of patience—the virtue opposite the vice of anger. (Each of the deadly sins or principal faults has a corresponding virtue.) As we will see, humility is often mentioned alongside patience, and the two are fundamental qualities that underlie the healthy spiritual life, as Cassian and the later *Rule of Benedict* make clear. In the case of anger, this patience allows the heart to be "widened" in order to diffuse anger.

We have already noted that Gregory *mentions* a kind of silent response in place of anger—a restraint that is not counter-productive but is part of an interior discipline. Cassian seems to be referring to the same thing when he teaches those who become even slightly disturbed by another person to keep lips and the "depth of his breast" unmoved—to "keep himself in by entire silence" (appealing to Pss. 39:1–2 and 77:4):

> And he should not pay any heed to his present state, nor give vent to what his violent rage suggests and his exasperated mind expresses at the moment, but should dwell on the grace of past love or look forward in his mind to the renewal and restoration of peace, and contemplate it even in the very hour of rage, as if it were sure presently to return.[54]

This silence, then, is not the kind of unhealthy suppression that allows the subject to stew until the pressure can be retained no longer, nor is it the kind of silence that is likely to further offend the other party. It requires a disciplined memory and a rather robust hope in order to settle the quake that threatens to destabilize one's spiritual and emotional equilibrium. But this is only the beginning of what Cassian is really after as one cultivates patience.

Toward the end of *Conference* 16 on the topic of friendship (in which we find one of two sustained treatments of anger in Cassian's writings, the other being *Institute* 8), Cassian indicates how anger should be disciplined by describing metaphorically what patience, long-suffering, and courage accomplish. Again, employing clever medieval hermeneutics—this time of Romans 12:19 (specifically, the phrase "but give place to wrath," NKJV)—he argues that our patient restraint "enlarges" the heart so that it has "safe recesses of counsel" to receive, diffuse, and thereby do away with the "foul smoke of anger." Following the advice of Proverbs 12:16, Cassian prescribes temporarily covering up anger for the moment in order to destroy it forever:

> For the nature of anger is such that when it is given room it languishes and perishes, but if openly exhibited, it burns more and more. The hearts then should be enlarged and opened wide,

lest they be confined in the narrow straights of cowardice, and be filled with the swelling surge of wrath, and so we become unable to receive what the prophet calls the "exceeding broad" commandment of God in our narrow heart.[55]

The imagery here might be likened to water passing through a narrow pipe with increased pressure, over against water passing through a widened pipe with decreasing pressure and movement. Cassian is arguing that the pressure of anger waiting to be released (and even to remain if unreleased) dissipates when our hearts are widened by, for instance, past memories of God's forgiveness of and patience with *us,* or by visions of future reconciliation.

In other words, the temporary restraint of our anger accompanied by intentionally focused mental exercises might mollify our anger toward another person. Certainly this is what some psychological prescriptions entail today when, for example, they teach an empathetic response in the moment of passion whereby, so to speak, the heart is enlarged. In some psychological circles this technique is referred to as "cognitive reappraisal" or "reframing"—a reinterpretation of an event. For example, I might say, "He did not intentionally cut me off in traffic to be mean to me or because he is a reckless driver or because he was preoccupied using his car phone to be the sixth caller in a local radio station contest. Perhaps he just received some tragic news and he is now in a hurry to attend to the situation." By delaying my angry response and withholding my typical verbal venting ("What a jerk!"), I can enlarge my heart, and further widen it as my mind works to realize how many times *I* have been the "jerk" on the highway and the object of people's wrath or forgiveness. Indeed, Mallick and McCandless's study concluded just that: "Reasonable interpretation of a frustrator's behavior is strikingly effective in reducing both behavioral and verbal aggression toward him."[56] Discretion and discernment are once again called for.

My wife's attempt to first understand the intention of the man's comment in the checkout line was an effort to reframe the event. Perhaps she could have paused longer to ask herself if there were other circumstances in this man's life that helped to explain his attitude toward the bagger. But at least her pause and attempt to reappraise the situation had the effect of reducing her subsequent verbal aggression. Besides that, my wife is just blessed with a lot more patience than someone like me.

Now, this patience is not something that we can develop "in thirty days or our money back." As in the cultivation of all virtues in the monastic tradition, this requires training over a long period of time in the company of like-minded individuals. Each of the eight principal thoughts has a specific cure. In the case of sloth, for instance, one must return to his cell and attend to spiritual readings and prayer. In the case of lust, as we explained, one must run from the object of desire. But in the case of anger, the one thing a person should *not* do, according to Cassian, is to leave those with whom she is angry because she thinks that solitude and Psalm-singing is what will ameliorate her angry feelings. Though such people think they are softening the bitter thoughts that have arisen by seeking solitude, they are actually losing the opportunity to obey Christ's command in Matthew 5:22–24, to demonstrate care and humility, to offer a "well-timed expression of regret," and so forth.[57]

Cassian insisted that a monk must be trained in the *coenobium* (monastic community) before he ventured forth into the desert alone. Only those who are

> perfect and purified from all faults ought to seek the desert, and only when such people have thoroughly exterminated all their faults amid the assembly of the brethren, should they enter it not by way of cowardly flight, but for the purpose of divine contemplation, and the desire of deeper insight into heavenly things, which can only be gained in solitude by those who are perfect. *For whatever faults we bring with us uncured into the*

desert, we shall find to remain concealed in us and not to be got rid of.[58]

Solitude only intensifies uncorrected faults. A person in solitude appears to himself to be patient and humble and loving when not interacting with others (which may explain, in part, why people are often surprised at the "failure" of public figures whom they have only known in the "solitude" of their conference speaking or professional position), but the person quickly reverts to his untrained nature when the opportunity comes to display it. Qualities such as patience and humility and love can only be developed with practice in community. Cassian wisely observes that the mere shadow or pretense of patience that the untrained displays out of respect and publicity is lost altogether through sloth and carelessness.[59]

One of the important ingredients in the cultivation of patience and humility that the angry person will miss if she retreats into solitude is the "common consent" of like-minded people and the advice of the elders. Even equipped with Scripture, what sounds good to two friends in the community may be a case of poor judgment and misuse of Scripture. Special revelation certainly must be the norm and source for a Christian psychology, but there is also the indispensable need for advice and admonition from our traditions and our elders in order to understand and apply Scripture. This is an important ingredient in monastic spirituality as it emphasizes obedience. In other words, in order to avoid self-deception and to check Satan's attempts to confuse and obscure our thoughts (à la 2 Cor. 11:14), Cassian warns us not to trust our own judgments more than the community's advice. We must receive advice "in a humble and gentle heart" and submit our own ideas for consideration by those more experienced and approved. Cassian has in mind operating under the rubric of Philippians 2:1–3, thinking more of the knowledge and holiness of one's partners and believing that "the better part of true discretion [which, again, anger blinds us from seeing] is to be found in the judgment of another" rather than in one's own. In fact, Cassian insists that this applies even to the most keen and learned, since "no one however learned he may be, should persuade himself in his empty vanity that he cannot require conference with another."[60] Once again, we see the connection between the eight *logismoi* or seven deadly sins: avarice, sloth, vainglory, and pride will do us in if we do not cultivate patience and humility in a community of like-minded friends. And anger precludes such friendships, which is why the ascetics can refer to it as the traitor of virtue.[61]

It should now be obvious why Cassian prescribes taking responsibility for one's own anger rather than blaming others. The person who blames others for her anger places herself in a position of solitude—either voluntarily or involuntarily. It is difficult to blame others for one's own anger and still seek out others for help in overcoming anger. Blaming others for our impatience and therefore seeking solitude where no one will provoke us to anger will not improve us. Cassian wisely says,

> The chief part then of our improvement and peace of mind must not be made to depend on another's will, which cannot possibly be subject to our authority, but it lies rather in our own control. And so the fact that we are not angry ought not to result from another's perfection but from our own virtue, which is acquired, not by somebody else's patience, but by our own long-suffering.[62]

Cassian compares people who lack virtue but blame others for their anger (and other faults) to people who are affected by some bodily malady but blame their cooks and attendants for the delicacy of their stomach and weak health: "they ascribe the grounds of their upset to those who are in good health, as they do not see that they are really due to the failure of their own health."[63]

Then if one is to accept responsibility for the management of his anger, what might help along the way? Cassian and Gregory offer some advice.

Practices, Preparation, and a Precept

There are *practices* one can engage in, such as *negative exercises* that ward off sins related to anger. Cassian recommends contempt for material or worldly possessions, which, as we have noted, might ward off the avarice that so often leads to anger.[64] For instance, a neighbor told me that his method of dealing with anger at a motorist who "took his space" on the highway was to remind himself that none of the highway was really *his* space to begin with. By cutting out his avaricious attitude regarding the highway, he was able to cut off anger at the pass. Another negative exercise that Gregory recommends has the effect of fostering the humility that is needed to counter pride and vainglory: one should refuse to imagine herself to be a wise and experienced person who prefers her own opinions to her neighbors. Likewise, when tempted to be angry at the transgressions of others, she must recall her own.[65] When our son lost his glasses in the lake one summer due to a lack of forethought, my anger didn't stand a chance when I remembered the two times during high school when mine ended up in muddy waters. When our son nicked another car as he maneuvered into a parking space with inexperienced judgment, my anger didn't stand a chance when I remembered the time I backed my mother's little car into my father's Impala in the driveway.

Positive exercises which Evagrius prescribes have been mentioned. They involve the ascetics' common ploy of countering vices with the opposite behavior. In this case Evagrius observes, "Turbid anger is calmed by the singing of Psalms, by patience and almsgiving."[66] Later, he echoes his almsgiving prescription by noting that "a gift snuffs out the fires of resentment."[67] Indeed, it *is* difficult to remain angry when you joyfully give a gift or sing a psalm of praise.

So much for practices on the spot. Gregory recommends a way whereby anger's hold on the mind can be relaxed. It involves *preparation*—a preemptive strike whereby one anticipates all the insults he might experience, keeping in mind at the same time the treatment of Jesus: "For he that forecasts impending ills in a spirit of earnest heedfulness, as it were, watching in ambush, awaits the assaults of his enemy. And he arrays himself in strength for the victory in the very point wherein he was expected to be caught in entire ignorance."[68]

Anticipating the assaults of anger means that one needs to gain some self-knowledge, monitor the patterns of past episodes, and plan ahead a course of action that will keep anger from arising. This is precisely the first step in anger management recommended by psychologist Roy Novaco: the individual must "become an expert on his or her anger" in order to see patterns—people, situations, provocateurs; he suggests keeping a journal to track triggers, frequency, intensity, duration, and mode of expression of one's anger.[69]

Finally, there is a *theological precept* that must be kept in mind: eschatology. In typical fashion, Cassian's last prescription for curing one's anger is this:

> The last is certainly decisive in regard to all vices in general— namely, that a person reflect daily on the fact that he is going to depart from this world. This conviction not only does not permit any annoyance to remain in the heart, but it even suppresses all the movements of every wrongful desire and sin. Whoever holds to this, therefore, will neither suffer nor inflict the bitterness of anger and discord.[70]

As he eludes to here, Cassian is *always* reminding his readers of the eschatological perspective that must pervade our thinking about life. It is an emphasis that is glaringly absent from practical theology and Christian psychology, yet in the Christian narrative it is the only thing that ultimately makes the story we have been baptized into worthwhile if Paul is to be believed in 1 Corinthians 15:14. In the light of God's assessment of our lives, Cassian reminds us that despite our sexual purity, renunciation of possessions, and fasts and vigils, none of this will mitigate God's judgment of our anger and hatred. In light of God's assessment of our works and the resurrection promise that our work is not in vain (1 Cor. 15:58), perhaps some things are not worth the wrath.[71] And when Cassian adds to it a soteriological concern, theology must pull the reins on our anger because God wishes all to be saved, and anger does not accomplish the righteousness of God. As Carol Tavris puts it in a secular context, "the ultimate purpose of thinking twice about anger is to enhance the long-term benefit of the relationship, not the short-term relief of the individual."[72] In this light Cassian insists that we try to cure the anger another has against us, since it is as harmful to us as our own self-destructive anger.

What about Abusive Relationships?

This leaves us with one vexing issue: What should we do about the extreme cases, particularly those involving abuse? This issue comes home to roost when we read in Cassian's conference on friendship that we are to preserve tranquility of heart no matter what evil transpires, not only to keep ourselves from the anger that disturbs us, "but also, by submitting to their injuries, compel those, who are disturbed by their own fault, to become calm, when they have had their fill of blows; and so overcome their rage by our gentleness."[73] This sometimes works, as it did in my high school experience when Rocky (his real name!) hit me in the left jaw (that still pops to this day) and later apologized in public because I had not retaliated. But rage is not often overcome by gentleness when there is a case of spousal abuse, for instance. Cassian is to be commended for trying to translate Romans 12:21 into our lives, and it ought to give the Anabaptist quadrant of our Christian sensibilities some hope. In a sense Cassian certainly is correct when he also says that "in general he plays a stronger part who subjects his own will to his brother's, than he who is found to be the more pertinacious in defending and clinging to his own decisions," because the latter must be pampered and petted. And only the strong can bear and restore to health the weak (after Gal. 6:2). But what if the weak one does not come around?

Cassian says that when two people are not like-minded in their spiritual goals, there will come a time when the weak will no longer be borne:

> The great frailty of the weak, which is sustained by the forbearance of the person who is well and which is daily declining to a worse state, was going to lead him to the conclusion that he himself ought no longer to be put up with or else that it would be better for him to depart at some time or other, once he has become aware of his neighbor's remarkable patience and the deterioration caused by his own impatience, rather than to be constantly put up with because of someone else's magnanimity.[74]

Perhaps Cassian would admit that the same rules do not apply when the friendship of like-minded individuals who seek virtue breaks down. This requires further reflection, and perhaps same-gender monastic communities are not the best source of wisdom here.

Nonetheless, we have seen that in the case of anger management modern secular psychology has not progressed beyond the insights of these ancient Christian psychologists and that moderns have in a few cases reversed their theories only to "arrive" at the conclusions reached by ascetic theologians 1,500 years ago.[75]

6

＊

Envy

The Silent Killer

Silent envy grows in silence. . . .

Nietzsche,
Collected Works, 2:37

The Bloody History of Envy

Following a long tradition attributed to Satan's initiation and perpetuated by the biblical likes of Cain, Jacob, Joseph's brothers, Saul, and Judas, on January 30, 1991, thirty-six-year-old Wanda Webb Holloway was arrested in Channelview, Texas, for what the *New York Times* described as "a purported murder plot born of big envies and small ambitions."[1]

Mrs. Holloway, a regular church attender and organist, had been frustrated for a couple of years because her thirteen-year-old daughter, Shanna Harper, had been bested in cheerleading tryouts by her rival and neighbor, thirteen-year-old Amber Heath. Though the case was retried on appeal, Mrs. Holloway was found guilty on September 3 of trying to hire someone to kill Amber's mother. It seems the $7,500 price tag for murdering Amber *and* her mother was a bit steep, so Wanda settled for a $2,500 bargain: she could rid herself of pesky Verna Heath and simultaneously grieve daughter Amber to the point that Shanna would be a shoo-in as a Channelview High School cheerleader on the freshmen squad. (Channelview's squads had won national championships, so the stakes were high!) Besides the obligatory television docudrama that later exploited the story, folks surrounding the case were quick to share their perspective. A police investigator described Mrs. Holloway's *modus operandi*: "She was cold, calculating and persistent about her intentions over an extended period of time." The school principal shared his *mea culpa*: "We are all guilty of standing back and watching what has been happening to her, because all of us—anyone who is a parent—can identify with her, at least to the extent that we all push our children to compete, that we all want our children to succeed." A detective tried to figure out this admittedly bizarre crime: "Reasonable people like you and me can't understand how in the world cheerleading can be so important, but I think these people are just a bubble off." And then there was the prosecutor's closing argument at the end of a six-day trial "replete with tales of jealousy, frustrated ambitions and conniving ex-spouses": "This ain't about cheerleading, folks. It's about someone who hated someone so much that it gnawed at her night and day." Before her sentencing, Mrs. Holloway denied she had solicited someone to murder Mrs. Heath (though she was caught on tape suggesting the intended victim be whisked away to Cuba for fifteen years—the rationale for the jury's sentence of fifteen years in prison), but she admitted she was "totally humiliated"; she claimed that in her secretly recorded conversations she never seriously wanted to hurt anyone, but Shanna's failures and Amber's successes had driven her to an irrational jealousy.

Such irrational jealousy—or "envy"[2]—can apparently get both the envier and the envied killed; it is a very serious thought to entertain, though Evagrius never really deals with it, and Cassian does not include it in his list of principal faults. Cassian does recognize its severity in one conference and, as we will see, considers it to be one of the most dangerous sins we confront. Perhaps this recognition led Gregory to add it to the infamous list of seven.[3]

We mentioned at the outset that, as a killer, envy has been around a long time. It is given as the reason for which Satan fell in Wisdom of Solomon 2:24, an observation made by Cassian and Gregory, as well as by Tertullian and Basil (in his wonderful sermon on envy). Gregory suggests the specific object of envy was what Satan lost in heaven that he subsequently begrudged to humans, damning himself further by ruining others.[4] Tertullian and Basil attribute the envy to Satan's rage against God for making humans in the image of God or for his "great bountifulness" to humans; since the adversary was powerless against God, he avenged himself on humans.[5] And so, Cassian concludes that because of envy "the very first to perish and to fall was the one who is the source of everything deadly."[6]

With that act the dominoes fell. Cain, whom Basil calls "the first disciple of the devil,"[7] committed the first homicide (Gen. 4:2–8). For envy of Abel's acceptable sacrifice Cain "wholly cut off from life him whom he was grieved to see better than himself."[8] The biblical story continues with Jacob who connived with his mother to steal his elder brother's birthright, Joseph's brothers who sold the favored sibling into slavery, and Saul whose envy burned brighter as the pursued David heaped kindnesses upon him (a very significant phenomenon we will recall later).[9]

Of course, Gregory and Basil locate the pinnacle of the biblical story about envy in the betrayal of Christ by the priests, scribes, and Pharisees (Matt. 27:18; Mark 15:10). As Gregory plays back and forth between the story of Job (e.g., 1:17) and the story of Christ's enemies, he reiterates his complaint that the "flames of envy" came down from the rulers and "consumed" the ignorant masses so that "all that was of good springing up in the people" was burnt up.[10] Gregory cites their envy of the truths Jesus taught. Basil cites their envy of his miracles. Both warn against the destruction to which we are liable if we associate with such enviers—those who destroy the Author of life, scourge the Deliverer of humans, and condemn the Judge of nations.

Basil concludes the narrative:

> So do the evils of envy reach to all things. And so from the beginning of the foundations of the world until the end of time, the Devil, the Destroyer of life, by means of this sole weapon, wounds and strikes down all men. He who rejoices in our destruction, he who fell himself through envy, is preparing the same path for us by means of this same vice.[11]

The Characteristics of Envy

Thomas Aquinas defined envy as a kind of sorrow for *another's good* that a person perceives to be *her evil*.[12] More specifically, it is not sorrow for the other's good when that good *is* an occasion of harm to the sorrower; in that case we would be speaking of fear, and that may not even enter the category of a sin.[13] Envy is grieving over another's good when it seems to lessen the envier's own good name or esteem. It is a self-inflicted wound in which one is racked by the prosperity of another person.

While Gregory and Aquinas believe that envy "manifestly" springs from vainglory,[14] and while Benedict appears to connect it with avarice,[15] envy has at least two characteristics it can call its own.

120

First, when we *covet* another's possessions, status, or reputation, we do not begrudge them having what they have; we just wish we had it, too. But when we *envy* what another possesses we not only want it for ourselves, we usually want to dispossess them of it in the process. It is their possession of that which we envy which drives us mad, as Aquinas's definition implies. The envier seems more interested in depriving, humiliating, or hurting the envied than in possessing what the envied has. In fact, even though the envier knows that despoiling the other will probably not result in her possession of the spoils, and even though the envier might know that the possessor has what she has due to hard work (though that is certainly not always the case), nonetheless, the envier seeks to deprive the other.[16]

Second, envy differs from avarice in another respect: a person often covets what is completely outside his reach, but he would rarely if ever envy someone who is far distant from him in place, time, or station. As Schoeck puts it, "Envy is above all a phenomenon of social proximity."[17] I might covet Shaquille O'Neal's fame or fortune, but I do not envy his fame or fortune, let alone his talent. A superior college basketball player might envy Shaquille O'Neal for all these things, yet he would not envy Joe DiMaggio. As Aquinas put it, a commoner does not envy the king unless he is out of his mind.[18] It is interesting that centuries later social scientists have substantiated Basil's and Aquinas's observations with a research-backed phenomenon called "domain relevance." In a relationship that is meaningful to us, when comparisons are made in domains that are crucial to how we define ourselves and we are outperformed by the other person, we experience envy. The discrepancy reflects badly on us, calling attention to our shortcomings or our inferiority.[19] So an enormous inequality arouses less envy than a minimal inequality.[20] We might covet what is outside our reach, but we can only meaningfully envy a relative equal. It makes no sense for me to envy the fame of Karl Barth, but it would be meaningful (though regrettable) for me to envy a contemporary, well-published theologian who is simultaneously popular on the lecture circuit.

Of course, it is likely that my peer did not gain his reputation merely by winning the theological lottery. He probably was diligent in his studies, his writing, and his speaking. On the other hand, I might have been content to have settled down into middle-class academic or ecclesiastical complacency. In this way envy is similar to sloth: as sloth is grief for a divine spiritual good without satisfying the demands of attaining it, so envy is grief for a neighbor's good without working for it.[21] The more another's reputation grows because he has earned it, the more ludicrous the envy is shown to be. This is why Cassian says that envy is the incentive of the sarabaites to act the way they do. Sarabaites are monks whom the *Rule of Benedict* describes as disobedient.[22] In other words, instead of submitting to authority and obeying monastic discipline, the envious sarabaite is the lukewarm independent soul who wants the name and reputation of faithful monks but lacks the urge to really be like them. He wants the praises that are heaped on those who prefer Christ's poverty to the world's riches, without taking on the poverty.

What is tragic about envy is precisely what is entailed in its definition: the more another succeeds in life, the more pain the envier feels. Like an engorged tick, envy is a parasite that swells to the degree that the other prospers. Worse, the envier begins to look for faults amid the good qualities of the righteous and becomes disheartened when the envied one makes further progress.[23] This is a person who will not rejoice with those who rejoice, but is eager to hypocritically weep with those who weep.[24] The envier figures he will climb in stature to the extent that the envied is dethroned. Gregory puts it graphically:

> Whether he goes after the things of earth, or applause, he grudges those things to others, which he pants to have awarded to himself, and strives to make others appear wicked in proportion

as he desires to appear more holy to all the world, so that by means of this, that others are rendered contemptible, he may himself at all times appear more worthy of respect. Whence it comes to pass, that as touching his credit with his neighbor, he spreads out the nets of his tongue before the judgments of his fellow-creatures, that he by himself may catch the good opinion of those whom he seeks to please.[25]

As Gregory insightfully concludes, since we cannot envy any but those who are better than ourselves, the one who is slain by envy bears witness against himself that *he* is the "little one," "in that except he himself proved less, he would not grieve for the goodness of another."[26]

So Cassian, Gregory, and others anticipate what recent psychologists and sociologists have come to recognize: at the heart of envy is a social context—a social comparison that powerfully influences one's self-concept.[27] As we have mentioned, it must be a comparison involving comparable folks resulting in a discrepancy that reflects badly on the envier. And this fits nicely with contemporary paradigms of human behavior, such as Tesser's "self-evaluation maintenance" (SEM) model: people are motivated to maintain or increase their self-esteem—to promote a positive view of themselves, for which much of the feedback comes in social interactions with similar people. We can either be bolstered by the superior attributes and performances of others by basking in reflected glory (not unlike a cure for envy that Gregory prescribes, as we will see) or be threatened in our self-esteem by the comparison.[28]

In the end, envy is a reproach to God. This is what Gregory means when he suggests that envy is as detestable as pride, for with envy we imitate Satan "because he loathes to submit to him who is placed over him by Divine ordinance."[29]

Though there is nothing to corroborate its truth, in Rimsky-Korsakov's opera *Mozart and Salieri* (an adaptation of a Pushkin text) the latter composer compares Mozart's musical skills to his own. The envious Salieri is afraid that his rival's gift is in reality destructive to musical tradition, so his only recourse is to poison Mozart, ostensibly to ensure the future of music. Mozart dies. Salieri is sad, yet relieved. Salieri anguishes in his monologue during the opening scene of this play: "Where is justice when the holy gift of immortal genius is bestowed not as a reward for fervent love of art, self-sacrificing labour, prayer and zeal, but lights upon the head of a dunce, an idle gadabout?" As Richard H. Smith points out on the basis of contemporary psychological research, one of the most important variables predicting an aggressive and hostile response by an envier like Salieri is his belief that the envied person's advantage is unfair, even if the injustice is the result of a hand dealt by God.[30] This belief is based on "equalization of lots" or the "ought force"—an expectation that reflects the envier's *subjective* requirements of justice: folks who are similar in most respects *ought* not to have native abilities, inherited wealth, or physical beauty such as those that are "arbitrarily" doled out to the envied and beyond the envier's control.[31] The effort and pain that went into Salieri's art were commendable, but spoiled by his disdain for God's providential work.[32] The envier detests divine dispensations of grace—of good gifts—when that grace is dispensed on another. That is why Cassian concludes that, "like the poison spurted out by the snake, the bane of envy shuts out the very life of religion and of faith before the wound can ever be diagnosed in the body."[33]

The Remedy for Envy

With his tongue in his cheek, Basil says that the envious person looks for "but one remedy for his affliction: to see one of those he envies fall into misfortune."[34] But his tongue does not remain long in his cheek; there is little to laugh about. For he assures us that there is nothing more destructive to the soul and there is no more implacable form of hatred than envy. To understand why this is, we must turn to Cassian, since before we can find the cure for envy, we must understand just how incurable it is!

In fact, Cassian spends a good deal of chapter 16 in *Conference* 18 telling us why envy is the "most dangerous and hardest to cure" of all sins. In this conference he is foreboding: "I would say that someone stricken by its poison is almost beyond healing." Why is the diagnosis so bleak? There are at least two reasons.

First, of all the sins on our list, this one is actually provoked or stimulated by the cure—by the remedies with which other faults are destroyed. The problem is this: to cure a fault you need a wise physician of the soul, but in this case you will envy the very one who comes to treat you. In fact, the better the physician, the deeper the envy burrows. Such a person, Cassian writes, has "barred all the efforts of the holy exorcist": "This deadly menace is so utterly incurable that it is worsened by soothings, inflamed by serious treatment, and irritated by gifts. . . . What can you do with a man who, the humbler and kindlier you are, feels increasingly angry with you?" Like Basil, Cassian slides his tongue over and adds: "But who is there who in order to satisfy one who envies him, would wish to fall from his good fortune, or to lose his prosperity or to be involved in some calamity?"[35] Is it so bad that the only cure is for the physician to become worse than the patient?

It is fascinating that studies in psychopathology bear out this ancient wisdom. Cohen describes it as a "no-win situation": you envy your friend's fur coat, so she gives it to you and you enjoy wearing it; but now you envy your friend's generous nature.[36] As Smith points out, the studies demonstrate that the crowning advantage of the envied who "have it all" is that they are also *good* people, and for some this seems to fuel the intensity of hostile envy.[37] In fact, Schoeck summarizes the findings of psychopathology by noting that even if the envied strips herself of all possessions, such a conciliatory gesture would only bring about the opposite of what was intended—namely, resentment of the character of the one whose possessions were formerly envied, since the envier still feels humiliated and inferior.[38]

The second reason the diagnosis is so bleak is that envy hides. It has to, because hiding is inherent in its very nature. Its bite is silent. As Cassian wisely observes, since envy relishes the faults and not the prosperity of another, the envier is ashamed to display the real truth, since calling attention to his envy will result in the exposure of his fault over against the other's virtue.[39] Basil drives home the point:

> And the worst of this sickness of soul is that the sufferer cannot make it known; but with bowed head and downcast eyes he suffers torment, he grieves, he perishes of his affliction. Asked of what he is suffering, he is ashamed to reveal his disease and confess, "I am envious and bitter: the gifts of my friends are a torment to me. I grieve at my brother's happiness, I cannot endure the sight of another's good fortune." For this is what he must say if he would tell the truth. But unwilling to speak out, he conceals in the depths of his mind the sickness that smolders within, consuming him.[40]

Certainly this was the behavior of Wanda Webb Holloway as she secretly asked another to get rid of her nemesis. And the shame that Cassian and Basil mention is echoed in her words before sentencing when she confessed she felt "totally humiliated."

This silent, secretive nature of envy is recognized in contemporary research as one of envy's more distinctive features.[41] For instance, while jealousy usually elicits more intense affective reactions than does envy, envy is significantly more intense when responding to the statement: "others would disapprove if they knew what I was feeling." Indeed, as Schoeck argues, research shows that society sees envy as a serious disease, even though from Schoeck's perspective no society could exist without it.[42]

Smith summarizes the findings and the attitude in a manner that echoes Basil:

> Indeed, one of the reasons why few people will admit to envy is that to do so betrays such inappropriate hostility. Ordinarily, unfair treatment is a good cause for anger and protest, but when the standard used to determine such unfairness is unsanctioned or dubious (as in the case of envy), open anger and protest are less likely. Furthermore, if others are likely to label the envious person's hostility as inappropriate . . . , then this form of hostility will remain concealed and harbored rather than openly expressed.[43]

In fact, to hide what is socially prohibited, one might over-compensate with something opposite like excessive praise to hide the ill will.[44]

While Cassian focuses on the internal silent killer, Gregory, who admits that you cannot always recognize an envier outwardly, not only recounts the heinous crimes of biblical characters we mentioned in the beginning, but gives an almost morbid description of the exterior appearance of the one whom envy has corrupted: "For paleness seizes the complexion, the eyes are weighed down, the spirit is inflamed, while the limbs are chilled, there is frenzy in the heart, there is gnashing with the teeth, and while the growing hate is buried in the depths of the heart, the pent wound works into the conscience with a blind grief."[45] It seems that Gregory's description picks up where Cassian's leaves off—the final demise of one within whom envy has been silently at work until what one was once too embarrassed to reveal cannot be held in check any longer—and the serpent speaks to the woman, Cain kills Abel, Jacob rips off Esau, Joseph's brothers raffle the one Dad always liked best, Saul uses David for target practice, and Jewish leaders frame a popular teacher.

So the first step in curing envy is to admit the silent killer is at work in our lives. This is the point of ascetic "therapy"—the manifestation and discernment of thoughts.[46]

Along with this recognition Gregory helps us to see that when it comes to temporal things, particularly possessions, it is hard *not* to envy the other when we desire to obtain these things *because there is only so much temporal stuff to go around.* In fact, Betsy Cohen builds on anthropologist George Foster's belief that the cause of envy is the fear of limited goods and suggests that this fear is exacerbated in a postindustrial society like ours because the have-nots are not isolated from the haves and are told they can become everything they want to be, only to find out social mobility is not as easy as thought.[47] But it is precisely for people in the same social space that Gregory provides a very insightful antidote that is worth quoting at length. If one wants to be "wholly and entirely void of the bane of envy," he should set his affections on the inheritance

> which no number of fellow heirs serves to stint or shorten, which is both one to all and whole to each, which is shown so much the larger, as the number of those that are vouchsafed it is enlarged for its reception. And so the lessening of envy is the feeling of inward sweetness arising, and the utter death of it is the perfect love of Eternity. For where the mind is withdrawn from the desire of that object, which is divided among a multitude of participators, the love of our neighbor is increased, in proportion as the fear of injury to self from his advancement is lessened. And if the soul be wholly ravished in love of the heavenly land, it is also thoroughly rooted in the love of our neighbor, and that without any mixture of envy. For whereas it desires no earthly objects, there is nothing to withstand the love it has for its fellow . . . no man perishes by this sickness of this plague [envy], except that is still unhealthy in his desires.[48]

Deconstructing Gregory we find several layers to his prescription for cure.

First, we must desire that which when possessed is not lessened. Preeminently these are nontangibles, such as love. But one might extend the principle to include many tangible gifts as well. While Gregory's comment about there being only so much temporal stuff to go around might apply to currency or commodities, there are tangible objects which may be "possessed" by many. As I sat writing this chapter at St. John's Abbey in Minnesota, a young man came in view outside my window and plucked a couple of the roses that load the bushes in the middle of the courtyard. In doing this he denied me and all other guests whose windows face the courtyard the beauty of a full splay, for each one of us can "possess" those roses if we share them. In fact, our delight in their display is increased when we can confer with each other about our aesthetic experiences. In Pushkin's tale, Salieri *could* have had his musical talents *and* the pleasure of Mozart's; instead, his envy reduces the aesthetic pleasure available not only to him but to others.

This is the irony in envy: it ultimately hurts the envier without improving her situation. In fact, the greatest damage of envy is to the envier who, with "an utterly destructive, uncreative and even diseased state of mind," is willing to hurt one's self if it can injure the other.[49] As the advice columnist Ann Landers once remarked about holding a grudge, it's like burning down a house to kill a rat! Or, as Betsy Cohen's mother put it, envy does more harm to the vessel in which it is stored than the object on which it is poured.[50] Envy is simply stupid, for it hurts the envier without improving her situation in her attempt to dispossess the envied. The envier will not only fail to possess that which she wishes to have, but she will also deny to all others the benefits of the gifts, talents, and goods of those who have them and wish to share them. The flipside of this irony is what Gregory observes: "the good things of others which these people cannot have, they would be making their own if they but loved them." This is particularly true of those in the church. Because we are all members of one body,

> those things are ours which we love in others, even if we cannot imitate them, and what is loved in ourselves becomes the

possession of those who love it. Wherefore, let the envious consider how efficacious is charity, which renders the works of another's labour our own, without any labour on our part.[51]

If we could learn to love what others have rather than to envy their having it, we would perhaps find that we vicariously possess and enjoy what our envy would otherwise have destroyed. Indeed, as Gerrod Parrott points out, this *does* involve learned character: confronted with another's superiority, one is either predisposed to feel inferior and resentful because she construes the other's success as personal loss, or to be inspired and motivated to improve because she construes the other's success as a gain in a larger whole of which she is a part.[52]

A second layer in Gregory's prescription has to do with the assessment of our desires. They should be healthy desires. The detective quoted in the Holloway case was right: those folks who so value cheerleading that they will kill for it *are* a "bubble off"—maybe a bubble and a half off! But with some reflection the detective should have realized that we are *all* at least a bubble off. Does it make any more sense to kill in mass quantities for oil, land, or national reputation? Are we right on plumb when we expend our lives and sacrifice our families to have not only what others have, but to have more than they have? James is right: "For where there is envy and selfish ambition, there will also be disorder and wickedness of every kind. . . . Those conflicts and disputes among you, where do they come from? Do they not come from your cravings that are at war within you? You want something and do not have it; so you commit murder" (James 3:16; 4:1–2a). Basil is then right when he suggests that the initial step in curing envy is

> that we should not look upon anything in the affairs of men as either great or impressive: neither their wealth nor their perishable glory nor their health of body. Let us not believe that our highest good consists of these so fleeting things, but rather remember

that we are called to the enjoyment and possession of real and eternal blessings.[53]

Envy thrives in a hedonistic and materialistic culture whose desires are unhealthy. Salovey and Rothman cite research that suggests the experience of envy in a domain is "dependent upon the value that a society ascribes to that domain."[54] This means that if Basil's curative suggestion is to have force we will need to be enculturated by an alternative society like the church rather than the prevailing culture.

What will also help us to maintain sound desires is a third theme in Gregory's advice—one that frames the ascetic agenda. Our perspective must be eschatological: "the utter death of [envy] is the perfect love of Eternity." In that light Aquinas is right to observe that there is a good kind of envy which we might refer to as emulation or admiration. This is a zeal for virtuous goods and is praiseworthy (cf. 1 Cor. 14:1). It is a nonmalicious dissatisfaction or longing engendered by a rival who is not seen as an enemy, but as one whose example stimulates us to improve ourselves—to possess what the other possesses without the self-seeking, spiteful, or hate-filled desire to dispossess the other.[55] We should keep in mind that those temporal goods we are tempted to envy are nothing compared to the "goods to come," so that envious sorrow over the earthly success of others is forbidden. Aquinas wisely commends us to Psalm 73 (especially compare vv. 2–3 with vv. 17–20, 27).

In the end, Aquinas concludes that envy can be a kind of punishment in itself. Self-consciously he is echoing Gregory who concluded that the envious person who is consumed by this "inward plague" winds up destroying whatever good he may have of his own. And the oft-cited Proverbs 14:30 is called to our attention.[56] The envier becomes, in Basil's words, "an enemy of his own profit."[57] Indeed, as Shanna Harper's mother learned, envy *is* the "hollow way"! It leaves one with nothing—like rust that corrodes metal or rot that eats away wood . . . or a murderous plot that destroys a soul.

Is there hope for those whom the snake of envy threatens? The antivenom has been hinted at all along by the ascetics: the cultivation of charity. We must celebrate that which others have when we are tempted to do nothing but possess and dispossess. In that way we can cultivate thoughts and attitudes that are incompatible with envy.[58] We can obey Paul's imperative to the Philippians by nurturing within us the same mind that was in Christ: to do nothing from selfish ambition or conceit, but in humility to regard others as better than ourselves; to look not to our own interests, but to the interests of others (2:3–4).

This does not come easily, particularly for those of us in the academic world. Our fallen nature needs to be repeatedly injected with acts of obedience to Paul's imperative until we find ourselves immunized against envy's bite. For instance, I needed such an inoculation a few years back when I felt the nip of envy over the success of a colleague's well-received book on Emily Dickinson. Before the wound could fester I knew what I had to do: I purchased a copy in our college bookstore, took it over to my colleague's house, and had him inscribe it to my son who was particularly fond of Dickinson's poetry. Though I am far from being fully immunized, the joy my son expressed in receiving this gift allows me to savor this one act of submission to Paul's injunction when I am similarly tempted to envy a peer's success.

Even better, Solomon Schimmel suggests we might emulate a hero of biblical proportions who must have conquered envy before it ever gained a foothold in his life—Jonathan.[59] If anyone had a "right" to envy it was Jonathan. His rival should have been David. Who was David that he should be a claimant to succeed Saul, compared to Saul's son Jonathan who had every right to be the next king? An upstart young shepherd is pitted against a privileged heir. Yet Jonathan somehow had the character to accept the decision of divine providence, and love won out over envy.[60] Indeed, David will eulogize:

> Jonathan lies slain upon your high places.
> I am distressed for you, my brother Jonathan;
> greatly beloved were you to me;
> your love to me was wonderful,
> passing the love of women. (2 Sam. 1:25b–26)

Wanda and Saul are cut from the same cloth, woven of threads of envy. Only the grace of God can weave daughter Shanna into the same bolt as son Jonathan.

7

✳

Sloth

Running from Love

> The other demons are like the rising or setting sun
> in that they are found in only a part of the soul. The
> noonday demon, however, is accustomed to embrace
> the entire soul and oppress the spirit.
>
> Evagrius, *Praktikos* 36

Of all the chapters in this book, this one threatens to be a speed
bump. In fact, like a speed bump on an evenly paved road, the
contours of this chapter have to be a bit different from the rest.
It involves the most complicated evolution of the primary concept, *acedia*, that lies behind our modern word "sloth," and
it is cousin to the related condition of depression which has a
history equally as complicated.

Introducing Sloth

Evagrius referred to *acedia*—the "noonday demon" (Ps. 91:6)—
as the worst of all the demons.[1] It begins its attack on the solitary

monk around the fourth hour (10:00 a.m.) and keeps it up until the monk finally gets to eat his single meal of the day at the hour of *none* (the ninth hour, or 3:00 p.m.). From morning to afternoon the day grinds on. The monk keeps poking his head out of his cell to check the sun's position. He grows restless, hates his place, despises his life, and tires of manual labor. He mopes, convinced that "no one cares." The grass looks greener elsewhere where, perhaps, he could procure life's necessities more easily and make a success of himself. Evagrius says *acedia* "leaves no leaf unturned to induce the monk to forsake his cell and drop out of the fight." He imagines the cure is to leave his cell and visit everyone.[2]

Evagrius was the first to describe the temptation of *acedia* in detail, and he did so in the context of his singular monastic life—the hermit-like existence of many of the desert monks. (In fact, we get the word "hermit" from *eremos*—the Greek word for *desert*.) By the time John Cassian comes along and brings Evagrius's ideas into the *coenobium* (the *koinos bios*, or "common life," of the monks who live in community), he is able to describe in greater detail what Evagrius was communicating. It is worth quoting at length:

> Once [*acedia*] has seized possession of a wretched mind it makes a person horrified at where he is, disgusted with his cell, and also disdainful and contemptuous of the brothers who live with him or at a slight distance, as being careless and unspiritual. Likewise it renders him slothful and immobile in the fact of all work to be done within the walls of his dwelling: it does not allow him to stay still in his cell or to devote any effort to reading. He groans quite frequently that spending such a long time there is of no profit to him and that he will possess no spiritual fruit for as long as he is attached to that group of people. He complains and sighs, lamenting that he is bereft and void of all spiritual gain in that place inasmuch as, even though he is edifying no one and being of no help to anyone

through his instruction and teaching. He makes a great deal of far-off and distant monasteries, describing such places as more suited to progress and more conducive to salvation, and also depicting the fellowship of the brothers there as pleasant and of an utterly spiritual cast. . . . Thereupon he says that he cannot be saved if he remains in that place. He must leave his cell and get away from it as quickly as he can, for he will perish if he stays in it any longer. Then the fifth and sixth hours arouse such bodily listlessness and such a yearning for food that he feels as worn out as if he had been exhausted by a long journey and very heavy labor or as if he had put off eating for the sake of a two- or three-day fast. Next he glances around anxiously here and there and sighs that none of the brothers is coming to see him. Constantly in and out of his cell, he looks at the sun as if it were too slow in setting. So filled is he with a kind of irrational confusion of mind, like a foul mist, and so disengaged and blank has he become with respect to any spiritual activity that he thinks that no other remedy for such an attack can be found than the visit of a brother or the solace of sleep alone . . . it also prescribes certain pious and religious tasks . . . it behooves him to expend his pious efforts rather than to remain, barren and having made no progress, in his cell.[3]

No wonder that centuries later Thomas Aquinas would refer to this malady as "an oppressive sorrow."[4] In fact, what became "sloth" by the time Gregory listed the seven capital sins was something of an amalgamation of both *acedia* and another passion that was on the original list of eight—*tristitia*, or what we might translate as "sadness" or "dejection." Cassian likens it to what is mentioned in Proverbs 25:20—a moth that eats away at the garment or a worm that destroys wood. He finds it described in Psalm 119:28 where the Psalmist cries, "My soul melts away for sorrow." *Tristitia* gets hold of the mind such that the monk can no longer say his prayers with gladness, be comforted in sacred readings, work with patience, treat people with civility, seek good counsel, or go through the day with energy. It is a "weariness or distress of heart."[5]

It should come as no surprise that moderns have compared *acedia* or its later designation "sloth" to depression. The *DSM-IV-TR* listed the telltale signs of major depressive episodes. They include: feelings of sadness or hopelessness; loss of interest in pleasurable or daily activities; changes in sleep patterns and appetite; fatigue; agitation; feelings of worthlessness or guilt; inability to concentrate; and suicidal ideation. Obviously *acedia* and depression have been bedfellows.

While there might be reason to think that these are the same concepts, it would be a mistake to equate the two as this chapter will make clear. For instance, in a popular article that includes some insightful comments, William Backus's treatment of sloth contains typical inaccuracies, generalizations, and misstatements, such as this opening remark: "The more we learn about *what the ancients called sloth*, the more it appears that *sloth is today labeled clinical depression*."[6] This statement is even more odd when it is juxtaposed to his *correct* observation that the word "sloth" derives from a Middle English term *slou* (i.e., "slow"). It is difficult to see how "what the ancients called sloth" could have come from Middle English! Worse, he does an injustice to both the ancient literature on *acedia* and the modern literature on depression when he sets out his course with the declaration, "As the trait originally called *sloth* is today called *depression*, I will treat the two words as synonymous," and then later remarks, "No doubt it comes as a shock to us today that Christians of old were taught to see what we call depression as sin."[7] What Aquinas will call "sloth" in the thirteenth century is *not* synonymous with what moderns label depression, nor is what moderns label depression necessarily what Christians would call a "sin." Once we examine the meaning of *acedia* in early monastic thought and the meaning of sloth in Aquinas it will be obvious that the 1 to 4 percent of US preschoolers (estimates vary) who are clinically depressed are *not* suffering from what early ascetic monks called *acedia* or from the "oppressive sorrow" over God's love which Aquinas identified as sloth.

The Evolution of *Acedia* and *Tristitia*

To demonstrate this and to lay the groundwork for unpacking the sin of sloth we should take a slight detour and recount the evolution of the concepts *acedia* and *tristitia*, after which we will examine current thinking about the rather complicated malady of depression.

In an intriguing article comparing *acedia* to burnout (rather than to depression), Rainer Jehl finds similarities in symptoms but not in treatments.[8] Jehl begins by tracing the etymology of *acedia*, a term that first appears in Cicero, from the root *kedos* (care; hence, *acedia* as carelessness with associated connotations).[9] But a significant turn is made in the early Christian era:

> Only in patristic literature does *acedia* turn into a frequently used designation for an important spiritual phenomenon, characterized by exhaustion, weariness, sluggishness, as well as sadness and hopelessness . . . [all integrated as] *acedia* became a *terminus technicus* in monastic terminology. As such, it designates the occupational vice of monks, and among them especially of anchorites: a lack of care for spiritual goods, even "amplified to an emotion of weary aversion to ascetic life."[10]

Working from Wenzel's comprehensive survey of the concept,[11] Jehl gives credence to psychotherapist Schimmel's treatment of sloth as the most explicitly religious of all the deadly sins,[12] pointing out that *acedia* is "a strictly theologically conceived sin which concerned specifically the yearning of human beings for God and the religious duties that resulted from this desire."[13] As he points out, this is one reason why this sin sounded strangely inappropriate from the Renaissance on, and why it is *not* the *same* thing that heirs of the Renaissance and Enlightenment have come to mean by depression.

What makes this complicated is the subsequent "semantic overburdening" of the concept that Jehl traces as *tedium vitae* or sadness (*tristitia*) which got "absorbed into the tradition of the concept of melancholy."[14] Other elements of *acedia* were orphaned while modern concepts such as Kierkegaard's "despair" and Nietzsche's spirit of heaviness were added. The result: "The hidden stream of the *acedia* tradition has spread out since the Renaissance like so many tributaries of a delta whose original unity is apparent only with a second look."[15]

Coming at it from a slightly different angle, Stanley Jackson would concur with Jehl (and profoundly disagree with those such as Backus):

> Some modern authors have viewed *acedia* as little more than a medieval term for what we would call depressive states or as a symptom for melancholia in its own time. Others have thought of it as merely a term for sloth or laziness. These are clearly misleading simplifications. This troublesome state was not merely dejection or sorrow. Nevertheless, from its beginnings it was associated with *tristitia* (dejection, sadness, sorrow), and this connection continued; there were frequent references to *desperatio* (despair) in writings about *acedia*; and it was intermittently brought into association with *melancholia* in the late Middle Ages. Similarly, despite having come to be referred to as 'the sin of sloth' in the later medieval period and subsequently, *acedia* was not merely sloth. Nevertheless, lassitude, weariness, inaction, carelessness, and neglect were all aspects of *acedia* to varying degrees in various instances.[16]

To some extent due to the needs of a penitential system and standard guidance for confessors and preachers—occurring at the same time that the standard English term for this sin became "sloth"—the emphasis shifted to behavioral neglect and reprehensible idleness. With the Renaissance the cardinal sins became less significant and *acedia* lost its prominent place in the scheme of sins: the behavioral side became more and more the focus "and the trend toward the use of sloth and related terms became more predominant." The result was that in later centuries "*acedia* received much less attention in the Western world as a distinct condition, and sloth became the usual denotation of the sin when it was mentioned"[17] (as we have seen in Backus).

These comments help us begin to see why *acedia* has a complicated history as a concept and why it is facile to quickly identify it with depression. The scenario is even more obscure when all of the dimensions of depression are taken into account.

Depression

There is probably no more comprehensive discussion of depression in one volume than Andrew Solomon's *The Noonday Demon*. Up front he admits that depression is a complicated issue:

> The hard numbers are the ones that lie. . . . The most accurate statement that can be made on the frequency of depression is that it occurs often and, directly or indirectly, affects the lives of everyone. . . . Depression, under various names and in various guises, is and always has been ubiquitous for biochemical and social reasons. . . . Diagnosis is as complex as the illness.[18]

He goes on: "We don't really know what causes or constitutes depression, why some treatments may be effective, or why one gets depression from circumstances that do not trouble another."[19]

It could be that this is complicated because of the sheer number of those in the population who are depressed. Though the statistics are always in flux (in part due to changing definitions), generally speaking about 3 percent of Americans suffer from chronic depression, and at least a tenth of those are children.

One of the leading causes of death among both males and females is manic-depressive illness (what is known as bipolar). And Solomon makes this astounding claim:

> Worldwide, including the developing world, depression accounts for more of the disease burden, as calculated by premature death plus healthy life-years lost to disability, than anything else but heart disease. Depression claims more years than war, cancer, and AIDS put together. Other illnesses, from alcoholism to heart disease, mask depression when it causes them; if one takes that into consideration, depression may be the biggest killer on earth.[20]

As many as 10 percent of all Americans now living can expect to have a major depressive episode during their lifetime, while about 50 percent will experience some symptoms of depression.[21] And it's getting worse: "The climbing rates of depression are without question the consequence of modernity." By this, Solomon is referring to the modern pace of life, technological chaos, alienation of people, the breakdown of traditional family structures, loneliness, and the failure of systems of belief. On the other hand, we have developed medications and therapies to cope.[22]

Before we move on to the treatment of *acedia* and sloth in our early monastic sources, for purposes of comparison we should briefly survey the symptoms and causes of depression, remembering the list from the *DSM-IV* that we mentioned above.

Major depression is usually exhibited by withdrawal, especially from what were once pleasurable activities. It upsets sleep, appetites, and energy. There is an increased sensitivity to rejection, and it may be accompanied by a loss of self-confidence and self-regard. Causes are found in both hypothalamic and cortical functions—that is, that part of the brain that controls body temperature, thirst, hunger, and other homeostatic systems affecting sleep and emotional activity and that part of the brain that has to do with philosophically interpreting experience. So, depression can drain one of energy or, atypically, leave one agitated, symptoms at two extremes that are manifestations of *acedia*.[23]

What triggers depressive episodes, at least initially, are usually life events, such as loss (of a person, a life role, a self-concept). The life event may even be a positive change, such as marriage, birth, or job change. The stress from loss or humiliation can exacerbate depression. And while classification used to be according to internal or external factors, now both are recognized as factors in all cases, though, granted, disordered biochemistry is an element in most cases.[24]

Sloth

As we return to our sources to learn more about the dynamics and remedies of *acedia* and sloth, determining along the way to what extent they are similar to what moderns call depression, it will help to keep in mind Solomon Schimmel's observation that, of all the capital sins, sloth is the most explicitly religious: it involves "the loss of one's spiritual moorings in life and the ensuing spiritual vacuum manifests itself as despondency, and flight from the worship of God and service to man."[25] This should caution us to refrain from making the kinds of remarks that Backus and others make.

Schimmel also correctly notes that a "paradox of sloth is its ability to mask itself in fervid but misdirected activity."[26] One can see this in the above description of *acedia* from Cassian. So what we have come to call sloth ends up being a spiritual condition with two different kinds of physical manifestations. On the one hand, it is what we have come to expect from sloth: laziness—those who stay in their cells and sleep. On the other hand, it is counterintuitive: feverish activity—those who leave their cells in restless wandering, perhaps even meddling in the affairs of others (as an excuse). Cassian describes the two extremes quite well:

And so the unhappy soul, preyed upon by devices like these of the enemy, is agitated until, worn out by the spirit of acedia as by the most powerful battering ram, it either learns to succumb to sleep or shakes off the restraints of the cell and gets in the habit of finding its consolation in the face of this onslaught by visiting a brother, although it will be all the more painfully vulnerable not long after having used this remedy as a stopgap.[27]

In essence, either way the slothful person is busy gratifying her self—her own desires—rather than busying herself serving others and God.[28] This is what Gregory concludes when he writes:

When the soul does not direct its efforts to higher things, neglecting itself, it stoops to concern itself with low desires, and when it does not restrain itself by aiming vigorously at higher things, it is wounded by the hunger of a base cupidity; and, consequently, as it neglects the constraint of discipline, it is the more distracted in its craving for pleasure.[29]

It is interesting that the second of these two manifestations is borne out by studies of pastors. They often neglect their spiritual reading and prayer life, substituting a task-oriented life.[30] The soul sleeps while the body is in motion. In this case, even good works get in the way of loving Jesus. Cassian puts it this way:

The same malady suggests that he should dutifully pay his respects to the brothers and visit the sick, whether at a slight distance or further away. It also prescribes certain pious and religious tasks: Those relatives male and female should be looked after, and he should hasten to bring his greetings to them more often; it would be a great and pious work to make frequent visits to that religious woman who is vowed to God and who, in particular, is totally deprived of her relatives' support, and a very holy thing to bring whatever might be necessary to one who was abandoned and disdained by her own relatives. On such things it behooves him to expend his pious efforts rather than to remain, barren and having made no progress, in his cell.[31]

The monks realized that, just as we do in the case of other capital sins, we can easily justify sloth with excuses. We can even find scriptural rationalization for our feverish activity, such as John 4:34 and 6:27, where Jesus instructs us that his and our "food" ought to be *doing* the will of the Father. Equally, we can justify our laziness: Gregory points out that the slothful person neglects what he *ought* to do, imagining to himself certain difficulties and harboring certain unfounded fears; when he discovers apparent reasons for having the fear "justified," he acts as if he is indeed justified in his inactivity and indolence.[32] A fairly recent popular book in a "seven deadly sins" series is a case in point, as it practically makes a virtue out of sloth, albeit it is a parody of self-help books.

In either case—whether listlessness or restlessness—the "disturbed heart has lost the satisfaction of joy within" and "seeks for sources of consolation without."[33] But the perceptive monks discerned that this search for external consolation can be one of the causes that leads to the *tristitia* that got linked with *acedia*. At this point it is good to recall one of the dynamics of the passions—they often come in pairs, or, in this case, in a trio.

Evagrius and Cassian noted that when our avaricious appetite is denied what it desires and we fail to get what we had planned on getting, whether that had to do with tangible goods or intangible purposes, we often get anxious and angry.[34] As we have already pointed out, depression is often triggered by a loss of some kind. While for depressives this deprivation related to avarice may not lead to anger as it did for the monks, it is interesting that there is some correlation between *acedia-tristitia* and depression at this point. Even the depressive's rejection of company ties in with Cassian's description here:

> But sometimes it follows upon the vice of anger, which precedes
> it, or arises out of the desire for some gain that has not been
> achieved, when a person sees that he has failed in his hope of

acquiring the things that his mind was set on. Occasionally we are even provoked to fall into this misfortune for no apparent reason, when we are suddenly weighed down with great sorrow at the instigation of the clever foe, so that we are unable to welcome with our usual courtesy the arrival even of those who are dear to us and our kinfolk, and we consider whatever they say in innocuous conversation to be inappropriate and unnecessary and do not give them a gracious response, since the recesses of our heart are all filled with the gall of bitterness.[35]

So the cause is in *us* according to these ancients; some sadness is even due to temperament, they tell us. At the same time, though, Cassian and Gregory recognize that the *situation* may expose or bring to the surface what was already there.[36] From what we have already noted, this sounds similar to what we know about the causes of depression—a predisposition (for whatever reason, genetics or nurture) *and* external circumstances.

But what makes the condition described by the monks unique is that this is the exhaustion of the soul through spiritual battle.

Overcoming Sloth

What, then, are the remedies? How may sloth be cured? Cassian tells us that *acedia* is overcome by conquering its partner, *tristitia*, through constant spiritual meditation.[37] One must eradicate the roots of dejection from the heart.[38] But that is easier said than done. How might one go about doing this?

The first thing to do is to deal with one's neighbor whom the slothful person has avoided and possibly offended. We must come to peace with those from whom we have turned, lest, after running away from those with whom we have been connected, we only change the cause of our dejection in our affiliation with others who reside where we think the grass might be greener.[39] This brings into play the humility, gentleness, and patience that are some of the incentives of the spiritual life—characteristics that ameliorate feelings of isolation and lack of understanding. In this respect Cassian Folsom makes the claim, "It can be argued from Cassian's text that friendship is a remedy for the spirit of dejection."[40]

Solomon echoes this ancient insight in his study of depression: "When you are depressed, you need the love of other people, and yet depression fosters actions that destroy that love. Depressed people often stick pins into their own life rafts."[41] In fact, he relates the story of one person who found a cure for depression in church services, such as evening prayer: "The Church is an exoskeleton for those whose endoskeleton has been eaten away by mental illness. You pour yourself into it and adapt to its shape. You grow a spine within it. Individualism, this breaking of ourselves away from everything else, has denigrated modern life."[42]

So to help the slothful sibling, we are admonished to encourage the one who is suffering (the kind of encouragement expressed in Ps. 42:5–6). But Cassian warns the encourager to be careful in the way he or she goes about this business, taking a cue from Proverbs 25:20 which reminds us that singing to a heavy heart is like applying vinegar to a wound. In fact, Cassian finds an exemplary case in Paul's first letter to the Thessalonians (4:9–12): first he praises, and only then does he gently administer the healing words.[43]

So much for the therapist's role. What advice is given for the one who suffers from *acedia* and its companion *tristitia*?

If love and encouragement is to be sought from one's peers, then the one who suffers from *acedia* and *tristitia* is to run away from those who encourage sloth. Cassian takes the Apostle Paul's admonition in 2 Thessalonians 3:6, 14–15 quite literally at this point: Have nothing to do with those who are disorderly, enjoy too much leisure, or are simply idle. Their complaints about life in the community and its daily grind are contagious. Cassian even relates the story of a slothful monk who was envious of a zealous new monk in the community and tricked the newbie into leaving the monastery, the latter finding out to his shame that the grass was not greener in the other pasture.[44] Anyone can relate who has experienced the effect that idlers, gossips, and busybodies have on the life of a church congregation, let alone any community.

But if one is to run away from such negative influences, in another most important sense, one is *not* to run away. (This is opposite the tactic prescribed for lust.) The slothful person *is* a runaway—a deserter. He is one who has become entangled in secular business so that he has forgotten his vocation. The way to combat sloth is to remain—to stay in one's cell with patience and resistance. Return to the cell that was despised in order to meditate on God's Word and pray—the very practices that the person suffering from *acedia* has found to be arduous. In fact, Evagrius warns that "to flee and to shun such conflicts schools the spirit in awkwardness, cowardice, and fear."[45] Instead, says Cassian, *acedia* is to be resisted:

> For the adversary will the more frequently and harshly try a person who he knows, once the battle is joined, will immediately offer him his back and who he sees hopes for safety not in victory or in struggle but in flight, until he is gradually drawn out of his cells and begins to forget the reason for his profession, which is nothing other than the vision and contemplation of that divine purity which is more excellent than anything else and which can be acquired only by silence, by remaining constantly in one's cell, and by meditation. Thus it is that the soldier of Christ, having become a fugitive and a deserter from his army, "entangles himself in worldly affairs" and displeases "him to whom he engaged himself."[46]

First Thessalonians 4:1 is appealed to for admonition, as Paul urges the disciples in that city to "more and more" do what they have already been doing—learning how to live and please God.

The monk is to focus on developing a deeper spiritual life and quit worrying about the latest gossip (or, perhaps in its modern idiom, Twitter, Facebook, and all their kin) and all else that might distract from what he is supposed to be doing. We seek instant gratification, but the way to combat spiritual sloth is to stay put—something like what Eugene Peterson called "a long obedience in the same direction."[47]

Like the monk whom Cassian described at the beginning of this chapter and who "makes a great deal of far-off and distant monasteries" that are surely more conducive to spiritual progress and occupied by brethren who are more pleasant and holy,[48] we are much like a class of monks that Benedict describes in the first chapter of his *Rule*—gyrovagues. The word combines Latin for "circle" and Greek for "wander." In other words, these fellows were moving around in circles. They roamed from abbey to abbey, their tenure lasting three or four days, leaving before the demands of the newly joined community might benefit them in their conversion. Benedict's description of them sounds too familiar: "Always on the move, they never settle down, and are slaves to their own wills and gross appetites."[49]

We modern-day gyrovagues believe the "grass is greener" in *another* marriage or church or vocation or geographical location. The trouble is that it often turns out to be about the same hue. But it's not just that the hue remains the same; *we* remain the same. Conversion and growth happen when we remain, not when we run (which is precisely what the ancients associated with *acedia*—a cowardly running away).

Hence, the oft repeated monastic mantra to combat the restlessness of *acedia*: "stay in your cell, and your cell will teach you everything."[50] As Gabriel Bunge interprets it, "The temptation of bodily vagabondage is the tangible manifestation of that fundamental evil which undermines any spiritual life: the vagabondage of thoughts. The anchorite therefore settles his body in his cell and his thoughts in remembering God."[51] Or, in terms of one of the three Benedictine vows, she is to practice "stability."[52]

"Stability of place" is much like a marriage vow. Monks and couples promise to stay with the same people for the rest of their lives. They may not always be in the same geographical location for various reasons, but like the icon on a GPS, "home" always leads them back to the same community. Stability is premised on the conviction that God places us in *particular* constellations of people so that we can speak to and hear from each other what is needed for our mutual growth into Christlikeness.

But it means more than simply remaining in place. We can live and work with the same people for years without being fully invested in their lives—or our own. Stability requires attentiveness—paying attention to those with whom we share common space and time. It means persevering in listening (the first word in the *Rule of Benedict*).

We need to remain confined to one "cell" of a church or marriage or vocation long enough for the depth and richness to take root. And here then is the other paradoxical nature of *acedia*: the remedy for the listless soul is to stay put. Change *can* be good, but often it can leave us untethered, uncentered, disoriented, and confused. When it comes to *acedia*, to get somewhere we need to remain where God has put us.

This brings us to the most important term associated with the cure for sloth in the monastic tradition—*hypomonē*, which is patience and perseverance. In one respect, as we will see, we might claim some similarities in the remedies for depression. But in another very important respect, this is a point at which the monastic description of *acedia* distinguishes itself from what moderns call depression.

Bernardo Olivera puts it succinctly: "In the last analysis, *acedia* is flight from God, and it can only be cured by the concrete, patient seeking of his face."[53] Appealing to Evagrius's *Praktikos* (chapter 28), Olivera stresses what we have intimated above:

The time of temptation is not the time to leave the cell on any pretext, no matter how plausible. Rather one must stay put (*hypomonē*) in his cell and humbly receive all attacks, but especially those of the demon of acedia, because it constitutes the worst threat of all, the highest test of the soul. For to simply flee and avoid such a battle makes the soul awkward, cowardly and timid.

Jesus himself makes this virtue of patience almost an absolute condition for eternal salvation: "The one who remains steadfast (*hypomonē*) will gain life" (Luke 21:19).[54]

In other words, *acedia* is a threat to the whole soul.[55] The struggle against passionate thoughts (or *logismoi*) is a struggle against *specific* disordered passions or inordinate desires rooted in thoughts such as lust, greed, envy, and vainglory. And *specific* virtues are cultivated against these vices, as we have seen—virtues such as chastity, generosity, and humility. But none of these can withstand sloth because sloth attacks the basic strategy for dealing with all these sins: the disciplines necessary to grow more closely to the one upon whom we meditate in *lectio* and with whom we converse in prayer. This is also why it is *hypomonē* that is required to combat sloth. This is not grit-your-teeth determination, but patient endurance motivated by a charitable disposition. And this virtue is linked with two other virtues Cassian mentions over against the vice of sloth: *zeal* in serving the Lord and others and *courage* that is developed through one's labor.[56]

So *acedia* is not simply fleeing the cell and the community, but fleeing from God (especially if we believe that it is by divine providence that we have been placed in a particular "cell," such as a vocation or a community). More specifically, having inherited the tradition regarding *acedia* and *tristitia*, Thomas Aquinas saw them paired into a sadness or sorrow that is opposed to the "divine goodness in which love delights," or, as Olivera sums it up: "the problem with acedia consists in its opposition to love, the queen of the virtues, which is a friendship of man with

God."[57] Aquinas (constantly citing Cassian) identifies sloth as an evil *in itself* when it is sorrow for an *apparent* evil that is in reality good, and evil in its *effects* when it is sorrow for a *real* evil if it so oppresses a person as to entirely draw him away from good deeds (as alluded to in 2 Corinthians 7, especially v. 7).[58] In this sense, in the end sloth is contrary to joy about a divine good—a theological variation of envy which is contrary to joy about a neighbor's good. In both cases these are vices opposed to the joy of love, according to Aquinas.[59]

Ultimately, sloth is the vice opposed to the joy of love. It is, simply, running from God and all goodness. And that means it entails a degree of volition. We have a choice on the field of battle against the passions. At one end is a fundamental longing for God that unites us to him if we meditate on him and live as human creatures with feelings and yearnings that arise from this longing. But at the other end of the battlefield is forgetfulness of God and the accompanying personal disintegration—the origin of our sorrow and the thoughts that are directed toward anti-God objects and goals. "Every time we are overcome by these passionate wishes and desires, they overshadow the thoughts of God. We forget him and our inner life disintegrates. Our fundamental longing for God is weakened."[60]

It is the mundane routine of the daily office, fulfilling the quotidian tasks of everyday existence, following the "schedule," and returning day after day to the same place (such as a workplace) and community (such as a workmate or spouse or family) that provides the specifics for *hypomonē*.[61]

Returning day after day to the same "cell" has a way of turning us (literally *converting* us) little by little into someone different. It turns out that something like sticking to the routine is a remedy for depression as well. Solomon mentions several examples of this in his book on depression. He relates the story of a Vietnamese woman named Phaly Noun who developed three steps for female victims of the war to get on with life: to forget, to work, and to love. The second step of engaging in what might be labeled everyday tasks was an important ingredient in getting beyond their depression.[62]

Of another woman he writes: "I believe that she kept herself from ever experiencing a breakdown by regimenting and regulating her life; she was a woman of remarkable self-discipline. I believe now that her blessed rage for order was ordained by the pain she so fastidiously relegated to a place just below the surface."[63]

Again, Solomon recites the account of women who were involved in Poland's Solidarity movement and had abandoned their home life for activism; they eventually went back to traditional roles for women and nursed ailing men through the difficulties. One of them told Solomon, "In this way we found a sense of purpose and had an agenda of our own. We got such satisfaction out of our role, which had turned out to be so essential! The early eighties was a period in which women were less depressed than at any other time in recent Polish history, and the men were more depressed than at any other time."[64]

He accompanies these stories with advice after insisting that Prozac is not enough to cure depression and that listening and loving people are necessary to help the depressed see a future: "Be brave; be strong; take your pills. Exercise because it's good for you even if every step weighs a thousand pounds. Eat when food itself disgusts you. Reason with yourself when you have lost your reason. . . . The surest way out of depression is to dislike it and not to let yourself grow accustomed to it."[65] And, again, at the end of his comprehensive survey he advises, "The most important thing to remember during a depression is this: you do not get the time back. . . . Wait it out and occupy the time of waiting as fully as you possibly can. That's my big piece of advice to depressed people."[66]

This sounds very much like *hypomonē* and the volitional stance that Olivera described in relation to the battlefield. Of course, Solomon goes on to insist that, because depression is "the most horrifying loneliness," his advice to the friends and relatives of the depressed is to "blunt their isolation."[67] We have seen that that *can* be a *manifestation* of *acedia*, not a cure for it, unless those friends and relatives are the "cell" to which one is committed. Depressives say: "I used to go out with friends and do things, but now I just want to stay home." Such is a symptom of depression, but a remedy for monks with *acedia*!

More importantly, while the quotidian routines are a cure for depression and an important aspect of *hypomonē* in addressing *acedia*, the closest that Solomon gets to linking this with any resolution to cultivate love for God and his goodness is the example we referred to earlier—Solomon's reference to the person who connected with the church; she found evening prayer slowed her down and helped her keep the chaos of depression at bay: "I'm laying down these *rituals* to contain my experience. . . . Going to church is a set of attentional practices that move you forward spiritually." To which Solomon comments, "In some ways this seems pragmatic: it is not about belief but about scheduling."[68] The strategy is the same (including the "attentional practices" to which we will attend later), but the *telos* or goal is significantly different. In fact, it precisely *does* have to do with "belief."

The monk's routines include the manual labor (literally, work with the hands) that became a classic remedy for sloth in the monastic tradition. And this is not just for the sake of the sloth's soul, but to encourage the love from which the sloth is running. Appeal is made to tentmaker Paul's example in Acts 20:33–35 and his admonition to the church in 1 Thessalonians 4:11–12. Such labor may involve serving others, but not in feverish activity. It may be simply to ward off the manifestation of sloth as laziness. Cassian cites the story of one abba in Egypt as exemplary of the abbas who never allowed monks to remain idle, "estimating the purpose of their hearts and their growth in patience and humility by their diligence in work." Abba Paul burned the excess produce of his labors.[69] In our context this may seem extravagantly wasteful and certainly there was concern to be self-supportive and give alms,[70] but we should not lose sight of the end result of the soul's advancement in humility and patience in all of this, since the monk's goal was the *apatheia* that would lead to *agapē*. *The Karate Kid* comes to mind—"wax on, wax off." There is no expectation of instant gratification here.

In fact, instead of instant gratification, we are to maintain an eschatological perspective. Specifically, we are to live our soul-life as if we would die tomorrow (*momento mori*), but to treat our bodies as if we will live for many years to come.[71] This is good advice: to have a sense of urgency about our spiritual condition, but to keep the body physically fit in order to be able to *do* something in our spiritually healthy condition. Gregory puts it this way: "The slothful should be made to realize that often when we are unwilling to do what we can, soon after, when we are willing, we are not able to do it."[72] Though we are admonished to keep in mind God's final assessment of our work, Cassian is a realist. He knows that it might be difficult to maintain a focus on long-term consequences, so he suggests that we might be moved by the requirements of nature and *immediate* death.[73]

Keeping in mind this long-range view, both Gregory and Cassian encourage us to look to the future with joy and avoid being depressed by the bad things that happen to us in the present or overelated by any prosperity that comes our way. We should look at each condition as uncertain and likely soon to pass away. If we keep this perspective, they insist, God can break through any darkness we experience with his light. What they are encouraging us to do is what Paul admonishes in Philippians 4:8–13—to think only on those things that are "worthy of praise," instead of cultivating an "affection for this world." In other words, if one of the triggers for sloth (and depression) is loss of goods or position or relationships and if avarice is one of the vices that often leads to *acedia*, then we are wise to put a damper on our desires.[74]

Toward that end, there is one case of *tristitia* or sorrow that the monks and Aquinas applaud. It is the sorrow that leads to repentance of sin or comes from the passion to be perfect (i.e., complete), not having yet achieved our future state of blessedness. This is what is sometimes called "compunction"—a "sorrow for sin, a sorrow full of joy in God's mercy."[75] In the Evagrian tradition, Cassian refers to it in terms of a shedding of tears[76] and finds precedent in 2 Corinthians 7:10: "For godly grief produces a repentance that leads to salvation and brings no regret, but worldly grief produces death." Unlike the manifestations of sloth that we have recounted, Evagrius says that this godly sorrow shows symptoms of obedience, civility, humility, kindness, gentleness, and patience—the fruit of the Spirit.[77] This is because, instead of running from the goodness and love of God in the purest expression of self-love that is *acedia*, these tears of sorrow spring from the love of God and the desire for perfection.

8

✳

Vainglory

The Disease of Self-Esteemia

For often whilst human praise falls to the lot of a
good deed, it alters the mind of the doer, and though
not sought after, yet when offered it pleases; and
whereas the mind of the well-doer is melted by the
delight thereof, it is set loose from all vigorousness
of the inward intention.

Gregory, *Morals on Job* 1:4

Pride and Its Companions

By the time Gregory reconfigured the list of eight vices he had
inherited from Evagrius and Cassian, pride took top billing as
the queen of all. Of course Evagrius had already concluded
that pride was "the basic substance out of which every passion is made," as Bunge continues to spell out: "A passion,

quintessentially, is a selfish distortion, a being dominated by one's own self. In all things, it seeks only itself, and in everything it loves only itself. Since it is not capable of achieving anything by itself, it turns this love of self into a blind hatred of everything."[1]

So where does *vainglory*, the subject of this chapter, fit in? It fares no better. In fact, it is pride's bedfellow. At one point after he lists the prodigy of vainglory, Gregory insists that this capital vice is itself the first offspring of pride.[2] But that does not prevent Gregory from using the terms "pride" and "vainglory" interchangeably, and, in fact, he speaks of them together as rendering obedience to the will of Satan, lifting up the infected in his own conceit above the rest of his fellow creatures "by pursuit of the gifts of fortune, . . . by the desire of dignities, . . . through greediness of honor."[3]

There is reason, then, to use the terms somewhat synonymously, though pride has more of a vertical reference (our relation to God) while vainglory's is more horizontal (our relation to fellow human beings).[4] And it will become clear that the two dimensions are inseparable so that interchanging the terminology will not be entirely misleading.

Perhaps a more intriguing issue with which to begin is why we would associate pride with self-esteem. Edward Katz provides a brief history lesson that helps launch our discussion. While Aristotle could make pride virtuous as a mean between extremes, religious thought—especially Christianity—made it a sin: "Pride came out of the Middle Ages a prancing steed, but under moral rein."[5] Eventually, the misuse of Darwin's thought provided the fertile soil for pride to grow into something of what it means today—"pride of winning and success"; "competitive victory" was seen as not only worthwhile, but rooted in the laws of nature.[6] The problem for the victorious self-made successful industrialists of the late nineteenth century was this— pride was still considered immoral, sinful: "How could this dilemma be solved so that they could be proud and proclaim their pride without feeling guilty and sinful?" The solution was at hand: "make what was formerly spiritually unpalatable now respectable and psychologically wise and valid. . . . If pride had an old bad name, what could be easier than to give it a new good name? . . . The new name of pride after 1890 was *self-esteem*."[7] It was William James who gave pride this new reputation by reconceptualizing it as self-esteem (though he used the phrase "his own regard" instead of "self-esteem"), and so he is credited with being the most influential in the origins of the concept. During the twentieth century "esteem became a standard, if not the standard, self-concept," being defined in terms of the importance Social Darwinism gave to competition and winning.[8]

Katz observes that even Webster now defines pride and self-esteem almost synonymously as "a justified feeling of one's assets and also as conceit or vainglory."[9] (Again, pride and vainglory are being used interchangeably.) It is only when self-esteem is qualified by something like the adjective *inordinate* that it is considered bad. And that brings up another definitional issue that we must consider before charging ahead.

Christopher J. Mruk has written both survey and proposal in the third edition of *Self-Esteem: Research, Theory, and Practice: Toward a Positive Psychology of Self-Esteem*.[10] The contention that leads to his revised consideration of self-esteem is the recognition that the way in which one defines "self-esteem" determines in large part how one assesses self-esteem. Some have a very negative assessment while others have a more positive appraisal. But he admits that the concept is complex, that there exists a "definitional maze," and that there are contradictory findings and assertions.[11] He distills three definitions that he finds throughout the field of research: self-esteem as competence, as worthiness, and as competence *and* worthiness.[12] We will be helped by the kinds of academic research that Mruk surveys, but the waters are muddied further by more popular definitions of self-esteem, such as that put forward by the National Association for Self-Esteem: "The experience of being capable of meeting life's challenges and being worthy of happiness." Not to be misunderstood, they add, "We also believe in personal responsibility and accountability."[13]

In fact, it is this more popular treatment, along with what is called the "dark side" of self-esteem, that could be labeled "self-esteemia"—a condition that corresponds in various ways to what Evagrius, Cassian, and Gregory described as pride and vainglory. These aspects of self-esteem are rather recent, and some historical orientation will help us put things in perspective.

The academic study of self-esteem all but disappeared after James's work from 1890 to the mid-1960s, interrupted only by the work of Mortimer Adler and Karen Horney; but then came Stanley Coopersmith, Carl Rogers, Morris Rosenberg (with a ten-item self-esteem survey), and Nathaniel Branden's popular *The Psychology of Self-Esteem* (1969).[14] Branden said that self-esteem was the single most important facet of a person, and the belief that we must do whatever we can to boost self-esteem became a movement.[15] As evidence of this, from 1970 to 2000, there were over 15,000 scholarly articles relating self-esteem to all aspects of life.[16] The self-esteem movement of the '80s and '90s included an initiative introduced by the California legislature to create a self-esteem task force, especially for children. It was assumed (not substantiated by research) that this would generate personal and social responsibility. Competition was frowned upon, and every child was given the blue ribbon. (I even got on the bandwagon as a youth pastor, leading a workshop at a national Presbyterian youth conference on the trend of noncompetitive cooperative games that I had been using exclusively in my youth group meetings.) This task force disbanded in 1995 and was replaced by the nonprofit organization NASE (National Association for Self-Esteem) to which we have already referred.[17] Encouraging everyone's sense of self-worth had become a national pastime.

All of this led to a backlash in the late 1990s. The results of research had been inconclusive; there was little, if anything, to demonstrate that boosting self-esteem led to success in school or good citizenship. Roy Baumeister, a leading authority in this area, had concluded that only 200 of the studies reported in the previous three decades were good science (such as people not rating themselves). This led to new research and theoretical advances in the psychology of self-esteem. Now it became apparent that there are various *types* of self-esteem, some associated with negative outcomes (narcissism, aggression, and the like—the "dark side" of self-esteem), and some associated with desirable qualities.[18] We will come back to this distinction as we unpack what the monks taught about pride and vainglory.

What Is Pride?

If there is no single, simple definition of self-esteem dominating psychological research and theory,[19] the obverse is true for pride in theology. Evagrius says it is "the cause of the most damaging fall for the soul."[20] It is the first and the last, declares Cassian: the eighth and last in the combat; "it is nonetheless first in terms of origin and time. It is a most savage beast, fiercer than all those previously mentioned, greatly trying the perfect and ravaging with its cruel bite those who are nearly established in the perfection of virtue."[21] It is, he says, "the beginning of all sins and faults."[22] Gregory gave it separate status as the queen of sins, "the root of all evils" that fully possesses a conquered heart and gives it over to the seven principal sins.[23] This prominent position is echoed through the centuries (Augustine, Dante, Aquinas, Luther, Calvin), and it becomes a *deadly* sin because, as we will see, it keeps us from submitting to God.

But our contemporaries seem not to agree. In one survey of clergy, pride came fourth on the list in the order of seriousness (above greed, anger, gluttony, and envy; melancholy had been added to make it a list of eight), but on the bottom in a survey of New Jersey residents. And Simon Wessely opines, "For the rest of us it does not even rate a place. Pride is 'in.'" Psychologists and sociologists link it with love, joy, gratitude, happiness, and satisfaction. Equating it with self-esteem, he editorializes: "'No matter what ails you, self esteem is the cure' [*Journal of Personality and Social Psychology* 1995]. Money cannot buy you love, but self esteem guarantees money, love, health, and fulfillment. In the film Wall Street the motto 'greed is good' became the epitaph of the 1980s. A 1990s remake would have Michael Douglas as a psychologist telling us that 'Pride is good.'"[24]

Actually, this attitude was recognized by Gregory. He notes that there are those who fall into the sin of pride without knowing it because they did so through gifts of received virtues and the grace of good works bestowed on them. And even though it is usually more serious to sin in one's silent thoughts that are born of deliberate pride than to engage in a bodily sin, "when pride is *believed* to be less disgraceful, it is less avoided." And that is why Gregory suggests that, as we mentioned in a previous chapter, God sometimes allows us to fall into sins of which we are more ashamed, such as lust, to call attention to the fact that the pride we had underestimated is misplaced: "Behold! he who prides himself on his virtue, through *sin* comes back to humility."[25]

But giving pride its place—fourth, last, not at all—doesn't quite define it. Ultimately, pride is our craving for superiority and the beliefs we harbor about ourselves that fuel such a craving. Added to this is our tendency to accentuate our neighbor's evil while we give greater weight to our own good (without God's help) and ignore our own evils. And as we will see, this is precisely what the "dark side" of self-esteem looks like as well. Evagrius put it well: pride's demon "induces the monk to deny that God is his helper and to consider that he himself is the cause of virtuous actions. Further, he gets a big head in regard to the brethren, considering them stupid because they do not all have the same opinion of him."[26]

In other words, it is self-exaltation with a correlative depreciation of others, grounded in a denial of the necessity of God's help. Much like Evagrius, this is the way that Robert Roberts has defined it. It is the need to excel over others in order to think well of ourselves: "We are committed to building our egos on a foundation of inferiority—the inferiority of others." It is the *comparison* that builds up the self.[27] (This is one reason why Baumeister did not think self-reporting made for good science.)

In this sense, pride is a "communal" sin or a sin of the *coenobium* (the monastic community). Though he admits that vainglory in a backhanded way affects those who go into solitude,[28] Cassian describes the novice as one who impresses himself with his good singing voice, his body emaciated from fasting, and his renunciation of military honors and worldly possessions; he even imagines pleasurably such accolades from other monasteries so that his soul "cannot even look at things present or the brethren."[29] In fact, Gregory says that vainglory and pride disqualify the monks from community with those on earth and in heaven, because they look down on the righteous with whom they are placed, yet are far from being united to the citizens above: "They neither keep equality of brotherhood in this lower world by charity, nor yet are able to attain the world above by setting themselves up."[30]

One other feature that distinguishes pride from the others is that, as Schimmel notes, we are often unaware of our arrogance, but we tend to know when we are angry, gluttonous, greedy, and so forth.[31] And even when we are aware of it or it is called to our attention, it is difficult to admit, simply because we imagine ourselves to be more important than we are—something we have already heard from Cassian and Gregory.

The Etiology of Pride

In several places Cassian makes a distinction between two kinds
of pride or vainglory. (He makes the same distinction under
both headings, further supporting our contention that a sharp
differentiation between the two is not apparent.) There is pride
or vainglory that assaults "carnal" persons (usually beginners)
and has more particularly to do with our relations with fellow
human beings, and there is pride or vainglory that tries the
"best and spiritually minded" and has more particularly to do
with our relation to God. The former has to do with our self-
importance when it has to do with our possessions, position,
and the like; the latter, when it has to do with our desire to be
praised for spiritual attainments.[32] But, making the same distinction, Gregory insists that "one and the same thing is going
on before the eyes of God, though as it seems to the hearts of
men, it is clothed in their sight with a different garb."[33]

No one of us is immune. Cassian constantly reminds us that
anyone can acquire vainglory and pride at any time and in any
place on any occasion, but it especially plagues those who are
triumphant over the other evil thoughts. In other words, like the
"Shapeshifter" in *Star Trek VI*, vainglory takes many shapes.
It is so subtle that it is difficult to see through and recognize
even with the keenest spiritual vision. Cassian says that those
who cannot be deceived by carnal vices that attack in the open
and in daylight are easy prey for the vainglory that attempts
to conquer the soul under the appearance of the virtues. Such
vanity tries to injure the soldier of Christ *in* his silence, obedience, work, dress, vigils, prayers, fasting—even in his humility—like a rock under the waves that shipwrecks those sailing
with a fair breeze:[34]

> We may be puffed up by our successes, stumble with the feet
> of our soul in bonds, and fall shackled, due to the traps of
> vainglory. And so it happens that, although we could not be

overcome in direct combat with our adversary, we are conquered by the loftiness of our triumph, or else (and this is another form of deceitfulness) we exceed the limits of our abstinence and of our capability and, with the onset of bodily exhaustion, we no longer persevere on our course.[35]

As this comment of Cassian's implies, this vice especially attacks those who have made the greatest spiritual progress. Similarly, Gregory points out that the other vices assail particular virtues, but pride is not satisfied with extinguishing only one virtue. Like a staph infection it attacks the whole body.[36] Various analogies are used to make this point, most having to do with battle. It is a tyrant that besieges the city and treats the wealthier more harshly, and when the "lofty citadel of the virtues has been taken, utterly destroys and lays waste the whole city; and leveling with the ground of vices the once high walls of saintliness . . . it will strip the soul it has subdued of all its powers of virtue."[37] The one who has overcome bad habits is brought low by the very things he brought under, "as if he died under the enemy he lays low, who is lifted up by the sin that he subdues."[38] We are brought low by the very things that brought us so far.[39] Pride lays low the proud one by his own "spear." The virtues of the one whom pride attacks are simply supplying the soul with "new fuel" for vanity. It is a vice "interwoven" with our virtues, as Evagrius puts it: "Vainglory is an irrational passion and it readily gets tangled up with any work of virtue."[40] The one who has forsaken the world and abandoned temporal honors and sought humility is wounded by the "shaft" of vainglory and falls the more fatally from on high.[41] Again, Evagrius gives us a graphic image of just this when he suggests that vainglory is "an underwater rock; if you run against it you lose your cargo."[42] And perhaps a contemporary analogy would be this: dealing with the vices that clergy and New Jersey residents rated more highly than pride only affects the software, while the one they underestimated—pride—attacks the hard drive.

Biblically, Cassian cites Hezekiah (2 Kings 20; 2 Chron. 32:24–26) as one who was barely recovered from a single act of pride that threatened to ruin this man of virtue, faith, and devotion. And he cites Uzziah (2 Chron. 26:15–16) who was injured by prosperity rather than adversity, proving that we can "fall before our own trophies and triumphs."[43] In his "commentary" on Job, Gregory reprimands Elihu for representing every person in the church who professes right belief but lives in pride; and this echoes a theme we see elsewhere in Gregory when he compares the inwardly empty persons who seek temporal glory outwardly to a hollow reed that "makes a fitting place for this Behemoth to rest within them."[44]

When my daughter was given an assignment in high school to list people she admired and the traits for which she admired them, she had a long list of traits for her mother, but only one for me. She told me she admired me because when I spoke I really thought people wanted to hear what I had to say. Despite my incredulity she thought that was admirable, but Gregory might have thought otherwise. At one point he says,

> For it is peculiar to the arrogant, that they always believe, even before they speak, that they are going to say some wonderful thing, and that they anticipate their own words by their own admiration, because, with all their acuteness, they are not sensible how great a folly is their pride.[45]

By way of contrast, elsewhere Gregory writes about two kinds of preachers: the humble and the arrogant. There are those who meditate on the secrets of wisdom silently and rejoice when they perceive it, not when they are obliged to make it known (which carries so many temptations); and when they *do* make it known, "charity steps in, and they rejoice at the progress of their hearers, and not at their own display." But when the arrogant gain any knowledge they "think that they have gained nothing, if it so happens that they keep it concealed. For they place their happiness nowhere but in the praise of men." In other words, the proud desire not to possess knowledge, but to make a display of it.[46] Though we may not be in a position to discern their motives, it is certain that Gregory's estimate of preachers in his day would apply equally, if not more, to some preachers in our own day—perhaps even to a daughter's father. And it certainly applies to those children mentioned in *NurtureShock* who are averse to taking risks or putting in the effort to try harder because they are not only overconfident but want to maintain the appearance of being innately "smart."[47]

Now, it may seem strange, if pride often strikes the person who has mastered the virtues over against the lesser vices, that *this* vice (pride) involves turning away from God. In fact, *only* pride has *God* as its adversary, says Cassian. The Bible does not say that God is opposed to the gluttonous, the covetous, and so forth, but only to the proud. "For those vices only turn back upon wrongdoers or seem to be committed against those who have a part in them—that is, against other human beings. This one, however, of its very nature touches God, and therefore it is specially worthy of having God opposed to it."[48]

Perhaps that is why the supreme example is Lucifer, whom Cassian identifies as one who turned from the Maker who had endowed him with splendor and purity, even though Lucifer believed he had acquired these qualities (similar to those cultivated virtues) through the power of his own nature. So, bolstered in the belief that he needed no divine assistance in order to maintain these traits, he assumed he was godlike, in need of no one; and, trusting in the power of his own will, he thought he could give himself whatever was needed to bring his virtues to their ultimate end. For this he fell, forsaken by God and finally aware of the weakness of his own nature and the loss of God's gift of sustaining grace.[49]

Cassian says the same about us when we are guilty of vainglory: polluted by the vice of pride as we glory in our purity, we believe we have won bodily chastity through human virtues when, in reality, it was a special gift of God.[50] (Recall what we said about chastity vis-à-vis willful abstinence in our discussion of lust.) And Gregory concurs when he notes that those who presume on their own goodness do not have recourse to the help of their Maker, "and it is brought to pass that the sinner perishes so much the worse, for that even this very thing, that he is a sinner, he is ignorant of."[51]

Aquinas follows Gregory's enumeration of the vices with pride as the queen of all and vainglory as its immediate offspring, and he helps us to see another aspect of pride's presumption that ignores divine aid. Arguing that vainglory renders a person overconfident so that he gradually is disposed to lose his inward good, Aquinas characterizes pride as an *inordinate* desire of excellence, "so that this vice seems to exercise a kind of causality over the other vices."[52]

Even though Cassian has always been suspected in the West of being at least a semi-Pelagian, in his thoughts about pride he insists on the necessity of God's grace. Human effort is needed, but without the grace of God no one can be altogether cleansed of carnal sins. One learns this, he insists, by his own experience, for without grace, no effort in fasting, vigils, readings, or solitude will be sufficient.[53] (At one point in the *Conferences* he asks whether good weather or the farmer's toil is necessary for a good crop. Of course, the answer is both.)

The effusive self-praise that is presumptuous and, in the end, a denial of God's grace, is likened by Gregory to the locusts that plagued Egypt—"the tongues of flatterers, which corrupt the mind of earthly men, if they ever observe them producing any good fruits, by praising them too immoderately."[54]

This is very much like what Katz suggests about self-esteem insofar as it entails narcissism or self-glorification—"being in love with [one's] idealized image."[55] As Bronson and Merryman point out in *NurtureShock*, ironically, a growing body of research indicates that giving children the label of "smart" may be causing them to underperform. That is to say, by praising them immoderately for their "intrinsic" ability or natural intelligence, they fail to learn from their mistakes, opting to look smart and not risk failure. Furthermore, excessive praise also distorts motivation so that children begin performing just to hear the praise (much like Gregory's arrogant preachers), although, again, this leads to risk avoidance and a lack of perceived autonomy.[56]

Like those whose esteem is based on virtuous effort, Aquinas argues that it is not a sin to know and approve of one's good or to approve of one's good works so long as that approval leads others to glorify God, leads others to become better, and leads the praised one to persevere in goodness.[57] Interestingly, it is perseverance or persistence that is lacking in those children who have received rewards too frequently and will quit when the rewards disappear. Again, this requires that legitimate self-esteem be built on praise of effort, not on resting on one's laurels. (The missing ingredient in this good side of self-esteem from the perspective of our monastic psychologists would be not only effort—the farmer's toil—but the necessity of God's grace—the good weather—as well.)

So, in an ultimate sense, the sin of pride begins when one defies and turns his heart away from his Creator (Hos. 7:10). As such, pride transgresses the limits imposed by God. In fact, the creature wants to be like God, so Aquinas reminds us the Latin word for pride is *superbia* (arrogance). In this sense pride is related to the deadly sin of *avarice*, only this time with reference to God: the desire to be what we were not meant to be.

In the Genesis story, the fall began as a lie about who we are and an attempt to be what we were never meant to be. The resulting endeavor to make ourselves God was a form of idolatry. But the irony is that in trying to become what we were never meant to be we become less than what we could be. And centering ourselves on self, we get off our true center, and everything around us becomes off-center (as we will see in the case of self-esteem's "dark side").

In our presumptuousness and self-exaltation, pride entails the denial of our finitude, creatureliness, and contingency—an illusion we often sustain by human ingenuity and technology, but which is shattered by death. Paul argues this in Romans 1: sin is rooted in *self-glorification* (vv. 21–25, 30).

When we inordinately exalt ourselves in this way, we refuse to acknowledge or fear God for who God is in relation to his creatures (Ps. 10:4). The result is God's judgment for such presumption—a theme that recurs in Scripture (Prov. 6:16; 16:5; Jer. 13:9–11; Luke 1:50–52; 16:15; Rom. 1:18, 24, 26, 28).

So, pride becomes a deadly sin—an obstacle to salvation, for salvation requires what pride cannot allow: an admission by the fallen creature of his nonsuperior sinful standing before God, of his *need* for grace, and of *faith*, which is absolute trust in God, not in self (see Rom. 3:27; 4:2–5; James 4:6). For Cassian, as he repeatedly says and as we have seen, this is the essence of pride: failure to recognize the necessity of divine help for such virtues as charity.

"Self-Esteemia" and the "Dark Side" of Pride

We have already indicated that pride is based on comparison, whether it is riches, power, status, or whatever else makes us feel superior. Self-esteem can be similarly characterized. Edward Katz argues that, at its heart, self-esteem is "an hierarchical ordering . . . rooted in open warfare and ceaseless competition." Human beings are sacrificed to a "mechanical accounting system" whereby they produce in order to achieve a higher self-esteem score. And it doesn't help to turn the focus on good deeds, since that just plays into the "competitive success-based criteria."[58] Gregory would concur, arguing in one place that though the proud one does not put in effort to cultivate virtue, he imagines himself to be righteous by *comparison* to the brother who can't control his anger since he, ignoring his pride, can.[59] (Is it any wonder that pride is encouraged in our society that rates competition so highly?)

Indeed, Bronson and Merryman point out that "frequently-praised children get more competitive and more interested in tearing others down. Image-maintenance becomes their primary concern."[60] In other words, pride tends to poison human relations and consume the other, or, as Robert Roberts puts it, pride is a kind of *cannibalism*.[61]

This follows from our account of pride as presumption—as exaggerated love and concern for the self. It makes the self absolute and central, ignoring or using others in order to achieve one's own ends. Gregory identifies its most insidious characteristic as the arrogance that despises others; the proud one looks down on all the good others do and admires himself and his own doings.[62] The self can become so absolute that when pride masters the person, he considers the *coenobium* to be a hindrance to his advances in patience and humility, leading him to seek a solitary cell or build a monastery *he* can run, devolving, says Cassian, "from being a bad disciple [to] a still worse master."[63]

That pride is so destructive of human relationships should not surprise us when we not only remember that Gregory and Aquinas declare it to be the source of all other capital sins, but also that these sins give birth to "daughter" sins (let alone that they gang up on us). So pride often comes with envy if one feels entitled to gain something at the expense of another; pride comes with anger if one does not think he gets the recognition he deserves; pride comes with sloth if self-satisfaction keeps one from pursuing his goals. The list of symptoms that accompany pride or vainglory is extensive in Cassian, Gregory, and Aquinas, as a sampling illustrates. The proud one is a tyrant, loud, impatient, bitter, lacking clarity, insulting, disobedient, unable to receive admonition, stubborn, preferring his own opinion to that of his elders, boasting, hypocritical, contentious, obstinate, provoking, and out of sort with other inhabitants of the monastery.[64]

What is remarkable at this point is how these manifestations of pride and vainglory line up with what contemporary research has found with regard to high self-esteem. While it is true that *low* self-esteem is related to twenty-four mental disorders in the fourth edition of the *DSM*,[65] and while it is true that studies have shown a *correlation* between *high* self-esteem and happiness, positive interpersonal dynamics, improving persistence in the face of failure, dealing successfully with stress and avoiding anxiety, and helping with job performance and problem solving,[66] there is also what we have referred to as the "dark side" of high self-esteem.

Before elaborating on the "dark side" it is important to say something about the context in which discussion of this other side of self-esteem occurs. The backlash which we mentioned earlier is apparent in the book *NurtureShock* by Bronson and Merryman who depend heavily, among others, on the research of Roy Baumeister. Chrisopher Mruk, a leading authority on self-esteem along with Baumeister, argues that, given a certain definition of self-esteem, one may or may not arrive at negative behaviors and attitudes associated with self-esteem. His claim is that Baumeister defines self-esteem as "worthiness" (e.g., "feeling good about oneself") and that others define it as "competence." Basing self-esteem on the former can lead to the "dark" states (which Mruk argues is what most research has been based upon), while basing it on the latter can mean that one would be constantly vigilant and looking out for threats against which one would act.[67] Mruk constructs a definition that combines "worthiness" *and* "competence," arguing that such a definition leads to fruitful and positive results in research, theory, and application. While this is not the place to go into further

detail about Mruk's proposal (and it *does* lead to some helpful paradigms, among which is a chart differentiating "types"
of self-esteem), Baumeister's contentions about self-esteem do
not seem to me to be based solely on "worthiness"; in fact, as
already mentioned, he accepted as legitimate scientific research
only 200 studies among thousands, insisting that self-reports
about how one felt about oneself was not good procedure. So
the claims made by Baumeister (and *NurtureShock*, among other
books and articles) about self-esteem are not to be dismissed.
And what is striking is that manifestations of high self-esteem
can end up looking much like what our monastic psychologists
have described as the socially debilitating effects of pride and
vainglory.

It seemed commonsense and empirically verifiable that high
self-esteem would lead to a flourishing life and society (recall
the California task force) and that low self-esteem was responsible for all that ails us. But what has been demonstrated by
research is that, apart from inferences about causality, having
high self-esteem does *not* necessarily improve grades, test performance, or career achievement. It does not reduce alcohol usage
nor lower violence. Furthermore, while there is no empirical
support for the claim that children with *low* self-esteem are
aggressive, there is evidence for the claim that those with *high*
self-esteem are more aggressive and more narcissistic. So, while
for decades psychologists believed that low self-esteem was an
important cause of aggression, a review of assorted studies led
Baumeister and others to the conclusion that "perpetrators of
aggression generally hold favorable and perhaps even inflated
views of themselves. . . . [And] high self-esteem does not lessen a
tendency toward violence, that it does not deter adolescents from
turning to alcohol, tobacco, drugs, and sex, and that it fails to
improve academic or job performance. . . ."[68] Even though there
is a *correlation* (but only that) between self-esteem and happiness, as we have mentioned, Baumeister and fellow researchers

also admitted that they could imagine a heightened sense of self-worth could prompt one to demand preferential treatment or to exploit others.[69]

Granted that Mruk is skeptical of the findings only because of the definition of self-esteem used, still, he admits that, *given* that definition and the accompanying research, a "dark side" of high self-esteem may elevate success over well-being, manifest more group favoritism, blame others for one's own shortcomings in relationships, put others down by comparison, think more highly of their value to others in relationships than is actually deserved, tend to overvalue the contributions they make to the group, exhibit some antisocial behavior such as bullying, and be defensive, narcissistic, arrogant, conceited, egoistic, and aggressive.[70] In other words, the "dark side"—what we've labeled "self-esteemia"—looks much like what Evagrius, Cassian, Gregory, and Aquinas referred to as the vice of vainglory and pride.

Before moving on to the "cure" for pride and vainglory, it is important to recognize that the vice is not confined to the individual. In fact, it is epitomized in the Bible by the autonomous ruler of a people who is hostile to God or by groups of people in a society who oppress others such as the poor or widows, and against whom the prophets rail.[71] Such "collective egotism" (as Reinhold Niebuhr called it) manifests itself in racism, nationalism, class snobbery, and the like. God finds such group pride abominable and culpable, and it leads to the proverbial fall of the individual or nation.[72] By way of an application that hits close to home, columnist and political pundit George Will put it poignantly with reference to the first Gulf War:

> A peculiar kind of patriot today says that by this war America "will get its pride back" . . . since when has American pride derived primarily from military episodes? A nation that constantly worries about its pride should worry. It is apt to confect

military occasions for bucking itself up, using foreign policy for psychotherapy.[73]

The Cure

Much like envy (with which vainglory shares some features), pride is very difficult to cure. Evagrius points out that it is escaped only with considerable difficulty. For one thing, as we have seen, while other vices are attacked by virtues, vainglory is interwoven *with* the virtues. Just as the envier envies the spiritual maturity of the person who can help another overcome that vice, so "what you do to destroy [vainglory] becomes the principle of some other form of vainglory."[74]

What is essential is the countervailing virtue of humility, a virtue that was not recommended in pagan philosophy at the time of Christianity's rise. In the spirit of Evagrius's *Antirheticos*, Cassian lines up a list of Scripture passages commending humility (such as Phil. 2:6–8) to counter an equally substantive list of passages condemning pride (such as Isa. 14:13).[75] That which is destroyed by pride is restored by humility. He continues later in the same conference to insist that the perfection and purity we seek cannot be obtained other than through humility which requires being convinced that God's protection and aid are needed at all times (the opposite attitude expressed by the proud).[76] Furthermore, just as pride destroys all virtues, so humility is the "mistress and mother of all virtues," especially of love, but also of obedience, patience, and kindness.[77] A "wonderful pitifulness," which consists of "lives walled in by the knowledge of [our] own weakness"—a "cage of humility"—is something that Gregory insists we can be brought to through sin! It is worth recalling here Gregory's insightful comment that we cited in an earlier chapter:

> Behold! he who prides himself on his virtue, through sin comes
> back to humility. . . . One who is puffed up with his virtues is

wounded with a remedy. Because, therefore, we make a wound of our remedy, He makes a remedy of our wound; in order that we who are wounded by our virtue, may be healed by our sin. For we pervert the gifts of virtues to the practice of vice; He applies the allurements of vices to promote virtues, and wounds our healthy state in order to preserve it, and that we who fly from humility when we run, may cling to it at least without falling.[78]

Cassian and Gregory insist that this humility requires self-denial, or at least a recognition of one's own nature and "present and past infirmities." More specifically, humility requires an *awareness* of our true nature.[79] For self-deception is symptomatic of pride, as the parable of the rich farmer reminds us (Luke 12:19–20).

Being made aware of their true nature is something that mothers had to do in an experiment reported in *NurtureShock*.[80] Students were given the first part of a test which was then scored before they met with their mothers. They were divided into two groups—American and Chinese. In the American group each mother avoided making negative comments and praised her child for their performance on the test whether or not they did well. In the Chinese group each mother suggested her child needed to put more effort into the second half of the test. After scoring the next part of the test the Chinese test takers had increased their scores by 33 percent—more than twice the gain of the American students. In other words, self-esteeemia (just feeling good about oneself) did not lead to markedly improved performance over against those who were made aware of the reality of their human condition. Or, as Gregory put it, "It is therefore prudent not to look at the good one has done, but at what one has neglected to do."[81]

This is not unlike Gregory's description of the pride that has become self-secure and hardened in its inevitability such that it does not realize it has been abandoned by the Creator; it no longer remembers from what it has fallen and no longer dreads punishment to come: "it knows nothing how deeply it is to be bewailed." But, then like the Chinese students,

> if it be touched by the inspiration of the Holy Spirit, at once it wakes up to the thought of its ruin, rouses itself in the pursuit after heavenly things, glows with the hot emotions of love towards the Highest, takes thought of the ills which every way beset it round about, and she weeps while *making progress*, who before was going to ruin in high glee.[82]

So, crucial in the cure for pride and vainglory is a healthy self-examination and self-criticism that leads to an accurate self-assessment. As Gregory says, those who want to rise to the heights of virtue must immediately recall to mind their own faults whenever they hear of the faults of others.[83] Otherwise, the proud "make light of reproof, considering themselves to be much wiser than their reprovers."[84] Real knowledge, says Gregory,

> influences without elating, and makes those whom it has filled, not proud, but sorrowful. For when anyone is filled therewith, he is in the first place anxious to know himself; and conscious of his own state, he acquires thereby a greater savour of strength, the more truly sensible he is of his own weakness therein. And this very humility opens to him more widely the pathway of this knowledge, and when he beholds his own weakness, this very knowledge opens to him the hidden recesses of sublime secrets; and pressed down by this knowledge, he is made more subtle to press forward into things hidden.[85]

This is precisely why Baumeister was correct when he suspected and rejected thousands of self-esteem studies based on self-reports of feeling good about oneself, not unlike the study of high school students I once heard of in which 70 percent rated themselves above average. (At least 20 percent had an inaccurate assessment!) And it is why, based on studies and theories such as his, the authors of *NurtureShock* warn against excessive, inauthentic, and indiscriminate praise of children. As Thomas Buchanan put it, "For some reason the proponents of such ideas [that we must give praise to a child even if not deserved] think it is more important to have an inordinately high regard for oneself than a proper one. Self-respect and a *proper* sense of self-worth are not sins, but holding oneself in high esteem is."[86] So, for this, brutal honesty is required; we might even have to listen to our enemies whose accusations often contain a kernel of truth. Enemies notwithstanding, unfortunately, people do not typically go to a psychologist or pastor to obtain guidance for avoiding pride and acquiring humility. But better to seek out those who define self-esteem as "competence," as deficient as Mruk thinks such a definition is, since they at least would focus on behavioral outcomes and the degree of discrepancy between the "ideal" and the "real" self—hopes and desires and aspirations vis-à-vis competence in realizing them.[87]

So a proper understanding of oneself that neither blames nor praises oneself unduly is what is called for, and this is truly what humility entails. It is sinful to deny or depreciate God's gifts to us, though their source must be acknowledged and their use must be for service rather than for self-aggrandizement. Of course, there is no place for a false humility, which can even serve as a pretext for sloth. Even pride can be disguised as humility (and, as we have seen, humility can even lead to pride about one's humility).

This proper understanding of oneself is enhanced by recalling a constant theme in the monastics—an eschatological perspective. Such a perspective keeps in mind God's judgment against our service when preferring the praise of fellow humans rather than of God and when engrossed in "deceitful riches" while neglecting the "true riches of God" (Matt. 6:33).[88] Cassian also reminds us to have as mental models those who have come before us who exhibited true humility, including Christ who suffered in humility.[89]

This eschatological perspective gets personal when we keep before us our own mortality. I was reminded of this when, four years after his retirement from Wheaton College, one of the most significant professors the college had had for a half century who had also greatly influenced the wider Christian college community, was virtually an unknown to the student body. It was not that *he* was filled with pride (he was not!); but that he was so easily forgotten makes all the more poignant for those who *are* filled with pride Gregory's admonition that those who "were lifted up with honors, swollen with the things gotten by them, who looked down upon others, . . . while they never considered where unto they were going, they knew nothing at all what they were." Gregory's point, as he elaborates, is that many of us fail to remember that happiness in this fleeting life is uncertain, and the uncertainty of our demise has a way of putting self-esteemia in perspective.[90]

Maintaining an eschatological perspective requires some discipline which will enhance other ways in which we can "clothe" ourselves with (or "put on" in Paul's lingo) humility (1 Pet. 5:5–6). Cassian provides us with several strategies. Essentially he instructs us to take stock of the motives that lead us to take on certain tasks or refuse others. It helps to maintain the same care with which we began a task until we see it to completion, and avoid even beginning such a task if it is of very little use or value in the common life of the *coenobium* or if it would make us look remarkable among the others as if we were the only ones who could pull off such an activity.[91] In these cases he is concerned that we would be tempted to do something merely for show. There are those pastors, for instance, who act as if they are indispensable—as if a parishioner's life would be irreparably harmed if they are not available when other brothers and sisters in the community can meet the need.[92] In fact, those are the times when we have an opportunity to rejoice in the excellence of others (1 Cor. 13:6; Phil. 2:3).

Perhaps most significantly, to counter pride, vainglory, or self-esteemia, we are instructed to establish our self-worth on the basis of something other than our comparison with others. In suggesting a cure for pride, after Gregory exhorts us to realize that disobeying the commands of our Creator is to be haughty over against God, he instructs us to call to mind that we are made by God and "humbly return to the order of his creation"; one can find a curative if "he loves himself as he was at first created by God."[93] In other words, the measure of our worth needs to find its source outside of ourselves. As Mruk puts it in his insistence on linking worthiness with competence, concepts such as "good" or "bad" and the like imply significant interpersonal and social foundations. But more than that, for the Christian, concepts that have to do with our worthiness come from outside us in that we are created in the image of God and are so beloved by the Father to have been the beneficiaries of his Son's sacrifice and adopted as his children; and we are so loved by God as we are that he is not satisfied to leave us as we are.

In this respect, the most humble are the most secure and have the healthiest sense of worth. We can avoid both self-esteemia and self-degradation because the self is not the source and judge of our worth with all its manipulation and exploitation of others to make ourselves feel superior. In other words, Christianity provides self-esteem independent of subjective perceptions of a changing reality. In fact, if our worth rests outside of ourselves in a Reality that is unchanging, then we are free to engage life with confidence and even to risk failure.

Addendum

The Anthropology of Evagrius, Cassian, and Gregory

Scattered throughout this book are bits and pieces of what we will put together in this addendum, along with additional information about the Evagrian understanding of the soul and its progression to the full knowledge of God. Much of what is included here depends heavily upon two works that have been cited—those of Bunge and Joest.[1] Though this gets technical and can sound somewhat architectonic, we need to remember that Evagrius (whose anthropology Cassian and Gregory follow) was not building a consistent scheme. (Evidence of this is the presence of some variation in the language and explanations articulated by Evagrian scholars.) This is further complicated by questions of authorship regarding writings that have been attributed to Evagrius.[2]

To set the overall context, the monastic life is twofold: the life of virtue (the active life) and the life of prayer (the contemplative life). As Cassian expressed it, the monk seeks "purity of heart," which is penultimate and proximate to the ultimate and postmortem goal of the "Kingdom of God."

The soul that makes this journey is tripartite, a configuration borrowed from Platonic philosophy that Evagrius learned from Gregory of Nazianzus. (Platonic-Stoic influence would be more precise. Gregory of Nazianzus was also influenced by Origen's teachings.)

The two parts of the soul that comprise the irrational animal division from which arise the passions are the *epithymatikon* and the *thymatikon*. The first (*epithymatikon*) is the realm of the body—of desiring. It is the concupiscible or appetitive part of the soul where gluttony, lust, and greed thrive. The passions at this level are especially curbed by abstinence and moderation. The second element (*thymatikon*) is the realm of the soul and emotions. It is the irascible part where passions of the soul—anger, sadness (*tristitia*), and despondency (*acedia*)—are manifest. (Actually, *acedia* sits on a tension point between this part of the soul and the third part—the intellect.) Courage, patience, and meekness are virtues that address the passions in this arena.

The third and highest part of the soul—the realm of the spirit—is the *logistikon* or intellect (*nous*), where vainglory and pride threaten (envy being intricately associated with pride). Insight and knowledge are sought at this level. We humans are essentially mind or intellect (somewhere between the Triune God and animal existence), and our natural state is to be in prayer—in the contemplation of God. It is this (the contemplation of God) from which the *nous* has fallen such that we must regain this "knowledge" to be what we were intended to be.

When the soul caters to the passions and desires of its irrational parts, it functions contrary to its divinely created nature. Instead, the three parts of the soul are meant to work together in harmony toward the true knowledge of God and creation. When the soul functions in this way, in accord with the way that God made it, the soul is integrated and is "passionless" (*apatheia*). It is important to recognize that Evagrius is not calling for the suppression of the irrational parts of the soul;

they were created good and must function according to their nature. This is one reason why *apatheia*—the complete health of the soul—is not to be thought of as "apathy."[3] *Apatheia* is an inner tranquility of the soul—a feeling of deep peace that makes undistracted prayer possible.

How does the soul reach this state and even go beyond it?

The first step is the *praktike*, grounded in faith and employing self-control, perseverance, and hope. This is the stage of the spiritual life with which we have been primarily concerned in this book, the stage at which Evagrius is scrupulously concerned with the causes and effects of thoughts. The final battle in this arena is with *acedia* before one moves on to *apatheia* and *agapē*, which, in turn, opens the door to *gnōsis physike* (natural knowledge or contemplation)—the knowledge of creation and, beyond that, the knowledge of spiritual realities of which creation reveals traces. (Those familiar with Bonaventure's *Mind's Road to God* will recognize this progression.) This level is called *theoria* and sits at the threshold of *theologia*—the knowledge of God and blessedness.

At the stage of *praktike*, the appetitive part of the soul is being purified and healed. Evagrius refers to it as the stage at which the commandments are fulfilled. This is why self-control is essential at this point. It involves battles with demons who fight the monk using the thoughts (*logismoi*).

When the monk has reached the latter stages of *praktike* he has gained knowledge of the maneuverings of the enemy. Those who do not arrive at this knowledge are described as ones who suffer from *acedia*—the last all-embracing and most dangerous temptation. It is dangerous because the monk struggles without understanding because *acedia* confuses the *nous*.

Those who have "arrived"—who experience perfect *apatheia*—have surpassed the need for self-control because they no longer struggle with temptation.[4] The goal of the *praktike* actually goes beyond *apatheia* to love (*agapē*). This is the remedy for the self-love that made the appetites and desires go awry in the first place. It is this *agapē* that marks the transition from *praktike* and brings the *nous* to *gnōsis*. This is true knowledge characteristic of a lover.[5]

As mentioned above, the stage beyond *praktike* is *gnostike*. As the monk gains knowledge (*theoria*) of the inner meaning of the struggle that has taken place during the stage of *praktike*, he moves to *gnōsis physike* (natural knowledge) of all created things. Moving even beyond this stage of knowledge he then advances to yet a higher level labeled *theologia*. He now has reached beyond created realities to pure contemplation—a participatory knowledge of God, the *visio dei*. It is the stage at which a human being becomes *nous*, eventually becoming one with God. As Joest summarizes it, it is to know as one is known—an essential knowledge that affects one at the deepest interior levels and involves an ineffable intimacy in which archetype and image are united.[6]

Notes

Chapter 1 Getting Oriented

1. Source: http://www.imdb.com/title/tt0114369/quotes.

2. See Gabriel Bunge, *Despondency: The Spiritual Teaching of Evagrius Ponticus*, trans. Anthony P. Gythiel (Crestwood, NY: St. Vladimir's Seminary Press, 2012), 40–45 for material in this paragraph. Also see "On Thoughts," especially chapter 1 on "the three fundamental thoughts" in *Evagrius of Pontus: The Greek Ascetic Corpus*, trans. Robert E. Sinkewicz (Oxford: Oxford University Press, 2003), 153–82.

3. See John Cassian, *The Twelve Books of the Institutes of the Coenobium*, 5.1 for the list of eight principal faults. Cassian Folsom clarifies that these are not vices *per self-esteem*, but "fundamental attitudes or basic instincts in human nature which turn the heart away from God" ("Anger, Dejection, and Acedia in the Writings of John Cassian," in *The American Benedictine Review* [1989] 35:220). In *The Conferences* 5.16, Cassian calls them "sins." Cassian's writings can be found translated by Edgar C. S. Gibson in *The Nicene and Post-Nicene Fathers*, 2nd series, eds. Philip Schaff and Henry Wace (Grand Rapids: Eerdmans, repr. 1986), vol. 11. In most cases I have preferred this translation to a more recent translation because, strangely, the older one seems to be more readily comprehensible than the newer one. But when I have used the newer one I have indicated so with the initials *ACW* that stand for two volumes in the *Ancient Christian Writers* series: *John Cassian: The Conferences*, trans. and annotated by Boniface Ramsey, O.P. (New York: The Newman Press, 1997) and *John Cassian: The Institutes*, trans. and annotated by Boniface Ramsey, O.P. (New York: The Newman Press, 2000).

4. See Gregory, *Morals on the Book of Job*, 3 vols., trans. J. Bliss (Oxford: John Henry Parker, 1850), vol. 3, comments on 39:25. Also, see Solomon Schimmel, *The Seven Deadly Sins: Jewish, Christian, and Classical Reflections on Human Nature* (New York: The Free Press, 1992), 25.

5. E.g., see Aquinas, *Summa Theologica*, 5 vols., trans. Fathers of the English Dominican Province (Westminster, MD: Christian Classics, 1948), IIaIIae, Q 148, resp. 2. (Hereafter the *Summa* will be referred to as *ST*.)

6. See Gregory, *Morals on Job* 39:25. Aquinas lists these same offspring in *ST* IIaIIae, Q 148, resp. 6; obviously, he has imported this idea from Gregory.

7. "But they are, each of them, so closely connected with each other, that they spring only the one from the other" (Gregory, *Morals on Job* 39:25).

8. Cassian, *Conferences* 5.10.

9. Introduction by John Eudes Bamberger, lxxxii, in Evagrius Ponticus, *The Praktikos and Chapters on Prayer*, trans. J. E. Bamberger, OCSO (Spencer, MA: Cistercian Publications, 1970).

10. Schimmel, *Seven Deadly Sins*, 25.

11. See Bamberger's introduction to Evagrius's *Praktikos*; he suggests that in Evagrius the concept is more biblical than Stoic, something like the fear of the Lord—see lxxxiii and n233. Also, cf. Cassian, *Institutes* 4.43.

12. There *is* some language that sounds like this; e.g., see Evagrius, *Praktikos* 87. But the fact that the goal is the passion of love, as we will see, means that we must be careful how we understand this language.

13. See Bamberger, introduction to *Praktikos*, lxxii–lxxiii.

14. Cassian's favorite term for *apatheia* is "purity of heart"; e.g., see his *Conferences* 1.4. It is a state of undistracted prayer.

15. *Praktikos* 34, 64–67, 69.

16. We should mention that *apatheia* refers to the first half of spiritual development in ascetic theology—the active ascetic life, which begins in faith, diminishes the force of the passions "until they are destroyed" or purified and results in charity; this leads to the second phase—the contemplative, which begins with the contemplation of nature, diminishes ignorance, and results in theology. See Evagrius, *Praktikos* 84. The disciplines in ascetic theology have to do with the first step (viz., purgation) of the threefold assent that ends in union with God.

17. Evagrius, *Praktikos* 55.

18. Gregory, *Pastoral Care*, trans. Henry Davis, SJ (New York: Newman Press, 1950), 3.19.

19. Evagrius, *Praktikos* 81. He continues with his thought: "*Ascesis* consists in keeping the commandments. The custodian of these commandments is the fear of God which is in turn the offspring of true faith. Now faith is an interior good, one which is to be found even in those who do not yet believe in God."

20. Bunge, *Despondency*, 23–24. Coming at this from the discipline of psychotherapy Solomon Schimmel concurs: "The diatribes against traditional religion and morality that one encounters in psychological circles reflect a superficial understanding of sin, vice, and virtue and other concepts in the moral vocabulary of the past. The deadly sins are not arbitrary, irrational restrictions on human behavior, imposed by a remote deity indifferent to human needs. On the contrary, most sins or vices, and the seven deadly sins in particular, concern the core of what we are, of what we can become, and most important, of what we should aspire to be." See his *Seven Deadly Sins*, 5.

21. Bunge, *Despondency*, 15–16. He goes on to point out, "Evagrius's justly famous 'psychology' has one aim only: to make the human being capable of loving

again, and thereby capable of God" (17). Later in the book Bunge makes the bold claim that "the secret connection between psychic and physical diseases, of such concern to modern medicine, was known perfectly well to Evagrius" (70).

22. E.g., see Evagrius, *Praktikos* 43, 50.

23. See Thomas Oden, *The Care of Souls in the Classical Tradition* (Philadelphia: Fortress, 1984), chap. 2.

24. See "Hurting Helpers" in *Christianity Today*, September 16, 1996, 76–80.

25. Benedict Groeschel was one of the first to be heard in recent venues of Christian psychology. E.g., see his *Spiritual Passages: The Psychology of Spiritual Development* (New York: Crossroad, 1990). And years ago Thomas Oden documented and chastised clinical pastoral counseling's neglect of centuries of Christian wisdom having to do with counseling; see chap. 1 of his *Care of Souls in the Classical Tradition*.

26. For example, see Alan Jones's *Soul Making* (San Francisco: HarperCollins, 1985). Jones purports to unpack the desert tradition and demonstrate its relevance for today, yet curiously the book has few actual references to the desert fathers and mothers; it is more modern and psychoanalytic than desert. (Even a glance at the index demonstrates this.) As a result, the spirituality of the desert monks is distorted and misrepresented. For instance, compare Jones's comment about the perfection of the desert fathers with a paradigmatic quote of Cassian. Jones typically writes, "The perfection which he or she [the desert ascetic] seeks is of a very different order from that of worldly success. [True enough.] It comes only as a gift and *never* as an achievement" (p. 41; italics mine). But Cassian typifies the preceding desert tradition: "Consider therefore that you belong to the few and elect; and do not grow cold after the examples of the lukewarmness of many. . . . You should therefore realize that it is no light sin for one who has made profession of perfection to follow after what is imperfect. And to this state of perfection you may *attain* by the following steps and in the following way" (*Conferences* 5.38 [refer to n5]; italics mine). If Jones is correct, it is difficult to understand how Cassian (who summarizes the desert tradition he inherited) could ever have been accused (rightly or wrongly) of being semi-Pelagian.

Despite Jones's misrepresentations and sometimes careless use of words and categories, his book is still valuable; he has many good insights despite the problems.

27. *Seven Deadly Sins*, 5; see especially all of chap. 1.

28. We are also drawing upon Thomas Aquinas in this book because he adds some clarification, and, while he was not an ascetic theologian and came much later than our three monks, on these topics he drew heavily on the tradition.

Chapter 2 Gluttony

1. On the word "gluttony" see Deut. 21:20; Prov. 23:20; 28:7; Matt. 11:9; Titus 1:12. Typical Pauline exhortations include Rom. 6:12; 12:1; 1 Cor. 6:15–20; 1 Thess. 4:4.

2. Cf. Matt. 4:4; 6:25; Phil. 3:19 with Matt. 7:18; Rom. 14:3; 1 Cor. 8:8; Col. 2:23; 1 Tim. 4:2–4.

3. Until recently, Mary Louise Bringle's book *The God of Thinness: Gluttony and Other Weighty Matters* (Nashville: Abingdon, 1992) was the only book written by a contemporary theologian devoted to the topic of gluttony; she made the

same observation (on p. 16) about the disparity between the topic's importance and the dearth of theological treatments. A related book at the time Bringle wrote was Caroline Walker Bynum's *Holy Feast and Holy Fast* (Berkeley: University of California Press, 1987), but since that time only a couple serious books on the topic have appeared.

4. Part of the blame for the high statistical rates among women is to be placed on cultural expectations and images that are portrayed by the media and the food and diet industries. See Marlene Boskind-White, "Bulimarexia: A Sociocultural Perspective" and Susie Orbach, "Visibility/Invisibility: Social Considerations in Anorexia Nervosa—A Feminist Perspective" in *Theory and Treatment of Anorexia Nervosa and Bulimia: Biomedical, Sociocultural, and Psychological Perspectives*, ed. Steven Wiley Emmett (New York: Brunner/Mazel, 1985), 113–26 and 127–38, respectively. These and other statistics can be found on the websites of the National Association of Anorexia Nervosa and Associated Disorders (ANAD) and the National Eating Disorders Association (NEDA).

5. Admittedly, one must be careful when it comes to statistics about dieting and eating disorders. For example, Bringle stated that 150,000 women die of anorexia each year in the US. Psychologist Paul Vitz saved me from the error of including this in a first draft of what was at the time a paper presented before several other scholars by calling my attention to the fact that this number exceeded the number of annual traffic fatalities at the time. So on further investigation I discovered that the source and perpetuation of this widely inflated figure Bringle reported was ultimately traced to a *misquote* of a comment made at a conference—a misquote that had gone unchallenged as it made its way even into textbooks. See Christina Hoff Sommers, *Who Stole Feminism? How Women Have Betrayed Women* (New York: Simon and Schuster, 1994), 11–12. Besides political agenda, statistics are further complicated by secrecy and denial.

6. Eric Schlosser, *Fast Food Nation* (Boston: Houghton Mifflin, 2001).

7. This is according to *U.S. Weight Loss and Diet Control Market* (11th edition, 2011).

8. While Aquinas is not an ascetic theologian, on this topic he draws heavily on them.

9. Aquinas, *ST* IIaIIae, Q 148, art. 2.

10. In Cassian, *Conferences* 5.3, Cassian classifies gluttony as a principal fault that is natural to us (rather than one like covetousness that arises outside of our nature), cannot be completed without a bodily act (rather than one like pride that needs no bodily act), and is aroused by something external to us (rather than something like *acedia* which is aroused only by internal feelings).

11. See Cassian, *Conferences* 5.6. This is why it is important to distinguish in the previous note between faults which arise outside our nature (after the image is marred), "whereas those [temptations] which are natural to us do not cease from troubling even the best of monks and those who dwell in solitude . . . all their life long they have to fight against gluttony, and cannot be safe from it without striving with the utmost watchfulness of heart and bodily abstinence" (*Conferences* 5.8). This is a point we will make more clearly in the next chapter.

12. Cf. Aquinas's similar observation regarding temperance in *ST* IIaIIae, Q 141, arts. 4, 5, 7. Temperance is particularly needed due to the fact that "nature

has introduced pleasure into the operations that are necessary for man's life" (Q 142, art. 1).

13. Schimmel thinks so; see *Seven Deadly Sins*, 247n9. While Aquinas agrees that gluttony is not the greatest sin for the same reason (though certain grave sins are connected with it), he argues that intemperance is the most disgraceful of sins since it refers to pleasures common to us and lower animals, dimming reason's light and clarity. Cf. *ST* IIaIIae, Q 148, art. 3 with Q 142, art. 4.

14. See Cassian, *Institutes* 5.12–13 and *Conferences* 5.3, 6, 10. Aquinas notes the same kind of talk in Gregory; cf. *ST* IIaIIae, Q 148, art. 1 with Gregory's *Morals on Job* 39:7.

15. *Conferences* 5.18.

16. Overcome the earlier sins and the rest die down without difficulty; *Conferences* 5.10. Conversely, gluttony is harmful because it opens the door to all other passions, such as lust, covetousness, anger, dejection, and pride; *Conferences* 5.26. There is wisdom in the observation of this order, but one might question it today given what we know about the genesis of eating disorders.

17. "But they are, each of them, so closely connected with each other, that they spring only the one from the other" (Gregory, *Morals on Job* 39:25).

18. *Conferences* 5.10.

19. Gregory, *Morals on Job* 29:25. Actually, Gregory's observation about the pressure a full stomach exerts on the genitals may not really be that laughable to moderns. In a conversation with A. A. Howsepian at Notre Dame, he described the physiological mechanism of the gastro-colic response by virtue of which eating stimulates the passage of fecal material into the colon, where the resulting pressure on the prostate gland tends to excite sexual interest. Once again, this could be a case where these early ascetic theologians already knew what it has taken our modern social and natural scientists centuries to rediscover.

20. See Schimmel, *Seven Deadly Sins*, 151.

21. Gregory, *Morals on Job* 39:7; Aquinas, *ST* IIaIIae, Q 148, art. 1.

22. E.g., see Cassian, *Institutes* 5.23 and *Conferences* 5.11; Gregory, *Morals on Job* 39:7; Aquinas, *ST* IIaIIae, Q 148, art. 4.

23. See Cassian, *Conferences* 5.11. I have observed this communal emphasis at Benedictine monasteries. For instance, while working on this chapter at former Blue Cloud Abbey in South Dakota, one of the brothers told me that though he does not eat breakfast, he comes to breakfast because the abbot insisted that all the monks should be together at every meal.

24. See Cassian, *Institutes* 5.23.

25. Bringle, *God of Thinness*, 143, see also 38.

26. Schimmel, *Seven Deadly Sins*, 152–55.

27. See Cornelius Plantinga, *Not the Way It's Supposed to Be: A Breviary of Sin* (Grand Rapids: Eerdmans, 1995).

28. Gerald May, *Addiction and Grace*, 93.

29. *Morals on Job* 39:25.

30. See *God of Thinness*, 148–49.

31. "The past two decades have led to divergence in etiological formulations as well as convergence of opinion on the utility of certain practical intervention principles. In spite of these advancements, current knowledge has yet to yield

conclusive support for any one theoretical viewpoint or treatment modality" (275). "There is general disagreement in the literature about the psychological and developmental significance of eating disorders and their symptoms" (277). These comments in David M. Garner and Anna Gerborg, "Understanding and Diagnosing Eating Disorders," in Robert Holman Coombs, ed., *Handbook of Addictive Disorders: A Practical Guide to Diagnosis and Treatment* (Hoboken, NJ: John Wiley & Sons, Inc., 2004).

32. See Schimmel, *Seven Deadly Sins*, 233–34 for some of what follows; also, see Bringle, *God of Thinness*, 132. Garner and Gerborg ("Eating Disorders," 276–77) argue for the addiction model for thinking about eating disorders because "both substance abuse and poor impulse regulation are common features in bulimia nervosa." It also works with self-starvation "since periods of sustained calorie restriction can activate powerful neurochemical reward systems that may fuel further dietary restriction. Moreover, applying the addiction model to eating disorders makes sense since eating disordered behaviors appear to conform to the following three Cs often used to define addiction (i.e., compulsive use, loss of control, and continued use despite adverse consequences)." For a discussion of anorexia nervosa and bulimia in terms of biological causes and treatments, see Harrison Pope and James Hudson, "Biological Treatments of Eating Disorders" in Emmett, *Theory and Treatment of Anorexia Nervosa and Bulimia*, 73–92.

33. See May, *Addiction*, 192n1: *Apatheia* is not to be confused with *acedia*, which is closer to what *we* mean by "apathy"—a "dull, lethargic absence of caring and interest."

34. See Bamberger's introduction to Evagrius's *Praktikos*; he suggests that in Evagrius the concept is more biblical than Stoic, something like the fear of the Lord—see lxxxiii and n233. Also, cf. Cassian, *Institutes* 4.43.

35. There *is* some language that sounds like this; e.g., see Evagrius, *Praktikos* 87. But the fact that the goal is the passion of love means that we must be careful how we understand this language. See previous two notes.

36. See Bamberger, lxxii–lxxiii.

37. Cassian's favorite term for *apatheia* is "purity of heart"; e.g., see his *Conferences* 1.4. It is a state of undistracted prayer.

38. *Praktikos* 34, 64–67, 69.

39. See Bamberger, lxxxv–lxxxvi and Evagrius, *Praktikos* 60 and 77.

40. We should mention that *apatheia* refers to the first half of spiritual development in ascetic theology—the active ascetic life, which begins in faith, diminishes the force of the passions "until they are destroyed," and results in charity; this leads to the second phase—the contemplative, which begins with the contemplation of nature, diminishes ignorance, and results in theology. See Evagrius, *Praktikos* 84. The disciplines in ascetic theology have to do with the first step (viz., purgation) of the threefold assent that ends in union with God.

41. *Praktikos* 55.

42. Gregory, *Pastoral Care* 3.19.

43. *Praktikos* 81.

44. According to Aquinas, knowledge must have something to do with gluttony: If the quantity of food necessary for the body is exceeded not due to desire for food but because one misjudged what is necessary, such is not gluttony but

inexperience. Gluttony is *knowingly* exceeding what is necessary out of desire for pleasure of the palate. See *ST* IIaIIae, Q 148, art. 1. This might be difficult to apply in cases of anorexia nervosa, since one attitude often associated with it is a denial of the illness and a failure to recognize nutritional needs.

45. Bringle refers to "caloric Pelagianism": "I cannot heal an obsession with food by replacing it with a counter obsession with dieting" (*God of Thinness*, 147).

46. We are not really interested in the mechanics of fasting in this paper. Many books have been written about that. We are only interested here in the connection between *ascesis, apatheia,* and *agapē.*

47. See *Conferences* 5.4 and *Institutes* 5.14, 21. This dual remedy is an emphasis that could be better developed in Bringle's book. She implies that caring for the body itself necessarily gives energy to the soul.

48. Evagrius, in *Praktikos* 7, seems to equate such fear and mistrust with gluttony: "It [gluttonous thoughts] brings to his [monk's] mind concern for his stomach, for his liver and spleen, the thought of a long illness, scarcity of the commodities of life and finally of his edematous body and the lack of care by the physicians. These things are depicted vividly before his eyes. It frequently brings him to recall certain ones among the brethren who have fallen upon such sufferings."

49. Cassian, *Institutes* 5.19; *Conferences* 5.14.

50. Evagrius, *Praktikos* 15–16, 58; Dallas Willard, *The Spirit of the Disciplines: Understanding How God Changes Lives* (San Francisco: Harper and Row, 1988), chap. 9. It is interesting that Cassian (in *Conferences* 5.4) even suggests that the cure for gluttony is not only getting away from food, but in some cases a change of venue. Sometimes the treatment of eating disorders requires some isolation from family and friends, particularly if therapy is guided by family systems theories.

51. Note the opening sentence of the *Rule of Benedict*: "Listen carefully, my son, to the master's instructions, and attend to them with the ear of your heart." Such sounds like wisdom literature in the Old Testament.

52. *Institutes* 5.4.

53. *Praktikos* 43, 50; *Chapters on Prayer*, 133.

54. Aquinas defines temperance as moderation which reason maintains over against passions—particularly those that tend toward sensible goods. See *ST* IIaIIae, Q 141.

55. *Morals on Job* 39:7

56. *Pastoral Care*, 2.9.

57. *Institutes* 5.9.

58. See Johanna Dwyer, "Nutritional Aspects of Anorexia Nervosa and Bulimia," in Emmett, *Theory and Treatment*, 29: "Present evidence suggests that it is simplistic to regard dieting as necessary and sufficient in itself to cause anorexia. However, the mind sets, attitudes, and behaviors associated with dieting may predispose individuals to develop these disorders." Also, see Bringle, *God of Thinness*, 45, 129–30, 147.

59. *The Rule of St. Benedict in English*, ed. Timothy Fry, OSB (Collegeville, MN: Liturgical Press, 1982), chaps. 2, 27, 64. Aquinas insists that we cannot fix the same quantity of food in fasting for all due to various body temperaments; see *ST* IIaIIae, Q 147, art. 6.

60. *Institutes* 5.9.

61. *Pastoral Care*, 3 prol.

62. *Institutes* 4.5. The need for moderation and discernment on an individual basis is a repeated emphasis in Benedicts's *Rule*, chaps. 36–41: e.g., he prescribes meat for the sick, greater amounts of food when the work is harder, two kinds of cooked food at the table in case a person who is not able to eat one kind can partake of the other, and so on.

63. Bringle documents such standards in the third chapter of *God of Thinness*.

64. See ibid., 123–24 for Bringle's summary of this theory.

65. Cassian, *Conferences* 5.12. Unfortunately, Bringle seems to dismiss this intermediate step, perhaps falling victim to the very absolutist mentality she abhors in other contexts. See *God of Thinness*, 141–42. Evagrius makes the same suggestion as Cassian in *Praktikos* 58, but goes on to say that only when a vice is opposed by a virtue do you have proof of *apatheia*. Presumably, a vice countered by an opposing vice would not yet achieve the state of *apatheia*.

66. *Chicago Tribune*, May 29, 1994, sec. 2, 3. The debate between AA and RR raises an interesting question for ascetic theology: Is the reorientation of gluttonous habits and behavior more like RR's proposal rather than the total abstinence mandated by AA? For reasons that have to do with the necessity of eating, which we have noted before in this essay, perhaps gluttony fits better with RR's philosophy while AA's is more appropriate for other vices which have to be expunged, though, as we will see, the twelve-step therapy has been successfully applied in cases of sexual addiction. Still, with both food and sex total abstinence (as in the case of alcoholism) is not necessarily healthy. Garner and Gerborg are advocates of twelve-step therapy in cases of eating disorders, but recognize this distinction with alcoholism; see "Eating Disorders," 303.

67. See Evagrius, *Chapters on Prayer*, 97.

68. *Conferences* 5.19.

69. *The Sayings of the Desert Fathers*, trans. Benedicta Ward, SLG (Kalamazoo, MI: Cistercian Publications, 1975), 223; cf. Cassian, *Conferences* 11.14, 15. Recall Gregory's words above. Also, cf. Aquinas who argues that reason is not operative in one who abstains from *all* pleasures, since one cannot use reason unless the body is sustained, and the body is sustained through operations (like eating) that afford pleasure; *ST* IIaIIae, Q 142, art. 1. This is why Schimmel's constant refrain in *Seven Deadly Sins* about choosing happiness in place of pleasure is too simplistic.

70. Ref. Bringle, *God of Thinness*, 34.

71. *Morals on Job* 39:7.

Chapter 3 Lust

1. Cassian, *Conferences* 5.11; cf. *Institutes* 6. He lists five senses of "fornication" in *Conferences* 14.11.

2. Evagrius, "On the Eight Thoughts," 1.2 in *Evagrius Ponticus: The Greek Ascetic Corpus*, trans. Robert E. Sinkewicz (Oxford: Oxford University Press, 2003).

3. Cassian, *Conferences* 22.3, 6.

4. Aquinas, *ST* IIaIIae, Q 151, art. 3; Q 153, art. 3. In the former reference, Thomas works from Jerome's commentary on Titus 1:7; in the latter, from Aristotle's *De Gener. Anim.* 1.18.

5. Ibid., Q 154, art. 2.

6. Terrence Kardong, "John Cassian's Teaching on Perfect Chastity," in *The American Benedictine Review* 30 (1979), 252. Also see Patrick J. Carnes, Robert E. Murray, and Louis Carpenter, "Addiction Interaction Disorder," in Coomb, *Handbook*, 31–59.

7. For this and what follows, see Cynthia A. Power, "Food and Sex Addiction: Helping the Clinician Recognize and Treat the Interaction," in *Sexual Addiction & Compulsivity* 12 (2005): 219–34.

8. Patrick Carnes published a book in 1983 titled *The Sexual Addiction*. It was controversial because the idea that a behavior rather than a drug or alcohol could be an addiction was novel (though some would argue the notion is as old as Freud's theories about masturbation). Because the title was also embarrassing for purchasers, the title was changed to *Out of the Shadows*. (See *Out of the Shadows: Understanding Sexual Addiction*, 3rd ed. [Center City, MN: Hazelden, 2001].) This was the beginning of theories and research related to the concept of sexual addiction. But the field is still not without its critics and those who question whether the label is legitimate and to what it applies. There are many different terms used to describe problematic sexual behavior, some reflecting different theoretical perspectives, diagnostic assessments, and treatment modalities. There are references to obsessive sexual objectification, compulsive sexual behavior, obsessive hypersexual desire, and poorly managed sexuality, not to mention terms that are used such as impulsivity, deviance, promiscuity, and perversion. Jennifer Schneider argues that while the *DSM-IV* did not use the term "sexual addiction," it can be extrapolated from diagnostic criteria for substance dependence. She suggests it can be classified under one of three *DSM-IV* categories: paraphilia, sexual disorder NOS (not otherwise specified), and impulse control disorder. Many in the field that deals with sexual offenders do not support the sex addiction model, since it tends to excuse the behavior. Some think that it should not be used to pathologize socially inappropriate behavior at one end of the spectrum nor behaviors that are sociopathic verging on evil at the other extreme. For discussions of some of this, see for example: John R. Giugliano, "A Psychoanalytic Overview of Excessive Sexual Behavior and Addiction," *Sexual Addiction & Compulsivity* 10 (2003): 275–90; Jennifer P. Schneider, "Sexual Addiction & Compulsivity: Twenty Years of the Field, Ten Years of the Journal," *Sexual Addiction & Compulsivity* 11 (2004): 3–5; Jennifer P. Schneider, "Understanding and Diagnosing Sex Addiction," in Coombs, *Handbook*, 198–232; Bill Herring, "The Next 20 Years: The Developmental Challenges Facing the Field of Compulsive Sexual Behavior," *Sexual Addiction & Compulsivity* 11 (2004): 35–42; John R. Giugliano, "Sexual Impulsivity, Compulsivity or Dependence: An Investigative Inquiry," *Sexual Addiction & Compulsivity* 15 (2008): 139–57; and Bill Herring, "The Nether Reaches of the Addictive/Compulsive Paradigm," *Sexual Addiction & Compulsivity* 18 (2011): 191–94. There are those who reject the label "sexual addiction" altogether, such as Marty Klein, a sex therapist, marriage counselor, and psychotherapist. He argues that when most people refer to themselves as sexual addicts they are simply talking about a "narcissistic character structure," which he considers normal. Others who are in pain are really struggling with other issues, such as obsessive-compulsive disorder, post-traumatic stress disorder, and so forth. Furthermore, he contends that some of this has to do with "cultural definitions of normal sex" and points

out that there is still no consensus on a definition of "sex addiction." See his article "You're Addicted to What?" in *Humanist* 72, no. 4 (July 2012): 31–35.

Without immersing ourselves in this debate, there does seem to be agreement that what we are dealing with (between the extremes) are such behaviors as compulsivity and impulsivity, and while "lust" may not always involve such behaviors (or associated thought processes), as we will see, there are interesting intersections between what our ancient psychologists taught and what is being reported as the fruit of research by our contemporaries.

9. In one study, among 75 persons suffering from sexual addiction issues, 32 percent had an eating disorder. See Peer Briken, Niels Habermann, Wolfgang Berner, and Andreas Hill, "Diagnosis and Treatment of Sexual Addiction: A Survey among German Sex Therapists," *Sexual Addiction & Compulsivity* 14 (2007): 131–43. Carnes gives us an insight into how food and sexual addiction might interact: "the belief system and delusional thought patterns may support more than one addiction. Overeating, for example, is a way to minimize pain. The sexual addicts who become overweight add shame concerning their body image to their repertoire of pain. The two addictions start to reinforce each other. When the addicts believe that people are not attracted to them, their sexual addiction is partially rooted in the fear of rejection. Then they eat compulsively to kill the pain due to the fear of rejection, and as a result put on weight. The added weight, by their standards, makes them even less desirable. Also, one way to avoid the depression after sexually bingeing is to binge again—with food. The two processes become interdependent. Addicts who have both addictions report that at the height of their sexual addiction, they had their greatest weight problem" (*Out of the Shadows*, 29).

10. Cassian, *Institutes* 6.1.

11. Cassian, *Conferences* 22.7, 9–13.

12. Kardong, "John Cassian's Teaching," 253.

13. Cassian, *Conferences* 12.5.

14. Cassian, *Institutes* 6.22, 23.

15. Carnes, *Out of the Shadows*, 34.

16. Ibid., 189.

17. Gregory, *Morals on Job* 31:2; cf. Aquinas, *ST* IIaIIae, Q153, art. 3. Also, see Gregory, *Pastoral Care*, 266n304.

18. Aquinas, *ST* IIaIIae, Q153, art. 3. Cf. Aquinas's definition of "sin" in Q 153, art. 3: "A sin, in human acts, is that which is against the order of reason. Now the order of reason consists in its ordering everything to its end in a fitting manner. Wherefore it is no sin if one, by the dictate of reason, makes use of certain things in a fitting manner and order for the end to which they are adapted, provided this end by something truly good. . . . Wherefore just as the use of food can be without sin, if it be taken in due manner and order, as required for the welfare of the body, so also the use of venereal acts can be without sin, provided they be performed in due manner and order, in keeping with the end of human procreation."

19. Ibid., art. 4.

20. Ibid., art. 5. In Q 154, art. 2 Aquinas adds that human reason is right when it is ordered by God's will. And, of course, in the area of sexuality the divine will is reflected in the "natural order of the venereal act as becoming to the human race,"

so that sexual sins are acts inconsistent with the end for which intercourse exists and the relationships that God established among people. See arts. 1, 2, and 11.

21. Ibid., Q156, art. 1.

22. Ibid., Q151, art. 3. Aquinas attributes the fact that "venereal concupiscence and pleasure are not subject to the command and moderation of reason" to the notion that what was deserved as the punishment for the first sin—rebelling against God—was that the body should rebel against reason; ibid., Q153, art. 2 (appealing to Augustine's *City of God*, 13.13).

23. Carnes, *Out of the Shadows*, 8.

24. See Giugliano, "Sexual Impulsivity," 144–45. He lists seven criteria from the former *DSM-IV*, only three of which are necessary to diagnose "dependence," and some of the criteria fit the dynamics the Evagrian tradition describes.

25. Gregory, *Morals on Job* 31:2.

26. Cassian, *Institutes* 6.3. Columba Stewart refers to this as "gaining a reflective distance from the immediate experience of temptation." See his *Cassian the Monk* (New York: Oxford University Press, 1998), 266.

27. Kardong, "John Cassian's Teaching," 254n12.

28. Carnes, *Out of the Shadows*, 95, 140. "Like all other addictions, the sexual addiction is rooted in a complex web of family and marital relationships" (4).

29. Ibid., 25.

30. Ibid., 31.

31. See Cassian, *Institutes* 6.13. We rightly cringe at the attitude of women as the seducer such as Evagrius articulated when he cautioned, "Flee encounters with women if you want to be chaste, and never allow them the familiarity to be bold with you" ("On the Eight Thoughts," 2.8 in Sinkewicz, *Evagrius Pontus*).

32. Gregory, *Morals on Job* 6:18.

33. Ibid., 31:2.

34. Joanne Kaufman, "The Fall of Jimmy Swaggart," *People*, March 7, 1988, 9. Details mentioned here are from this article along with "Swaggart Plans to Step Down," in the *New York Times*, October 15, 1991.

35. See Kailla Edger, "The Lived Experiences of Evangelical Christian Men Who Self-Identify as Sexual Addicts: An Existential-Phenomenological Study," *Sexual Addiction & Compulsivity* 16 (2009): 319.

36. See Evagrius of Pontus, *Talking Back: A Monastic Handbook for Combating Demons*, trans. David Brakke (Collegeville, MN: Liturgical Press, 2009).

37. See Cassian, *Institutes* 6.1 for this list of spiritual antidotes.

38. Cassian, *Conferences* 12.5.

39. Power, "Food and Sex Addiction," 231.

40. Edger, "Lived Experiences," 307.

41. Stewart, *Cassian the Monk*, 72.

42. Cassian, *Conferences* 12.4, 16.

43. Ibid., 12.4 (*ACW*). Also, see *Institutes* 6.5.

44. See Kardong, "John Cassian's Teaching," 14.

45. Stewart, *Cassian*, 77.

46. Cassian, *Conferences* 12.10. Here is where one could apply Luther's evening and morning prayers. The first (in part) prays "and graciously keep me this night. For into your hands I commend myself, my body and soul, and all things. Let your

holy angel be with me, that the wicked Foe may have no power over me. Amen." The morning prayer asks for this continued protection in like manner. See *The Lutheran Book of Prayer* (St. Louis, MO: Concordia, 1970), 43–44.

47. See Schneider, "Sexual Addiction and Compulsivity," 3.

48. Cassian, *Conferences* 22.3 (*ACW*). He goes on to observe that beginners who are not far along in the ascetic disciplines are humiliated and left suspecting that the disciplined life itself is responsible for their "failure" at night.

49. Cassian, *Institutes* 6.7 (*ACW*).

50. Ibid., 6.11. Aquinas says something of the same sort when discussing "nocturnal emissions": they are not sinful *in themselves*, but are sometimes the result of previous sin, either in behavior, thoughts when awake, or lack of vigilance against the adversary. See *ST* IIaIIae, Q154, art. 5.

51. Cassian, *Institutes* 6.20. He at least wants the monk to strive for a condition in which, as we already pointed out, "the flesh satisfies its natural demands without arousing desire" (6.22). In *Conferences* 12.7, he says that absolutely pure chastity is such that semen is not even produced or emitted, and this he says is *very* rare.

52. Stewart, *Cassian*, 84; cf. Kardong, "John Cassian's Teaching," 254.

53. Cassian, *Conferences* 12.10; *Institutes* 6.4, 15. A helpful article (besides Kardong's) on what we are discussing is Kenneth Russsell, "John Cassian on a Delicate Subject," *Cistercian Studies Quarterly* 27, no. 1 (1992): 1–12.

54. We should point out that Aquinas has a discussion of this that somewhat parallels Cassian's. Under the rubric of "temperance" Aquinas locates "abstinence" with regard to food that is necessary for the preservation of the individual and "chastity" with regard to sexual intercourse that is necessary for the preservation of the species. "Continence" can be abstention from all venereal pleasure or resistance to evil desires; since virtue must be in accord with reason, one is properly and truly continent who thinks and acts in accord with right reason by abstaining from evil desires. It is a "certain curbing" whereby one refrains from following his passions (which work off of inclinations of nature). Continence resides in the will, not in the reason, and has to do with resisting the desire for the pleasures of touch, whereas temperance's role is to moderate those desires. Temperance comes closer to what Cassian means by chastity, since for Aquinas it is greater than continence: it tames the sensitive appetite by making it obedient to reason, so temperance has more to do with reason than does continence. Intemperance (i.e., lacking the virtue of chastity) is worse than incontinence: "Now in the intemperate man the will is inclined to sin in virtue of its own choice, which proceeds from a habit acquired through custom. Whereas in the incontinent man, the will is inclined to sin through a passion. And since passion soon passes, whereas a habit is a disposition difficult to remove, the result is that the incontinent man repents at once, as soon as the passion has passed; but not so the intemperate man; in fact he rejoices in having sinned, because the sinful act has become connatural to him by reason of his habit." (See *ST* IIaIIae, Q151, arts. 1, 3; Q155, arts. 1–4; Q156, art. 3.) The fact that temperance has more to do with habit squares nicely with Cassian's understanding of chastity vis-à-vis the constant battle that abstinence or mere continence must endure.

55. Cassian, *Conferences* 12.1; see Kardong, "John Cassian's Teaching," 254–55. Similarly, Gregory teaches that we need *all* the virtues, since one without another

is equivalent to none at all or only the very least one; they must be mutually supported by their alliance together because a person is really strong when she is not subject to any evil habits in *any* quarter. See *Morals on Job* 31:2.

56. Cassian, *Conferences* 12.6.

57. Ibid., 12.15; see Kardong, "John Cassian's Teaching," 259.

58. Carnes, *Out of the Shadows*, 53–54.

59. See ibid., 110, 151.

60. Stewart, *Cassian*, 71. The phrases are his.

61. Evagrius, *Praktikos* 8.

62. See Ronald J. Sider, *The Scandal of the Evangelical Conscience: Why Are Christians Living Just Like the Rest of the World?* (Grand Rapids: Baker Books, 2005), 23.

63. Cassian, *Conferences* 12.10–11 (*ACW*).

64. Carnes, *Out of the Shadows*, 6, 23, 36, 164–86.

65. Cassian lists many grades of chastity on the road to "full recovery"—that is, to inviolable purity. They are distinct stages, but Kardong insists that they are not to be thought of as a strict progression. They include: (1) keeping vigils without lustful thoughts; (2) not dwelling on lustful thoughts; (3) not moved to even the slightest desire at the sight of a woman; (4) during vigils not experiencing even the slightest movement of the flesh; (5) if something read or heard deals with human generation, keeping a tranquil spirit; and (6) having no fantasies about women while asleep. See *Conferences* 12.7 and Kardong, "John Cassian's Teaching," 259n20. In *Conferences* 22.6 Cassian mentions several very general strategies for assisting us in arriving at a "permanently peaceful bodily state."

66. Cassian, *Institutes* 6.19.

67. Ibid., 6.16, 18.

68. Cassian, *Conferences* 12.11.

69. See Kardong, "John Cassian's Teaching," 255.

70. Cassian, *Conferences* 12.5, 7.

71. Ibid., 12.16, 11.

72. Edger, "Lived Experience of Evangelical Christian Men," 315–16.

73. See Cassian, *Conferences* 22.7 and *Institutes* 6.18. See Kardong, "John Cassian's Teaching," 258. Also, see Michael Casey's book *Living in the Truth* for his thesis that humility really has to do with knowing one's self.

74. See sources in n34.

75. Gregory, *Morals on Job* 35:15.

76. Carnes, *Out of the Shadows*, 15.

77. Ibid., 19.

78. Gregory, *Morals on Job* 35:11.

79. Ibid., 39:1.

80. Gregory, *Pastoral Care* 3.28.

81. See Cassian, *Conferences* 2.13. In *Morals on Job* 6:18, Gregory refers to the awe of fellow monks who are impressed by the abstinence with which one of their own restrains his habit of immoderate bodily behavior, only for this awe to incite vainglory in the abstainer.

82. Gregory, *Morals on Job* 40:21. The italics are mine.

83. Edger, "Lived Experiences of Evangelical Christian Men," 309.

84. Ibid., 310.

85. Joan Chittester, *Wisdom Distilled from the Daily: Living the Rule of St. Benedict Today* (San Francisco: Harper & Row, 1990), 188.

Chapter 4 Greed

1. Citing research from Ronald J. Faber and Thomas C. O'Guinn in the *Journal of Consumer Research*, Gerhard Scherhorn in the *Journal of Consumer Policy*, and Rajan Natarajan and Brent C. Goff in *Psychology and Marketing*, Juliet Schor defines "compulsive buyers" as "people who engage in 'chronic, repetitive purchasing that becomes a primary response to negative events or feelings'; such purchasing 'becomes very difficult to stop and ultimately results in harmful consequences.'" These researchers "disagree about whether this is an addiction or a compulsion, although the terms are often used interchangeably." Studies do show that compulsive buyers are more likely to abuse drugs and alcohol, binge eat, and engage in other compulsive behaviors like gambling and shoplifting vis-à-vis the general population. Juliet B. Schor, *The Overspent American: Why We Want What We Don't Need* (New York: Harper Perennial, 1999), 139n158 and 240n160.

2. William Green, "The Master Passion," in *Worth*, May 1996, 97–103.

3. Rodney Clapp, "The Theology of Consumption and the Consumption of Theology: Toward a Christian Response," in Rodney Clapp, *The Consuming Passion: Christianity and the Consumer Culture* (Downers Grove, IL: InterVarsity, 1998), 171.

4. John Schneider, "On New Things," in Clapp, *Consuming Passion*, 130.

5. *ST* IIaIIae, Q 118, art. 1.

6. Ibid., Q 119, art. 1.

7. Ibid., Q 119, art. 3.

8. Ted Peters, *Sin: Radical Evil in Soul and Society* (Grand Rapids: Eerdmans, 1994), 126.

9. Green, "Master Passion," 140, 143–44.

10. Cassian, *Institutes* 7.14; cf. *Conferences* 5.11, where he essentially covers the same three categories.

11. Ibid., 7.1.

12. *ST* IIaIIae, Q 118, art. 2.

13. Gregory, *Morals on Job* 15:34.

14. Evagrius, "Letter to Anatolius," 14.

15. Aquinas considers the order of sins in two ways at this point (*ST* IIaIIae, Q 118, art. 5): (1) with regard to the good that is despised or corrupted by sin, so that the greater the good (in descending order—God, a person, an external thing), the graver the sin; and (2) with regard to the good to which the human appetite is inordinately subjected, so that the lesser the good (in descending order—divine good, soul's good, body's good, external things), the more deformed the sin, because it is more shameful to be subject to a lower good than to a higher good. So, in the first case, the gravity of the sin is to be judged from the point of view of the good corrupted.

16. Ibid.

17. Jacques Ellul, *Money and Power*, trans. LaVonne Neff (Downers Grove, IL: InterVarsity, 1984), 47.

18. Cassian, *Institutes* 7.2.

19. *ST* IIaIIae, Q 119, art. 2.

20. Gregory, *Pastoral Care*, 1.11.

21. Gregory, *Morals on Job* 19:23–24; 20:23.

22. See his *Institutes* 7.1–5 for what follows.

23. Peters, *Radical Evil*, 135.

24. Schor, *Overspent American*, 24 and 241n163.

25. See Clapp, "Theology of Consumption," 184–91 for what follows.

26. Quoted in William T. Cavanaugh, *Being Consumed: Economics and Christian Desire* (Grand Rapids: Eerdmans, 2008), 47–48.

27. Actually, the figures range from 3,000 to 17,000 depending on the source. And it would be difficult to get an exact figure given the proliferation of ads on web sites.

28. Cavanaugh, *Being Consumed*, 47. In *Still Following Christ in a Consumer Society* (New York: Orbis Books, 1991), John Kavanaugh echoes this formative influence of consumerism: "The Consumer Society is a formation system: it forms us and our behavior. It is also an information system: it informs us as to our identity as to the status of our world. Its influence is felt in every dimension of our lives, and each dimension echoes and mirrors the others" (4). "The Consumer Society is a formation system and training ground which educates us to a life of fragmented relatedness. . . . The consumer formation system, through its media, speaks to our souls and utters its pronouncement: 'We shall squeeze you empty, and then we shall fill you with ourselves'" (9–10). "Connecting all of the parts of our experience with an underlying frame of meaning and purpose, consumerism becomes a worldview of ultimate significance, a religion, in effect, supported by its own philosophy and leading to its own theory of behavior" (19). "The buying and consuming of material things has taken on religious, even theological significance. It serves as a 'way of life,' a truth about 'the real world,' a method of achieving meaning and fulfillment in our existence" (26).

29. Kavanaugh, *Still Following Christ*, 31–32.

30. Cassian, *Institutes* 7.21.

31. Ellul, *Money and Power*, 106.

32. Peters, *Radical Evil*, 127.

33. Schor, *Overspent American*, 39.

34. Ibid., 82.

35. Ibid., 68.

36. Ellul, *Money and Power*, 131.

37. Ibid., 144.

38. Cassian, *Institutes* 7.7.

39. Gregory, *Morals on Job* 15:31–34.

40. Ibid., 20:23.

41. Evagrius, *Praktikos* 17.

42. Green, "Master Passion," 100.

43. See *Institutes* 7.7 for what follows in this paragraph.

44. Ibid. Evagrius graphically portrays this hold that possessions have on the monk as he connects avarice to sadness: "But the monk with many possessions has bound himself with the fetters of his worries, as a dog is tied to a leash, even when he is forced to move off elsewhere. He carries around the memories of possessions

as a heavy burden and a useless weight; he is stung with sadness and is mightily pained in his thoughts. He has abandoned his possessions and is lashed with sadness. Even if death should approach, he is miserable in leaving behind present things and giving up his soul; . . . He is dragged away unwillingly, like a runaway slave: he is separated from the body but he is not separated from his possessions; the passion (for possessions) has a greater hold on him than those dragging him (towards death)" ("On the Eight Thoughts," 3.7, in Sinkewicz, *Evagrius of Pontus*).

45. Cassian, *Institutes* 7.16.
46. Schor, *Overspent American*, 98.
47. Ibid., 57–59.
48. Ibid., 150–52.
49. Ibid., 98.
50. Ibid., 13. Schor cites a 1991 study in which 85 percent aspire to be in the top 18 percent of US households; only 15 percent would be satisfied ending up as middle class. In a 1990 Gallup poll half of the women and two-thirds of the men surveyed and four-fifths of the people earning more than $75,000 annually indicated that they would like to be rich. ($75,000 in 1990 would be about $130,000 in 2013. More recent 2010 Gallup polls indicate that $75,000 has become a cut-off point beyond which happiness does not increase.) Half of the 250,000 entering collegians who were surveyed in 1971 said going to college "to make more money" was "very important"; that percentage increased to three-quarters in 1995. The same two surveys demonstrated a shift from 39 percent to 74 percent of those who said it was "very important or essential" that they be "very well off financially"—a goal that was first among nineteen objectives that included "becoming an authority in my own field," "helping others in difficulty," and "raising a family"; percentages were flip-flopped with regard to those who considered it important to "develop a meaningful philosophy of life." In 2011 a Gallup poll found 53 percent of those surveyed indicated they believed the main reason why students get an education beyond high school is "to earn more money," while 5 percent said it was "to become a well-rounded person," 3 percent "to learn more about the world," and 1 percent "to learn to think critically." Perhaps even more startling was that a nationwide survey of professors of economics who, despite having high salaries, were more than twice as likely as professors of other disciplines to contribute no money to private charities. See David Myers, "Money and Misery" in Clapp, *Consuming Passion*, 52–53.
51. *Institutes* 7.8–9. For Aquinas the excessive desire to receive that leaves the person restless in thoughts and violent in acts is one of greed's offspring. The other progeny is an excessive desire to retain that leads to insensibility in mercy, not unlike Schor's comments about the sweatshops that are created by our consumer culture. See Aquinas, *ST* IIaIIae, Q 118, art. 8; and Schor, *Overspent American*, 156.
52. Schor, *Overspent American*, 239n159; see p. 11.
53. Ibid., 104.
54. Cavanaugh, *Being Consumed*, 47.
55. Schor, *Overspent American*, 106. Schor suggests the strategy of emphasizing durability to foster *attachment* rather than novelty which encourages detachment (146).
56. Gregory, *On Pastoral Care*, 3.21.

57. Schor, *Overspent American*, 12.

58. Kavanaugh, *Still Following Christ*, 93, 112.

59. Ellul, *Money and Power*, 79. Developing this association with the selling of Jesus, Ellul states, "Only once did God submit to the law of selling. He allowed his Son to be sold. He agreed to pay the price of our redemption. Redemption is very literally the payment of Satan's price in order to free us. . . . But when God thus binds himself to the law of selling and agrees to pay the price, he freely *gives* his Son in order to *give* liberty" (87). "In this new world we are entering, nothing is for sale; everything is given away" (88).

60. Green, "The Master Passion," 141. Orville's son traces his father's treatment of family members to his father's own upbringing: "My father did not know how he could be accepted, understood, even loved. . . . Because love had never been shared with him, he could not share love with others" (147).

61. Cassian, *Institutes* 7.15. See Paul's stern warnings in 1 Cor. 5:11; 6:10; and Eph. 5:3.

62. Schor, *Overspent American*, 21 for this paragraph (italics mine). Later, she argues that our obsession with a "brand-oriented market" causes us to spend more than we need to on products, such that "the costs of status consumption in the US economy are considerable"; the extra money saved could fund public schools, retirement savings, or drug treatments. See p. 63. David Myers puts it like this: "Money may not buy happiness, but it would buy the poor good food, decent shelter, opportunities to learn, reduced family stress, a healthy neighborhood, preventive health care, healthy recreation and improved economic opportunity. And . . . it would do so at less cost than the long-term price that society pays in escalating crime, welfare and unproductivity" ("Money and Misery" in Clapp, *Consuming Passion*, 65).

63. See Clapp, introduction to *Consuming Passion*, 8, 12–14. Perhaps a recent example of this was the discussion that took place within the context of one of the largest mass killing sprees in US history at a movie theater in Aurora, Colorado, in July 2012 when concerns were raised about the effect this would have on the consumption of movies and Hollywood's economy. Granted this effect involved a community of people who needed to earn a livelihood, but the point is that much of the discussion was filtered in terms of our consumptive culture.

64. See Kavanaugh, *Still Following Christ*, 14–15. He continues: "The unified theme is that persons do not count, unless they are certain kinds of persons. If they are not endowed with value by power, affluence, productivity, or national interest, they may be sacrificed at the altar of 'our way of life.' What is 'ours,' what we possess, what we own and consume has become the ultimate criterion against which we measure all other values. As an ultimate, this criterion has become our functional god" (26).

65. Ibid., 52.

66. Schor, *Overspent American*, 139.

67. Ibid., 84.

68. Ibid., 83. Schor cites a survey of Telcom employees, 70 percent of whom described the "average American" as "very materialistic," while only 8 percent of the respondents felt that they themselves were materialistic.

69. Ibid., 24.

70. Ibid., 148–49.

71. Ibid., 154.

72. Gregory, *Morals on Job* 3:14.

73. Ibid., 20:20–21 for this and the rest of the paragraph.

74. Schor, *Overspent American*, 243n165. She cites many studies, including those of Marsha L. Richens in the *Journal of Consumer Research*, Tim Kasser and Richard M. Ryan in the *Journal of Personality and Social Psychology*, and Russell W. Belk in the *Journal of Consumer Research*.

75. Green, "The Master Passion," 98.

76. Myers, "Money and Misery," 57. He develops negative responses to three questions in his essay: Are people happier in rich countries? Are rich Americans happier? and Does economic growth improve public morale?

77. Ibid., 58–61.

78. Cassian, *Institutes* 7.10.

79. Clapp, "Theology of Consumption," 188.

80. Ellul, *Money and Power*, 54.

81. Cassian, *Institutes* 7.28.

82. Ibid., 7.21 (italics mine).

83. Schor, *Overspent American*, 158–60.

84. Gregory, *Morals on Job* 18:9. Cassian shares a similar sentiment about greed's insatiable appetite; see *Institutes* 7.10, 23–24, 28: The covetous person neglects spiritual "chores" in the process of laboring day and night to "satisfy the madness of avarice and supply his daily wants, inflaming the more the fire of covetousness, while believing that it will be extinguished by getting."

85. Schor, *Overspent American*, 18; see 14–18.

86. Ibid., 145.

87. Green, "Master Passion," 100.

88. Gregory, *Morals on Job* 20:20.

89. See Cassian, *Institutes* 7.22.

90. Schor, *Overspent American*, 57. See the discussion that begins on p. 48.

91. Ibid., 138–39.

92. Ibid., 140.

93. Kavanaugh, *Still Following Christ*, 25.

94. Jonathan Wharton, quoted in Schor, *Overspent American*, 141.

95. Ibid., 152.

96. See *RB1980*, prol.

97. Cassian, *Institutes* 7.29. This in contrast to the monk who hides his accumulated money (7.7).

98. Ronald Sider, *Scandal of the Evangelical Conscience*, 112–13.

99. Kavanaugh, *Still Following Christ*, 43.

100. Clapp says that modernity privatized "personal relationships" and religion and left only two public institutions—the state and the market. See his introduction in *Consuming Passion*, 7.

101. Clapp, "Theology of Consumption," 200. He is citing data from Wuthnow's *God and Mammon in America*.

102. Ibid., 200–1.

103. Evagrius, *Praktikos* 18.

104. Cassian says that we cannot bridle avarice once we have it; we can only end it through renunciation (*Institutes* 7.24). Renunciation is a kind of death.

105. Aquinas, *ST* IIaIIae, Q117, art. 1. Recalling what we said earlier about the possibility of greed inhabiting the character of a poor person, Aquinas reasons that since virtue is a habit, liberality consists not in the quantity given, but in the habit of the giver, thus a poor person can be liberal.

Describing this virtue further, Aquinas says, "Primarily and of its very nature it [liberality] tends to set in order one's own affection towards the possession and use of money. In this way temperance, which moderates desires and pleasures relating to one's own body, takes precedence of liberality. . . . For by reason of his not being a lover of money, it follows that a man readily makes use of it, whether for himself, or for the good of others, or for God's glory. Thus it derives a certain excellence from being useful in many ways" (art. 6).

106. Ellul, *Money and Power*, 110–12.

107. Kavanaugh, *Still Following Jesus*, 60–61.

108. Ibid., 127.

109. Cassian, *Institutes* 7.30.

110. Gregory, *Pastoral Care*, 3.20.

111. Green, "The Master Passion," 98.

Chapter 5 Anger

1. See Gregory, *Morals on Job* 39:25.

2. See Aquinas, *ST* IaIIae, Q 46, art. 6.

3. *Praktikos* 11.

4. Schimmel, *Seven Deadly Sins*, 83.

5. For example, in *Conferences* 16.7 Cassian writes: "As then nothing should be put before love, so on the other hand nothing should be put below rage and anger . . . because we should reckon nothing more damaging than anger and vexation, and nothing more advantageous than love." He commends to us Prov. 10:12.

6. *Praktikos* 11. Similarly, Aquinas defines anger as "the desire to hurt another for the purpose of just vengeance" in response to an injury received (*ST* IaIIae, Q47, art. 1; cf. Q 46, art. 1).

7. See Cassian, *Conferences* 11.4, where he distinguishes *thumos*, *orge*, and *menis*. Cf. Gregory's catalog of four categories of anger, depending on speed of onset and dissipation; anger that arises quickly and dies slowly is the worst, while anger that catches slowly and parts quickly is the best (*Morals on Job* 5.2). Aquinas lists three species of anger: the choleric (*akrocholoi*), the bitter (*pikros*, similar to Cassian's third), and the ill-tempered (*chalepoi*, similar to Gregory's worst). Interestingly, Carol Tavris deliniates a catalog similar to Gregory's in *Anger: The Misunderstood Emotion*, rev. ed. (New York: Simon & Schuster, 1989), 12.

8. Aquinas, *ST* IaIIae, Q46, art. 7.

9. Ibid.

10. Gregory gives us the most explicit and precise exposition of these connections; see *Morals on Job* 39:25. Here he reverses the etiological direction, so that envy gives rise to anger. But we should note that envy and avarice have some very similar qualities. For the connection between desire, avarice, and anger, see, e.g., Evagrius, *Praktikos* 99, quoting a monk: "I have this reason for putting aside

pleasure—that I might cut off the pretext for growing angry. For I know that anger constantly fights for pleasures and clouds the mind with passions that drive away contemplative knowledge." Cf. his *Chapters on Prayer* 27: "Armed as you are against anger do not submit to any powerful desire. For it is these which provide fuel for anger. . . ." Several times Cassian warns that regard for material things is the first ground of discord leading to anger; e.g., see *Conferences* 16.6, 9.

11. See Gregory, *Morals on Job* 39:25.

12. Tavris makes the same connection 1,500 years later in *Anger*, 108: "When anger is unsuccessful in averting danger or removing obstacles, when it does not restore your sense of control over the environment, you may eventually begin to feel apathetic. According to the *hopelessness theory of depression*, the key cognitions in depression are that nothing good will ever happen ('It's all hopeless'), and that the person is helpless in changing this bleak future. Depressed people tend to believe that negative events have internal, stable, and global causes ('It's my fault; it will always be my fault; and it will affect everything I do'). In such cases of depression, though, it is not quite right to say that anger has been 'turned inward.' More accurately, it has been extinguished." Tavris deliniates several relationships (and nonrelationships) between anger and depression.

13. *Institutes* 8.22.

14. *Institutes* 8.5.

15. *Institutes* 8.21.

16. At one point, Cassian employs what we consider higher critical tools to reprimand those who had added "without a cause" to Matt. 5:22 to justify anger for just causes. He argues that the phrase does not appear in X, B, Origen, or the Vulgate. (Compare the KJV, which retains the phrase, with the NIV and NRSV, which only footnote it.) Insightfully, he argues that "certainly nobody, however unreasonably he is disturbed, would say that he is angry without a cause." See *Institutes* 8.21.

17. *Institutes* 8.2–4.

18. See *Conferences* 16.17.

19. *Institutes* 8.9 (*ACW*).

20. See *Praktikos* 23, 42 (italics mine). Cf. Cassian, *Institutes* 8.7, where he seems to echo Evagrius intentionally, insisting that the only case in which anger is "excellently implanted in us" and is useful is when we "are indignant and rage" against the "lustful emotions of the heart."

21. *Morals on Job* 5:2.

22. Ibid.

23. See *ST* IaIIae, QQ46–48.

24. *ST* IaIIae, Q48, art. 3. According to Aquinas, reason needs certain sensitive powers to execute its acts, so it is hindered when the body is disturbed. I.e., any hindrance in the body, such as drunkenness or drowsiness, hinders the judgment of reason. It is anger *above all* that causes a bodily disturbance around the heart such that it even affects the outward members; hence, Aquinas's assessment of anger's debilitating effects. The physiological effects of anger are also recognized by the early ascetic theologians, and it is interesting to note that 1,500 years later this has become perhaps the most important area of research for studies about anger. E.g., see Margaret A. Chesney and Ray H. Rosenman, eds., *Anger and*

Hostility in Cardiovascular and Behavioral Disorders (Washington: Hemisphere, 1985), and Aaron Wolfe Siegman and Timothy W. Smith, eds., *Anger, Hostility, and the Heart* (London: Psychology Press, 1993). Also, see Tavris, 119–27: though overrated, there *is* a relation between anger and coronary heart disease.

25. *Praktikos* 24.

26. *Institutes* 8.6. Cf. *Institutes* 21 and *Conferences* 16.6, 16.

27. Cf. Tavris, *Anger*, chap. 3.

28. *Morals on Job* 1.5. Cf. his comments on 41:11: "For this smoke deadens in truth the keenness of the heart, because with the cloud of its darkness it disturbs the serenity of inward peace. But God cannot be recognized, except by a tranquil heart." We are commended here Ps. 46:10.

29. Evagrius, *Praktikos* 23.

30. *ST* IaIIae, Q46, art. 4; cf. art. 6. Ref. Evagrius vivid imagery in "On the Eight Thoughts," 4.6, in Sinkewicz, *Evagrius of Pontus*: "A passing cloud darkens the sun; a thought of resentment darkens the mind."

31. See 12–13, 21–22, 24, 26–27, 53, 64, 137. E.g., 53: "The man who strives after true prayer must learn to master not only anger and his lust, but must free himself from every thought that is colored by passion."

32. *Institutes* 8.6.

33. *Conferences* 16.6, 16.

34. *Institutes* 8.22.

35. *Institutes* 8.1.

36. *Morals on Job* 5:1.

37. Aquinas says something similar when he observes that, while anger can sometimes hinder reason from curbing the tongue, it can also go so far as to paralyze the tongue and bodily expression. See *ST* IaIIae, Q48, art. 4.

38. *Morals on Job* 5:2.

39. *Morals on Job* 36:18–21.

40. Cassian, *Institutes* 8.12.

41. *Anger*, chap. 2, esp. 33.

42. Ibid., 38.

43. Ibid., 45.

44. See Shahbaz Khan Mallick and Boyd R. McCandless, "A Study of Catharsis of Aggression," *Journal of Personality and Social Psychology* 4, no. 6 (1966): 591–96. They begin the article in this fashion: "Many of those interested, theoretically or practically, in personality theory, therapy, or general social psychology, for that matter, believe that aggressive acting-out behavior reduces aggression and hostility. Most theory of play therapy is still based on this hydraulic notion: the frustrated, angry, hostile child behaves aggressively, and this aggressive behavior reduces his level of hostility and aggression. Many parents and teachers accept the dictum that it is well to allow their children to blow off steam. Boxing, wrestling, and other intramural athletics are considered by some to provide catharsis for hostile aggression. . . . Freud spoke of Thanatos or a death instinct constantly working to return the organism 'to the quiescence of the inorganic world. . . .' Libido interacts with the death instinct, neutralizing its effect on the person, by directing it outward as destruction, mastery, and will to power, concepts which may be subsumed under the general term *catharsis*." Also, see the study done by

Tilmer Engebretson and Catherine Stoney, in *International Journal of Behavioral Medicine* (1996).

45. *Praktikos* 20. Cf. Cassian in *Conferences* 16.27: "We ought then to restrain every movement of anger and moderate it under the direction of discretion, that we may not by blind rage be hurried into that which is condemned by Solomon" [viz., Prov. 29:11].

46. *Morals on Job* 39:25.

47. *Morals on Job* 5:1.

48. *Institutes* 8.11 (ACW).

49. *Institutes* 8.12.

50. See *Morals on Job* 5:1 and *Conferences* 16.18, 20, 22, 27 for what follows.

51. Cassian says there is no difference between pushing a blind man down or neglecting to save him when it is in our power to do so; *Conferences* 16.18.

52. Cassian insists that the inward tranquility of the stricken must match her outward gentleness, since that is our only hope of reducing anger in both parties, "for it bears no fruit of righteousness to profit oneself by keeping calm and quiet if the other is spoiled in the process." *Conferences* 16.22; cf. 16.28.

53. *Institutes* 8.18. Cassian says, somewhat humorously, that there might be *some* advantage to the fact that inanimate objects cannot "talk back" and provoke worse fits of passion.

54. *Conferences* 16.26.

55. *Conferences* 16.27.

56. "A Study of Catharsis," 591, 596. Cf. Tavris, *Anger*, 290.

57. *Conferences* 16.15.

58. *Institutes* 8.18 (italics mine).

59. Ibid.

60. See *Conferences* 16.10–12.

61. See *Conferences* 16.6 for Cassian's description of how sins such as avarice and pride can poison a friendship with anger and preclude the growth in virtue that friendship affords. We should note here that Cassian begins the conference on friendship by distinguishing dissoluble friendships based on some expediency (such as one entered into on the basis of a recommendation, gift, bargain, nature, or instinct) and indissoluble ones based on a mutual commitment to virtue. The treatment for anger by the cultivation of patience in community is to take place in this latter kind of community. A modern-day parallel *might* be the church, *if* Christians today understood better the role of the Christian community in the moral shaping of its members. One would like to be able to ask Cassian if the same rules apply when we are not in a community of like-minded people who are seeking to reduce all of their desires to the love of God. He does not say much about dissoluble relationships, but it would help us to know what he thought about modern therapeutic relationships between counselor and client if he had had the opportunity to speak to this "friendship."

62. *Institutes* 8.17.

63. *Conferences* 16.3.

64. *Conferences* 16.6.

65. *Morals on Job* 5:2, 36:18–21.

66. *Praktikos* 15.

67. *Praktikos* 26.
68. *Morals on Job* 5:2.
69. Cited in Tavris, *Anger*, 289.
70. Cassian, *Conferences* 16.6.
71. *Institutes* 8.22.
72. *Anger*, 319.
73. *Conferences* 16.22–24 for this and what follows.
74. *Conferences* 16.26 (ACW).
75. See the similar conclusion of Simon Kemp and K. T. Strongman in "Anger Theory and Management: A Historical Analysis," *American Journal of Psychology* 108, no. 3 (Fall 1995): 397–417: "At the outset, it is interesting to note that despite the ubiquity of anger in everyday affairs and despite a proliferation of theory and empirical research on emotion in the last twenty years, psychologists do not, in general, have much to say about anger" (405). "In recent years, there has been a large discrepancy between practice and theory in anger control; practice has been rife and theory has been sparse" (411). "[P]erhaps it is not surprising that our knowledge of anger and its control has developed little in two millennia" (414).

Chapter 6 Envy

1. *New York Times*, March 17, 1991, I20. In addition, for what follows (including quotes) see stories on August 25, I31; September 4, A18; September 5, A18; and November 9, I8 (all 1991).

2. Envy and jealousy are often confused due to ambiguities in the English language, their joint occurrence, and some common features (such as some form of hostility, lowered self-esteem, and sadness). So we should distinguish envy from jealousy. Terrence Kardong suggests that jealousy "is the fear of losing a precious possession, while envy is the desire to possess what another has"; see Terrence G. Kardong, *Benedict's Rule: A Translation and Commentary* (Collegeville, MN: Liturgical Press, 1996), 94. Kardong is right to a point: envy would not make sense if it referred to something we already possess. But Kardong's definition of envy is incomplete, since without the desire to see the possessor dispossessed of what the envier desires, the desire to possess what another has would just be avarice. In fact, Schoeck alludes to this when he suggests that the "decisive difference" between jealousy and envy is that the former "is only directed against a definitive transfer of coveted assets or their removal elsewhere, never against the asset as such. Envy often denies the asset itself." (Helmut Schoeck, *Envy: A Theory of Social Behavior* [New York: Harcourt, Brace, and World, 1966], 14; cf. 96.)

While jealousy in relationships can also involve considerable envy, social scientists like Schoeck point out that jealousy never just involves two players, but always three or more, while envy not only is confined to two parties, but the envied may not even be aware of the envier's existence (Schoeck, *Envy*, 14, 710). While both may stem from a lack of self-esteem, jealousy involves a complex of human relationships, while envy revolves around a personal attachment or attribute. Also, the situations inducing envy and jealousy give rise to different cognitive assessments which result in different affective responses. Finally, while the envier feels guilty because of social disapproval of envy, jealousy often elicits publicly sanctioned feelings of self-righteousness. In fact, envy is sometimes disguised as socially sanctioned jealousy.

See W. Gerrod Parrott and Richard H. Smith, "Distinguishing the Experiences of Envy and Jealousy," *The Journal of Personality and Social Psychology* 64, no. 6 (1993): 906–8, 918; Richard H. Smith, W. Gerrod Parrott, Edward F. Diener, Rick H. Hoyle, Sung Hee Kim, "Dispositional Envy," *The Personality and Social Psychology Bulletin* 25, no. 8 (Aug. 1999): 1008; Richard H. Smith, W. Gerrod Parrott, Daniel Ozer, Andrew Moniz, "Subjective Injustice and Inferiority as Predictors of Hostile and Depressive Feelings in Envy," *The Personality and Social Psychology Bulletin* 20, no. 6 (Dec. 1994): 705–6; W. Gerrod Parrott, "The Emotional Experiences of Envy and Jealousy," in Peter Salovey, ed., *The Psychology of Jealousy and Envy* (New York and London: Guilford, 1991), 23–24; Peter Salovey and Alexander J. Rothman, "Envy and Jealousy: Self and Society," in Salovey, *Psychology*, 276; Richard H. Smith, W. Gerrod Parrott, Daniel Ozer, Andrew Moniz, "Subjective Injustice and Inferiority as Predictors of Hostile and Depressive Feelings in Envy," *The Personality and Social Psychology Bulletin* 20, no. 6 (Dec. 1994): 705–6; and Betsy Cohen, *The Snow White Syndrome: All About Envy* (New York: Macmillan, 1986), 23.

3. Aquinas speculates why Cassian did not consider envy to be a capital sin. Since a capital vice should have some principal reason for being itself the origin of several kinds of sins (Gregory, *Morals on Job* 31:45), "it is perhaps because envy manifestly arises from vainglory, that it is not reckoned a capital sin, either by Isiodore (*De Summo Bono*) or by Cassian (*De Instit. Coenob.* v. 1)." Aquinas, *ST* IaIIae, Q36, art. 4. Perhaps, but even this explanation would not be adequate for Aquinas, since elsewhere he suggests that a capital vice *can* arise from other vices, even though it must *frequently* be the source of others (*ST* IaIIae, Q118, art. 7). Furthermore, this still does not explain why Gregory *added* it to his list.

4. Gregory, *Pastoral Care* 3.10.

5. Tertullian, *Of Patience* 5; St. Basil, *On Envy* 3.

6. Cassian, *Conferences* 18.16.

7. *On Envy* 3.

8. Gregory, *Pastoral Care* 3.10. Basil notes that since Cain could not attack God, he turned his hatred toward his own brother; it is often the case that we take out our anger on God by attacking the one who is made in God's image.

9. See Gregory, *Morals on Job* 5:2. Basil deals with some of these same examples, particularly Saul and David; see *On Envy* 3–4.

10. *Morals on Job* 1:17. Cassian specifically links Judas with envy of Christ, though avarice is usually the motive cited for Judas's betrayal.

11. *On Envy* 4.

12. See *ST* IaIIae, Q36, art. 1. Aquinas depends on Gregory for his definition. Cf. Basil: "Envy is the pain that arises from another's good fortune." *On Envy* 1. Citing Neu and Salovey and Rodin, Parrott echoes Aquinas: "[Envy] occurs when the superior qualities, achievements, or possessions of another are perceived as reflecting badly on the self. Envy is typically experienced as feelings of inferiority, longing, or ill-will toward the envied person" (Parrott, "Emotional Experiences," 4). Contrast these essential affects of envy with jealousy's characteristic feelings—fear

of loss, anxiety, and suspicion and anger about betrayal. See Parrott and Smith, "Distinguishing," 906, 918.

13. Parrott insightfully suggests that there are strong similarities between malicious envy and anger. If the envier perceives the envied person's superiority to be the result of injustice, the quality of the envier's experience is predominantly anger, "righteous indignation," or resentment; if the envier's disadvantage is his own fault or not perceived as due to injustice, then the envier's most salient responses are feelings of inferiority and a motivation to self-improvement. See Parrott, "Emotional Experiences," 10–11, 15.

14. *Morals on Job* 39:25; *ST* IIaIIae, Q36, art. 4. Gregory finds envy to be a link between vainglory and anger: following vainglory, "because doubtless while it is seeking the power of an empty name, it feels envy against anyone else being able to obtain it"; preceding anger, "because the more the mind is pierced by the inward wound of envy, the more also is the gentleness of tranquility lost." With these two links (vanity and anger) Gregory anticipates contemporary social scientists for whom feelings of inferiority and hostility define the affective experience of envy. In fact, the latter is usually considered a *sine qua non* of the emotion of envy, distinguishing it from what might instead be labeled admiration or unhappiness. (See Smith et al., "Subjective Injustice," 706, and Smith et al., "Dispositional Envy," 1009.) With regard to the former (vanity and feelings of inferiority), see Robert C. Roberts's insightful connection between envy and pride in *Taking the Word to Heart* (Grand Rapids: Eerdmans, 1993), chap. 9.

15. See *Rule of Benedict* 55.21.

16. Schoeck puts it more forcefully when he suggests that envy is closer to arson than theft: "Beneath the envious man's primarily destructive desire is the realization that in the long run it would be a very demanding responsibility were he to have the envied man's qualities or possessions, and that the best kind of world would be one in which neither he, the subject, nor the object of his envy would have them" (*Envy*, 19; cf. 5, 14). Cf. Salovey and Rothman, "Envy and Jealousy," 280: "Indeed, the derogation of rivals when self-evaluation is threatened is considered the defining feature of envy by some theorists." This feature that distinguishes envy from avarice is what Betsy Cohen misses in her book *The Snow White Syndrome*. Her inadequate definition of envy ("the unpleasant feeling of wanting what another person has and feeling bad that you don't have it") leads her to misconstrue the tenth commandment as a prohibition against envy. See 16–17 of her book.

17. Schoeck, *Envy*, 20.

18. *ST* IIaIIae, Q36, art. 1. Basil makes the same point: "A Scythian is not envious of an Egyptian, but each will envy one of the same nation. And among people of the same nation, those not known are not envied, but those with whom we are familiar; and among these again, it arises between persons of the same age, the same kinship, among brothers. As red blight is a pest in the growing wheat, so is envy a pest among friends."

19. See Salovey and Rothman, "Envy and Jealousy," 271–74, 284; and Parrott, "Emotional Experiences," 7. Salovey and Rothman quote William James's *The Principles of Psychology*: "I, who for the time have staked my all on being a psychologist, am mortified if others know much more psychology than I. But I am contented to wallow in the grossest ignorance of Greek. My deficiencies there give

me no sense of personal humiliation at all. Had I 'pretensions' to be a linguist, it would have been just the reverse. So we have the paradox of a man shamed to death because he is only the second pugilist or the second oarsman in the world. That he is able to beat the whole population of the globe minus one is nothing; he has 'pitted' himself to beat that one; and as long as he doesn't do that nothing else counts. He is to his own regard as if he were not, indeed he *is* not."

20. Schoeck, *Envy*, 62. A colleague's new Rolls-Royce would arouse less envy than his new Honda. Elsewhere, Schoeck notes that in India the caste system leaves little room for envious feelings between social classes, but there is the possibility of a great deal of envy *within* a caste.

21. See Aquinas, *ST* IIaIIae, Q36, art. 4. Richard H. Smith cites "considerable evidence suggesting that one response to unflattering social comparisons can be depression" or a "depressive form of envy." This can result in hostility turned inward, leading to resignation and apathy. See Richard H. Smith, "Envy and the Sense of Injustice," 93 in Salovey, *Psychology of Jealousy and Envy*; also see Smith et al., "Subjective Injustice," 709–10.

22. See *Rule of Benedict* 1.6–9. For what follows, see *Conferences* 18.7.

23. See Gregory, *Morals on Job* 5:2, 15; *Pastoral Care* 3.10.

24. Basil, *On Envy* 2. Actually, the situation may be more complicated than this. While "envy is the one 'sin' that has no obvious pleasure joined with it," one study has demonstrated that the pain of envy creates the conditions under which the pleasure of *Schadenfreude* occurs; but because *Schadenfreude* is a socially disreputable emotion, "it may emerge as a lack of an appropriate sympathy for the sufferer rather than as a pleased feeling." Still, a downward comparison might give relief from envy, boost the envier's self-esteem, and produce "outright mirth." See Richard H. Smith et al., "Envy and *Schadenfreude*," *The Personality and Social Psychology Bulletin* 22, no. 2 (Feb. 1996): 166–67.

25. *Morals on Job* 15:33–34.

26. *Morals on Job* 5:2.

27. See Parrott, "Emotional Experiences," 7; Schoeck, *Envy*, 1–5. Schoeck goes so far as to say that strictly speaking there is no such thing as envy; it's a "directed emotion" such that "without a target, without a victim, it cannot occur." This is corroborated by the observation that a joyful or sad person can be depicted in isolation. See Schoeck, *Envy*, 7.

28. See Salovey and Rothman, "Jealousy and Envy," 272–73.

29. *Morals on Job* 38:15.

30. See Richard H. Smith, "Envy and the Sense of Injustice," 82, 93. Still, Schoeck suggests that recognition of a divine dispensation might ameliorate envy: "The path of inequality . . . is less rugged for the man living in a community whose culture has evolved conceptions, such as varying degrees of luck, which can assuage his own conscience and disarm the envious. A doctrine, highly successful in the suppression of envy, is that of predestination taught by Calvinism" (*Envy*, 353; cf. 237–38, 360).

31. See Smith et al., "Envy and *Schadenfreude*," 159, 167; and Smith et al., "Subjective Injustice," 705–6, 710. Why doesn't the envier right the perceived injustice? Societal norms require the acceptance of one's lot, crying foul due to another's superiority is forbidden, and the merit system of our efficient society

favors those who possess advantages based on uncontrollable attributes; see Smith et al., "Envy and *Schadenfreude*," 167. The pleasure an envier takes in a setback for the "unjustly" advantaged depends on how deserved the setback is and the envied's likeability; ibid., 159.

32. On this cf. Aquinas, *ST* IIaIIae, Q36, art. 2: unworthy envy includes grieving over another's goods because we deem the possessor unworthy of them, but by faith, says Aquinas, we must believe that such are distributed by providence, either for correction or condemnation. Still, this might be more difficult to take to heart in a culture characterized by one magazine's report on annual salaries wherein a comedian (viz., Jerry Seinfeld) makes $66,000,000, while a school teacher makes about $30,000.

33. *Conferences* 18.16. Mary T. Stimming makes a wise and insightful application of this focus on God's providence with regard to envy in cases of infertility: "Our envy of others is, at least in large measure, an expression of grief over our own barrenness. . . . [However] if God is the author of all life, then eventually our appreciation of life must override our sorrow at our inability to share in one particular way of perpetuating life" ("Childless in December: Endless Advent?," *Christian Century*, December 6, 2000, 1274).

34. *On Envy* 2.

35. *Conferences* 18.16. At this point it is worth noting that Aquinas also recognizes the severity of such envy, for the "kind of envy which is accounted among the most grievous sins" is "envy of another's spiritual good, which envy is a sorrow for the increase of God's grace, and not merely for our neighbor's good." Aquinas suggests this is a sin against the Holy Spirit, since the envy is directed at the One who is glorified in His works. *ST* IIaIIae, Q36, art. 4. This is precisely the attitude of the envier vis-à-vis his spiritual therapist.

36. Cohen, *Snow White*, 19.

37. Smith, "Envy," 96.

38. Schoeck, *Envy*, 21–22, 258–59.

39. *Conferences* 18.16.

40. *On Envy* 1.

41. E.g., see Smith, "Envy," 85, 88; also, Parrott, "Emotional Experiences," 26.

42. Schoeck, *Envy*, 105.

43. Smith, "Envy," 85.

44. Ibid., 88.

45. *Morals on Job* 5:2.

46. Cohen fits in nicely with the ascetics at this point. In her prescriptions for each "level" of envy on her continuum, she insists that in every case "awareness" is a prerequisite to "talking to yourself" realistically and taking counterpositive measures: "Envy comes in part from not looking deeply enough into yourself" (*Snow White*, 260).

47. Ibid., 42–43.

48. *Morals on Job* 5:2.

49. Schoeck, *Envy*, 22.

50. Cohen, *Snow White*, 20.

51. *Pastoral Care* 3.10.

52. Parrott, "Emotional Experiences," 8.

53. *On Envy* 5. Schoeck seems to be moving in Gregory's direction when he gets prescriptive: "The only activity that liberates from envy is that which fills us with new, different impulses, feelings and thoughts which, to be of help, have to be value-asserting, dynamic, and forward looking" (*Envy*, 351).

54. Salovey and Rothman, "Jealousy and Envy," 281. The fact that psychologists understand this amplifies Solomon Schimmel's indictment against his colleagues: "Because secular psychology does not challenge the prevailing materialist and hedonist values and our culture's nonspiritual and moral criteria for evaluating human worth, it cannot provide radical remedies for envy" (Schimmel, *Seven Deadly Sins*, 59).

55. Parrott has a good brief discussion of emulation, except that he fails to distinguish moral emulation from immoral avarice, *both* of which can be "nonmalicious envy." He *is* correct to point out that of the two types of envy—malicious and nonmalicious—only the former seems worthy of *envy's* membership among the seven deadly sins, even though both can be unpleasant to experience. See "Emotional Experiences," 9–10. Also, see Schoeck, *Envy*, 16; and Cohen, *Snow White*, 260, who distinguishes admiration from idealizing.

56. *Pastoral Care* 3.10.

57. *On Envy* 3.

58. Echoes of such virtue are expressed by Smith et al. in "Dispositional Envy," 1018: "Some people not only may feel little envy when confronted by another person's advantage but also may feel energized and challenged in a positive, nonhostile manner. They may have a benevolent response even when most people might typically experience invidious feelings. . . . As a result, they may be more disposed to use social comparison information as an opportunity to see possibilities for themselves, to learn new skills, or simply, to enjoy excellence, beauty, or good luck vicariously. . . ." The alternative is "dispositional envy" that lacks coping mechanisms needed to reframe one's response to the advantaged. People *disposed* to feeling envy often suffer from a "chronic sense of inferiority," unable to discount, ignore, or reframe negative implications of upward social comparisons; see Smith et al., "Dispositional Envy," 1008–9, 1018.

59. Schimmel, *Seven Deadly Sins*, 75. Jonathan can be set in stark contrast to the elder son in Jesus's parable of the prodigal.

60. In his own way, Schoeck connects belief in providence with the antidote to envy; see n30 above.

Chapter 7 Sloth

1. Origen was the first to link the "noonday demon" with *acedia*, after which Augustine and others linked the phrase in Ps. 91:6 with other maladies. See Rudolph Arbesmann, OSA, "The '*Daemonium Meridianum*' and Greek and Latin Patristic Exegesis," *Traditio* 14 (1958): 17–31.

2. Evagrius, *Praktikos* 12.

3. Cassian, *Institutes* 10.2 (ACW).

4. Aquinas, *ST* IIaIIae, Q35, art. 1.

5. Cassian, *Institutes* 9.2–3.

6. William Backus, "Sloth: Laziness or Depression?," *Cornerstone* 29, 120–24. Disappointingly, this same misunderstanding occurs in what is probably the most

comprehensive and in *many* ways insightful and helpful book on depression by one who has researched it thoroughly *and* experienced it deeply—Andrew Solomon's *The Noonday Demon: An Atlas of Depression* (New York: Scribner, 2001). In his chapter titled "History," he writes, "I have taken the phrase [noonday demon] as the title of this book because it describes so exactly what one experiences in depression" (293). I suspect this simple equivocation is due to a surface knowledge of the writings of Evagrius, Cassian, Gregory, and Thomas, for on the same page Solomon goes on to say, "The medieval Church defined nine deadly sins (they were subsequently compacted to seven). Among these was *acedia* (translated as 'sloth' in the thirteenth century). The word seems to have been used almost as broadly as the word *depression* is in modern times, and it described symptoms familiar to anyone who has seen or felt depression—symptoms that had not previously been counted as vice." As we have already discussed, Gregory compacted (so to speak) the *eight* that had been defined by the *early* church into *seven* at the *beginning* of the medieval period.

7. Backus, "Sloth," 25, 28.

8. Rainer Jehl, trans. Andrea Nèmeth-Newhauser, "*Acedia* and Burnout Syndrome: From an Occupational Vice of the Early Monks to a Psychological Concept in Secularized Professional Life," in *In the Garden of Evil: The Vices and Culture in the Middle Ages*, ed. Richard Newhauser (Toronto: Pontifical Institute of Medieval Studies, 2005), 455–76.

9. Gabriel Bunge admits that *acedia* is "overloaded with so many and various shades of meaning that it is nearly impossible to express it adequately with a single word." He lists other English equivalents: repulsion, boredom, inertia, indolence, lassitude, dislike, dejection, and his preference—despondency. See Bunge, *Evagrius Ponticus*, 45–46.

10. Jehl, "*Acedia* and Burnout Syndrome," 455–56.

11. Siegfried Wenzel, *The Sin of Sloth: Acedia in Medieval Thought and Literature* (Chapel Hill, NC: University of North Carolina Press, 1967).

12. See Schimmel, *Seven Deadly Sins*, 193.

13. Jehl, "*Acedia* and Burnout Syndrome," 457.

14. "Sadness [*tristitia*] and despondency are therefore not identical; but they are nonetheless so closely related to one another that what Evagrius says about the former applies to a large extent to the latter" (Bunge, *Despondency*, 54).

15. Ibid., 459.

16. Stanley W. Jackson, *Melancholia and Depression: From Hippocratic Times to Modern Times* (New Haven: Yale University Press, 1986), 66.

17. Ibid., 75, 77.

18. Solomon, *Noonday Demon*, 13–14.

19. Ibid., 29. At one point he says that the *DSM-IV* "ineptly defines depression as the presence of five or more on a list of nine symptoms. The problem with the definition is that it's entirely arbitrary" (19).

20. Ibid., 26.

21. Ibid., 25.

22. Ibid., 31, 32.

23. Ibid., 48.

24. Ibid., 62–63.

25. Schimmel, *Seven Deadly Sins*, 193.

26. Ibid., 201.

27. Cassian, *Institutes* 10.3.

28. Evagrius puts it succinctly: "A person afflicted with acedia proposes visiting the sick, but is fulfilling his own purpose" ("On the Eight Thoughts" 6.6, in Sinkewicz, *Evagrius of Pontus*).

29. Gregory, *Pastoral Care* 3.15.

30. One study found that while 65 percent of the pastors surveyed said they worked fifty or more hours a week, 52 percent indicated that they spent only one to six hours in prayer each week, and 5 percent reported they spent no time at all in prayer. See "Pastor Burnout by the Numbers," www.lifeway.com/Article /LifeWay-Research-finds-pastors-long-work-hours-can-come-at-the-expense-of-people-ministry.

31. Cassian, *Conferences* 10.2 (*ACW*).

32. Gregory, *Pastoral Care* 3.15.

33. Gregory, *Morals on Job* 39:25.

34. Evagrius, *Praktikos* 10; Cassian, *Conferences* 5; *Institutes* 9.4. In *Despondency* Bunge states "at the root of acedia lies the frustration of a desire" (54). "*Frustration* and *aggressiveness* combine in a new way and produce this 'complex' (that is, interwoven) phenomenon of acedia" (58).

35. Cassian, *Institutes* 9.4 (*ACW*). Working from the model that requires the rational part of a tranquil soul to be in command of the two lower parts (associated with desire and anger), Evagrius (in *Praktikos* 23) mentions the thought of fornication, as well as anger, as one that leads to *acedia*. In other words, the fantasy of sexual pleasure disturbs the prayer life. One might think that this would distinguish *acedia* from depression (for which a decreased interest in sex is symptomatic) in that the focus here is on the specifically religious aspect of early monastic thought about sloth.

36. See Cassian, *Institutes* 9.5; Gregory, *Pastoral Care* 3.3.

37. See Cassian, *Conferences* 5.10, 24.6; *Institutes* 2.14.

38. See Cassian, *Institutes* 9.13.

39. Cassian, *Institutes* 9.7; see Cassian Folsom, OSB, "Anger, Dejection, and Acedia in the Writings of John Cassian," *American Benedictine Review* 31 (1989): 230.

40. Folsom, "Anger, Dejection, and Acedia," 231. He's referring to Cassian's *Conferences* 16–17.

41. Solomon, *Noonday Demon*, 110.

42. Ibid., 132. Later Solomon points out that depression is "a disease of loneliness, and anyone who has suffered it acutely knows that it imposes a dread isolation, even for people surrounded by love" (214). The difference here with the early understanding of *acedia* is that *acedia* involves a disgust of the community, while the cure, as we shall see, includes returning to the isolation of the "cell."

43. Cassian, *Institutes* 10.7.

44. Cassian, *Conferences* 5.20.

45. Evagrius, *Praktikos* 28.

46. Cassian, *Institutes* 10.3 (*ACW*).

47. Eugene Peterson, *A Long Obedience in the Same Direction: Discipleship in an Instant Society* (Downers Grove, IL: InterVarsity, 2000).

48. Cassian, *Institutes* 10.2.

49. *RB1980: The Rule of St. Benedict in English*, ed. Timothy Fry, OSB (Collegeville, MN: The Liturgical Press, 1981), 1.11.

50. Evagrius puts it this way: "You must not abandon the cell in the time of temptations, fashioning excuses seemingly reasonable. Rather, you must remain seated inside, exercise perseverance, and valiantly welcome all attackers, especially the demon of acedia, who is the most oppressive of all but leaves the soul proved to the highest degree. Fleeing and circumventing such struggles teaches the mind to be unskilled, cowardly, and evasive (Evagrius, *Praktikos* 28, in Sinkewicz, *Evagrius of Pontus*).

51. Bunge, *Despondency*, 68. We must be careful with our understanding of what is meant by "cell" in these contexts. Bunge points out that it is clear from the sayings of the desert fathers and from Evagrius (a fourth-century monk who originally came up with the list of eight "thoughts" which included *acedia*) that they "visited one another gladly and frequently, above all to get advice from an older and more experienced monk" (73). In fact, he points out that refusal to do this would be a sign of spiritual pride. And we would not have the stories or sayings of the desert fathers if they had not been in some sort of community.

52. See *RB1980* 4.78; cf. 58.9.

53. Bernardo Olivera, OCSO, "A Sadness That Undermines the Longing for God," *American Benedictine Review* 60, no. 4 (December 2009): 359.

54. Ibid., 369.

55. Christoph Joest asserts that *acedia* is not just one temptation among many: "It is quite simply *the* temptation, the calling into question of one's entire existence, the major identity crisis, in which the very foundations of everything are severely shaken" (144). It can even drive to suicide. It is the endpoint of the sequences of vices, encompassing the other vices (see *Praktikos* 93), *especially sadness and anger*; it goes for the whole soul, and attempts to suffocate the *nous* (mind, spirit). See Christoph Joest, "The Significance of *Acedia* and *Apatheia* in Evagrius Ponticus," parts 1 and 2, in *The American Benedictine Review* 55, no. 2 (June 2004): 121–50 and 55, no. 3 (Sept. 2004): 273–307.

56. See Cassian, *Conferences* 5.23, and *Institutes* 10.25.

57. Olivera, "Sadness," 362. See Aquinas, *ST* IIaIIae, Q35, esp. art. 3.

58. *ST* IIaIIae, Q35.

59. Ibid. In this discussion Aquinas distances himself from Cassian's distinction between sorrow and sloth (see Cassian, *Institutes* 10.1), preferring Gregory's identification of sloth as a kind of sorrow.

60. Olivera, "Sadness," 367. The metaphor of the battlefield is his.

61. Interestingly, Joest points out that monastic elders made the observation that *acedia*-level temptations occur not only at the middle of the day, but especially in the *middle of life*. "Evagrius himself once said such a thing, writing that the young men have to battle against the temptations of *epithymatikon* [the concupiscible part of the soul] while the elders against those of the *thymikon* [the irascible part of the soul], that is, the emotional disgruntlement that first happens when one reaches an advanced age: 'Encourage the elders to master their anger, but the

young men their stomach. For the demons of the soul fight with the former, but the demons of the body, for the most part, fight with the latter.'" Johannes Tauler (d. 1361) used the conceptual framework of *acedia* in a sermon series, giving an exact description of what psychologists today call "mid-life crisis"—a time of disquiet and restlessness, using words reminiscent of Evagrius's. (See Joest, "*Acedia and Apatheia*," 140–41n94.)

62. Solomon, *Noonday Demon*, 34–37.

63. Ibid., 70.

64. Ibid., 201.

65. Ibid., 29.

66. Ibid., 430.

67. Ibid., 437.

68. Ibid., 131. Italics are mine.

69. Cassian, *Institutes* 10.7–25.

70. Cassian, *Institutes* 10.22.

71. Evagrius, *Praktikos* 29. Adalbert de Vogüe ("Keep Death Daily before Your Eyes," in *Monastic Studies* 16 [1985]: 25–38) cites Evagrius (*Praktikos* 29, 72) and Cassian (*Institutes* 5.4; 12.33) teaching that the daily reminder of death is the remedy against *acedia*. Death is "a source of spiritual freedom" that can free the soul from the passions because it "exposes all passionate attachment as erroneous and infantile."

72. Gregory, *Pastoral Care* 3.15.

73. Cassian, *Institutes* 10.12.

74. Cassian, *Institutes* 9.13; Gregory, *Morals on Job* 39:25.

75. Joest, "Significance of *Acedia* and *Aphatheia*: Part 2," 230. In Cassian this compunction is related to unceasing prayer which is synonymous with purity of heart; see *Conferences* 5.23, 27.

76. Bunge argues that tears are the first of the stronger remedies. "Tears" are intimately linked to prayer; praying meant shedding tears before God. These tears exert an influence on God and change us (*Despondency,* 104–5). "Despondency is the most malicious enemy of tears and of prayer coming from the heart. Thus to soften this inner hardening and brutalization, nothing helps so much as to have recourse again to tears" (106). Tears soften the inner hardening.

77. Cassian, *Institutes* 9.11.

Chapter 8 Vainglory

1. Bunge, *Despondency*, 62.

2. *Morals on Job* 39:25. Aquinas acknowledges this relationship in Gregory in *ST* IIaIIae, Q132, art. 4.

3. *Morals on Job* 19:23–24. He uses the terms interchangeably in *Pastoral Care* 3.33. Unlike the other vices, Cassian does not so much *define* vainglory as *constantly* remind us that it can affect anyone, anytime, and anyplace, especially, as we will see, those who triumph in virtue.

4. Thomas S. Buchanan translates *kenodoxia* in Cassian as "self-esteem" or "empty glory" (vis-à-vis *orthodoxia* or "right glory")—a sense of conceit, vanity, and excessive ambition—which he distinguishes from pride using Cassian's

description as "an evil beast that is most savage and more dreadful than all the former ones." See "The Sin of Self-Esteem," *Touchstone*, October 2000, 52.

5. Edward Katz, "Self Esteem: The Past of an Illusion," *American Journal of Psychoanalysis* (September 1998), 306.

6. Ibid.

7. Ibid., 307. Katz notes that this was a misuse of Darwinism which did not teach survival of the strongest, but survival of the *fittest*.

8. Ibid., 308–9.

9. Ibid., 309.

10. Christopher J. Mruk, *Self-Esteem: Research, Theory, and Practice: Toward a Positive Psychology of Self-Esteem*, 3rd ed. (New York: Springer, 2006).

11. See, for example, ibid., 10.

12. Ibid., 12–28. He favors the last, defining self-esteem as "the lived status of one's competence at dealing with the challenges of living in a worthy way over time" (28). He gets even more specific later when talking about self-esteem as "meaning making" in chapter 5; he charts various combinations on the axes of competence and worthiness. It is his way of locating the "dark side" of self-esteem vis-à-vis his more positive approach to the concept.

13. http://www.self-esteem-nase.org/. This has similarities to Mruk's definition, but he would not use "happiness."

14. Katz, "Self-Esteem," 312; Mruk, *Self-Esteem*, 4–7 (and for what follows).

15. Po Bronson and Ashley Merryman, *NurtureShock: New Thinking about Children* (New York: Twelve, 2009), 18.

16. Ibid. Mruk indicates that more than 23,215 articles, chapters, and books were written about self-esteem between James's introduction of the topic and 2006, though he says that between 1999 (the second edition of his book) and 2006, the ideas, research, and theories were out-of-date; see Mruk, *Self-Esteem*, 1.

17. See Roy F. Baumeister et al., "Exploding the Self-Esteem Myth," *Scientific American* 292 (2005): 85; Bronson and Merryman, *NurtureShock*, 18.

18. See Mruk, *Self-Esteem*, 5–7; Baumeister et al., "Exploding," 84; Bronson and Merryman, *NurtureShock*, 18.

19. See Michael H. Kernis, *Self-Esteem: Issues and Answers: A Sourcebook of Current Perspectives* (New York: Psychology Press, 2006), 1–2.

20. Evagrius, *Praktikos* 14.

21. Cassian, *Institutes* 12.1 (ACW).

22. Cassian, *Institutes* 12.6.

23. Gregory, *Morals on Job* 39:25. Commenting on 41:25 he cites Ecclesiasticus 10:13 and states that pride conceals itself, but "vices immediately shoot forth from it."

24. Simon Wessely, "Pride," *British Medical Journal, International Edition* (Dec. 21, 1996): 1594–95. The surveys he cites are taken from D. Capps, "The Deadly Sins and Saving Virtues: How They Are Viewed by Laity," *Pastoral Psychology* 37 (1989): 229–53, and "The Deadly Sins and Saving Virtues: How They Are Viewed by Clergy," *Pastoral Psychology* 40 (1992): 209–33.

25. Gregory, *Morals on Job* 40:21 (italics are mine).

26. Evagrius, *Praktikos* 20.

27. Robert C. Roberts, *Spiritual Emotions: A Psychology of Christian Virtues* (Grand Rapids: Eerdmans, 2007), 78. This is why the words for pride in the Old Testament (derivatives of *allh*) are usually translated "to become lofty" or "to be arrogant" (Prov. 3:34; Ps. 10:4). In the New Testament the word (used sparsely) is *hubris*, often translated "insolence" (Rom. 1:30; Heb. 10:29).

28. Cassian cites Abbot Macarius's insight that those living in the desert find it harder, for instance, to fast than do those in the *coenobium* "because, said he, 'here there is nobody to see your fast, and feed and support you with his praise of you: but there you grew fat on the notice of others and the food of vainglory.'" See *Conferences* 5.12.

29. Cassian, *Institutes* 11.15.

30. Gregory, *Morals on Job* 19:23–24.

31. Schimmel, *Seven Deadly Sins*, 36.

32. See Cassian, *Conferences* 5.11 and *Institutes* 12.2, 24–25.

33. Gregory, *Morals on Job* 41:25. He also distinguishes the way in which pride attacks rulers and subjects.

34. Cassian, *Institutes* 11.1–4.

35. Cassian, *Institutes* 11.6 (ACW).

36. Gregory, *Morals on Job* 41:25. Also, see Evagrius, *Praktikos* 13.

37. Cassian, *Institutes* 11.3; Gregory uses the same analogy.

38. Gregory, *Morals on Job* 29:15.

39. Gregory, *Morals on Job* 7:1.

40. Evagrius, "On the Eight Thoughts," 7.1, in Sinkewicz, *Evagrius of Pontus*.

41. Cassian, *Institutes* 11.7–9; Gregory, *Morals on Job* 40:16.

42. Evagrius, "On the Eight Thoughts," 7.9, in Sinkewicz, *Evagrius of Pontus*.

43. See Cassian, *Institutes* 11.10–11.

44. Gregory, *Morals on Job* 1:4; 39:25. Evagrius makes a similar observation in his "Letter to Anatolius" where he uses the symbol of bare hands for a life lived free of hypocrisy over against vainglory which "has a frightful power to cover over and cast virtues into the shade. Ever searching out praises from men, it banishes faith." See *Praktikos* Letter 13.

45. Gregory, *Morals on Job* 33:5.

46. Gregory, *Morals on Job* 32:8.

47. See Bronson and Merryman, *NurtureShock*, 12–17.

48. Cassian, *Institutes* 12.7 (ACW).

49. Cassian, *Institutes* 11.4. Cassian cites Isa. 14:13–14 and Ps. 52:6–9.

50. Cassian, *Conferences* 22.6.

51. Gregory, *Morals on Job* 31:28.

52. Aquinas, *ST* IIaIIae, Q132, art. 4.

53. Cassian, *Institutes* 12.11.

54. Gregory, *Morals on Job* 39:20.

55. Katz, "Self-Esteem," 310.

56. Bronson and Merryman, *NurtureShock*, 12–15 (on Carol Dweck's research) and 20–21.

57. Aquinas, *ST* IIaIIae, Q132, art. 1. Essentially, Aquinas is identifying what is "vain" about vainglory as opposed to legitimate glory. In art. 3 he argues that vainglory is a mortal sin only if it is contrary to charity.

58. Katz, "Self-Esteem," 313. He goes on to argue that "self-esteem concepts confuse our attributes, our assets and deficits, our title, income, achievements, looks, race, sex, etc., with our selves. If we are 'high' in these or other attributes, we are. If not, we do not exist. . . . If our being depends on success or failure, is conditional on good fortune or bad, as self-esteem proposes, then we cannot easily be with our selves or congruently with others. Self-esteem has produced a world of somebodies and nobodies, not a world of unique selves."

59. Gregory, *Morals on Job* 2:8.

60. Bronson and Merryman, *NurtureShock*, 22.

61. Roberts, *Spiritual Emotions*, 87.

62. Gregory, *Morals on Job* 32:8; 41:25, where he continues: "he walks with himself along the broad spaces of his thought, and silently utters his own praises."

63. Cassian, *Institutes* 12.30.

64. See Cassian, *Institutes* 12.27–29; Gregory, *Morals on Job* 15:20; 41:25; 39:25; Aquinas, *ST* IIaIIae, Q132, art. 5.

65. Mruk, *Self-Esteem*, 3. Poor self-esteem is also a risk factor in, e.g., certain eating disorders; see Baumeister et al., "Exploding," 90.

66. See Mruk, *Self-Esteem*, 84–86; Baumeister et al., "Exploding," 89–90.

67. Mruk, *Self-Esteem*, 17–18, 20, 23.

68. Baumeister et al., "Exploding," 89; Bronson and Merryman, *NurtureShock*, 19, 246n.

69. Baumeister et al., "Exploding," 90.

70. Mruk, *Self-Esteem*, 17, 86.

71. See Prov. 15:25; 16:19; Pss. 94:2; 140:5; Isa. 9:8–9; 16:6, 47:10–11; Hos. 5:5; 7:10; Jer. 13:17; 48:29–30; 50:32; Ezek. 16:49; 28:17; Zeph. 2:10; Zech. 9:6.

72. See Prov. 16:18; Jer. 50:32. This is the apologetic agenda in Augustine's *City of God*.

73. Quoted in Schimmel, *Seven Deadly Sins*, 28.

74. Evagrius, *Praktikos* 30.

75. Cassian, *Institutes* 12.8.

76. Ibid., 12.23.

77. Ibid., 12.31–32; Gregory, *Morals on Job* 33:1–2; 48:25. Gregory makes the point that humility begets love vis-à-vis pride that begets hatred; *Morals on Job* 6:7.

78. Gregory, *Morals on Job* 40:21; 10:16 for the line about "wonderful pitifulness."

79. Gregory, *Morals on Job* 33:1–2; Cassian, *Institutes* 12.32.

80. Bronson and Merryman, *NurtureShock*, 22–23.

81. Gregory, *On Pastoral Care* 4 (237). In *Morals on Job* 19:23–24, Gregory admonishes people to turn inward when they feel vainglory creeping up in order to realize what in themselves is condemnable by the Judge and the neglected good they have left undone—i.e., to have tears for the evil done and the good still owed. "After the manner of travelers we ought not ever to look how much of the way we have already gone through, but how much there remains for us to carry through. . . . Therefore we ought much more to survey what good things we have not yet done, than those good things which we are glad that we have already done." Here Gregory refers to Paul's "progress" report in Phil. 3:12–13. How similar this is to

the classic prayer of confession: "We confess that we have sinned against you in thought, word, and deed by what we have done and by what we have left undone."

82. Gregory, *Morals on Job* 10:16. Elsewhere (6:7), Gregory says that holy people begin to dread their prosperity and long for trials so that "fear and pain may discipline the unwary mind, lest" it get ambushed and "its self-security cause its greater downfall."

83. Gregory, *Morals on Job* 2:8.

84. Gregory, *Morals on Job* 32:8.

85. Gregory, *Morals on Job* 33:9–11.

86. Thomas S. Buchanan, "The Sin of Self-Esteem," in *Touchstone*, October 2000, 52 (italics mine).

87. See Mruk, *Self-Esteem*, 13.

88. Gregory, *Morals on Job* 15:27; Cassian, *Institutes* 11.18.

89. Cassian, *Institutes* 12.15, 32.

90. The quote is from Gregory, *Morals on Job* 13:12 and the elaboration, 15:20.

91. Cassian, *Institutes* 11.18.

92. Significantly, given what we said in the chapter on lust and the story of Jimmy Swaggart, it is worthwhile to point out Evagrius's warning about the danger of vainglory that leaves the monk to pride or sadness, and when one was a short while before a priest, he "is led off bound and is handed over to the demon of impurity to be sifted by him." See *Praktikos* 13. In *Morals on Job* 35:11, Gregory states, "pride has often been to many a seed-plot of lust," and argues that humility guards chastity; granted the stretched exegesis, in 40:7, he uses Adam and Eve as an example of the link between pride and lust.

93. Gregory, *Morals on Job* 33:17.

Addendum

1. Gabriel Bunge, *Despondency: The Spiritual Teaching of Evagrius Ponticus*, trans. Anthony P. Gythiel (Crestwood, NY: St. Vladimir's Seminary Press, 2012); Christoph Joest, "The Significance of *Acedia* and *Apatheia* in Evagrius Ponticus," parts 1 and 2, *The American Benedictine Review* 55, no. 2 (June 2004): 121–50 and 55, no. 3 (Sept. 2004): 273–307.

2. See Sinkewicz's discussions in the several introductions to texts in *Evagrius of Pontus*.

3. Bunge suggests that Evagrius's rejection of the condemnation or suppression of the irrational parts of the soul is where he counters Plato and fills the ancient ideal with Christian content (*Despondency*, 63). But a careful reading of Plato shows that he too considered the interrelation (not the suppression) of the parts performing the tasks for which they exist under the guidance of reason in order to be a temperate and just soul. For one thing, without the dark horse—the concupiscible—in Plato's metaphor of the soul in the *Phaedrus* the soul would never move toward the objects of knowledge to which reason (the charioteer) steers the chariot; and without the white horse—the irascible—the soul would never put up a fight to get to the object.

4. Joest calls attention to a distinction between perfect and imperfect *apatheia*, since it involves a developmental process with overlapping times of transition and various stages. "Imperfect *apatheia* belongs to a man who still experiences

temptations, but once he has overcome all demons, then is perfect passionlessness attained," even over memories and dreams ("Significance of Acedia, Part 2," 280–81).

5. Actually, Joest points out that *agapē* has been at work even before *apatheia* is achieved. He argues that the passions of the *epithymatikon* are restrained by self-control, while those of the *thymatikon* are restrained by love which turns imperfect *apatheia* into perfect *apatheia* and is the door to knowledge ("Significance of Acedia, Part 2," 285–88).

6. See Joest, "Significance of Acedia, Part 2," n64.

Index